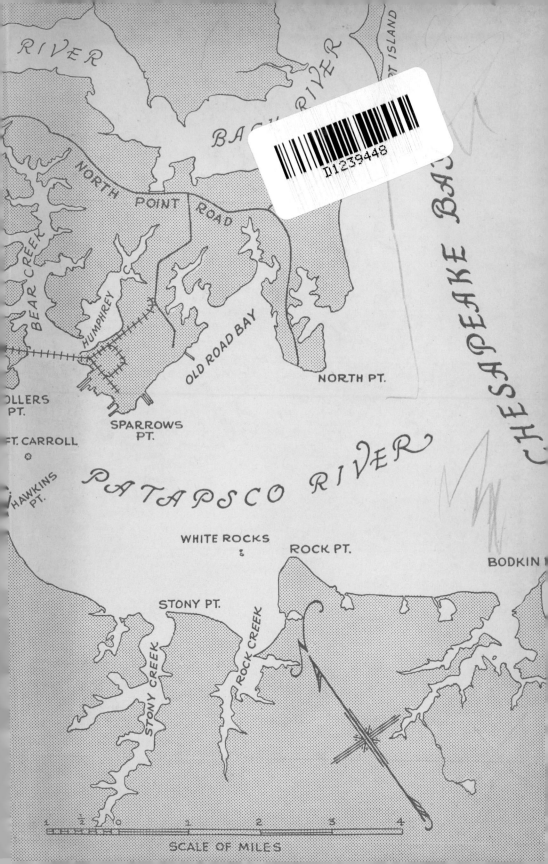

RIVER

BACK RIVER

T ISLAND

CHESAPEAKE BAY

NORTH POINT ROAD

BEAR CREEK

HUMPHREY

OLD ROAD BAY

NORTH PT.

OLLERS PT.

FT. CARROLL

SPARROWS PT.

HAWKINS PT.

PATAPSCO RIVER

WHITE ROCKS

ROCK PT.

BODKIN

STONY PT.

STONY CREEK

ROCK CREEK

SCALE OF MILES

1   ½   0   1   2   3   4

Baltimore on the Chesapeake

Baltimore

ON THE CHESAPEAKE

By

HAMILTON OWENS

ILLUSTRATED

Doubleday, Doran & Company, Inc.

GARDEN CITY, N. Y. 1941

PRINTED AT THE *Country Life Press*, GARDEN CITY, N. Y., U. S. A.

Acknowledgments

MOST of the main sources of the material in the following pages are mentioned in the text. It would be impossible
to list all the books, newspapers, magazines, doctoral theses,
family and business records on which I have drawn for in-
spiration as well as for detail. Certain individuals, however,
have been continuously helpful. Mr. Edgar Ellis, librarian
of *The Sun*, of Baltimore, did so much of the laborious
ferreting out and copying of ancient papers that I owe him
a special debt. Mr. Joseph L. Wheeler, librarian of the
great Enoch Pratt Free Library of Baltimore, and his
numerous assistants have been not only helpful but stimulating. Mr. Raphael Semmes of the Maryland Historical
Society, Mr. Louis H. Dielman, librarian of the Peabody
Institute of Baltimore, Mr. Richard Carl Medford, of the
Municipal Museum, have responded wholeheartedly to
every call. Mr. Howard I. Chapelle, of Cambridge, Maryland, has read and checked the chapter about the technical
evolution of the Baltimore clipper. My secretary, Miss
Ethel Armiger, has typed and retyped unflinchingly. My

Acknowledgments

wife has endured hearing each chapter read aloud and found something to praise in the dullest of them.

Indeed, if cooperation and encouragement could ensure the successful writing of a book this should be a masterwork. But as I have progressed painfully in the task of taking a complicated community apart decade after decade to see what made it tick I have conceived an ever-growing admiration for the skill and especially for the discretion of the professional historian who deliberately restricts his field as to both time and space. I am conscious of errors, omissions, and wrong deductions. The informed reader will doubtless find many of which I am not conscious. My generous collaborators, I hasten to assure him, are responsible for none of these. To me alone the blame.

H. O.

Contents

[vii]

Contents

Halftone Illustrations

LINECUT ILLUSTRATIONS

[ix]

CHAPTER I

Prologue

THE STORY OF BALTIMORE is a story of conflict.
There is dichotomy in every aspect of its history, in
every expression of its enterprise. Sometimes it seems that
several forces are pulling at it and that they will manage
to dismember it. Indeed, on occasion it has been all but dis-
membered and the citizens have engaged in violent struggle, the mob against the constituted authorities or one mob
against another. Yet despite these conflicts, some of which
have causes so subtle as to defy analysis, the city has grown
and throughout most of its years has prospered. It has
prospered because, in spite of man-made obstacles, Providence has been on its side. For Providence, working
through geography, made it a kind of funnel through
which the products of a large part of the middle-eastern
seaboard, of the great piedmont region behind it, and even
of the lands on the other side of the mountains inevitably
flow to the sea.

Man is set in his ways and, especially in Maryland, is
inclined to regard yesterday as more important and more

[1]

divine than tomorrow. At the very beginning Baltimore Town seemed an alien thing in the body politic of the palatinate on the Chesapeake Bay. The tobacco planters had a civilization of their own which seemed good to them. There was no allowance in their maturing scheme of things for something which was an excrescence, if not a cancer. To the planters, urban traders and workers seemed rude, grasping boors, not to be fitted into their gracious society which they had designed to mirror as exactly as possible the manorial life of England. That was the first great conflict and the most persistent one. It has never been resolved.

The traders, as they prospered, found it not always agreeable to give their allegiance to the sometimes stifling town which nourished them. Rather, they often gave first thought to the great country estates they acquired on the wind-swept hills and in the pleasant valleys to the north and west. They became gentlemen farmers and to that extent divorced themselves from those who were unable to leave the closely built-up streets. They even adopted, on occasion, the political doctrines of the planters and thus put themselves in temporary opposition to the source of their wealth and to the workingmen and small businessmen who contributed to it. This conflict, too, continues to express itself.

There are other conflicts, wider in scope and more tragic in their historical development. The tidewater country to the south of Baltimore is chiefly tobacco country and so up to the Civil War was dependent upon the labor of slaves. But all the rolling lands to the north and west are wheatlands and never did depend on slave labor. The two cultures first met and found their ways at variance in the narrow streets of Baltimore. That friction continued for a hundred years. In 1861 it burst into flame in those same narrow streets.

On the national scene the issue was decided in bloody battle. But in Baltimore, where the opposing forces were so nearly equal, it has never been decided and continues to rage, often inside the bosom of a single individual. The languid culture of the South dominates the social customs of its persistently manorial aristocracy. But in its commercial and industrial life it is often as bustling and as crude as a bumptious town in the Middle West.

There is a conflict also between the races. It is not an open conflict but it is there nevertheless. Baltimore has a reservoir of unskilled labor made of its vast Negro population. Such a reserve of labor fixes the wage scale. That scale can never move up rapidly because in addition to numerous Negro workers in Baltimore there is the still vaster reservoir of Negroes of the whole Southern coastal plain. These live at a bare subsistence level. If wages tend to move up in Baltimore it means a new influx of Southern Negroes to the town. The scale is thus forced down again. This makes for a kind of social stability, of course, but it does not necessarily make for wealth or happiness. Whether it is healthy or not depends on the point of view.

There is another element in Maryland which must not be overlooked in listing the conflicting forces which meet in Baltimore. This element is the Eastern Shore. Its culture is different from that of the tobacco country of southern Maryland and different, too, from that of the wheat country to the west and north. Its people's looks are different; they act differently and even talk differently. They are not wholly unified among themselves. Indeed, there is a marked distinction between those north of the Choptank River and those south of it. But in their differences with the rest of the state, and particularly in their differences with Baltimore City, they act as a unit.

Geography explains this in part, for the long, narrow peninsula which is the Eastern Shore is tied to the rest of the state only by bridges and ferries. Thus it is necessary for every Eastern Shoreman to be part mariner. It was the Eastern Shore which produced the first shipbuilders of the province of Maryland, and it was the Eastern Shore more than the rest of the state which developed the typical sailing craft of the Chesapeake. These craft came to their apotheosis in the Baltimore clipper, the type which in times of peace enabled Baltimore to compete on equal terms with the more maritime North and which in time of war gave Baltimore something very close to a monopoly on certain trade routes and in certain sinister undertakings. The Shore may not be a completely willing or complaisant partner in the enterprise of Baltimore but it is a full partner and a valuable one.

These conflicts and the many other related ones growing out of them, which will fit into their places in the narrative which follows, make for drama.

Yet even the discerning visitor could hardly find evidences of that drama. His first impression would be one of drabness, though he might be entertained by the long rows of red brick houses with their usually gleaming white marble steps. He would find the streets in the older parts of the town narrow, often ill kept, and leading to but few architectural climaxes. Here and there he might find interesting survivals of an age somewhat more gracious than our own but he would miss—if he were a Bostonian, for example—such dramatic episodes as the State House and the Common. Baltimore is not a capital. Even in the pretty little squares which dot the closely built-up sections he would see signs of neglect. It is hard to maintain beauty spots in the midst of a teeming varicolored population. Such a visitor would be put to it to discover the meaning of what lay before his eyes, to find the significant expression of the result of the effort of so many hundreds of thousands of individuals.

Nor could any Baltimorean point to such an expression, as New Yorkers, for instance, might point to their skyscrapers. But I like to think that Baltimore's ability to take its many conflicts as they come and to live, in spite of them, a casual and, on the whole, a charming life is due to the benign influence of the sea. If that is true, then the harbor, despite its being so well hidden from the visitor, is Baltimore's reason for being and its most significant achievement.

The town lies, of course, nearly two hundred miles from the ocean, but it is a salt tide which laves the docks and piers which line its nearly one hundred miles of foreshore. The hurried visitor would never know these docks and piers were there, so little are they in evidence. But if he will make but a small effort he can be carried in five or ten minutes to the top of Federal Hill, an eminence which lies on the southern side of the little basin which was the original haven of the town. After the Civil War, during which it was occupied by Federal troops under the command of General Ben Butler and sprouted big guns whose every muzzle pointed toward the restless city below, Federal Hill became a public park. Before that it bore the tower from which observers watched for the approach of ships and signaled their coming to the merchants in the town below.

From Federal Hill the visitor can see at a glance the surprising extent of the harbor of Baltimore and get some idea of the variety of the shipping which uses it. Just beneath him are the Light Street wharves from which ply the little steamboats which serve—to a diminishing extent, alas—the rivers of the bay. Next come the piers of the coastwise lines and the berths of the coffee, sugar, and banana boats from the West Indies and Latin America. After them, following the involuted shores, are the great terminals of the Baltimore and Ohio Railroad, the Pennsylvania Railroad, and the Western Maryland Railroad. Each of these terminals is equipped with huge elevators for the storage of wheat and corn for export, whose towering bulk dramatizes for the knowing observer the historic reason for Baltimore's existence. Farther out, getting now toward the distant horizon, he can see on the ever-widening river a great series of shipyards, with their steel ways and their cranes and derricks. And finally, on the horizon itself, he will see the belching stacks of the gasoline refineries which mark the ends of pipe lines bringing oil from the interior. He will see, too, the smoke and haze from the steel plants which contribute so largely to the economy of the community. He will know, in brief, that this is a major port and that despite all human conflict geography made it and still controls its destiny.

CHAPTER II

The Inland Sea

IN ALL NARRATIVES about this part of the world it is necessary to start with Captain John Smith. That brave, if boastful, adventurer did not discover the Chesapeake Bay. The Spaniards knew a great inland body of water which they called St. Mary's Bay and had some notions about taking it over. The Dutch knew it too. Smith was a man of restless energy and after he had got the colonists at Jamestown through their first winter, but long before the long list of their troubles had been half uncovered, he took a few men in a shallop—gentlemen and sailors—to see where this great bay really led. There is little doubt that he still cherished that hope which seems to have animated most explorers for two hundred years— that this might, after all, be the passage to the Indies.

The bay was much longer, much rougher, and altogether much more of an undertaking than he had counted upon. Contrary winds, drenching and long-continued rains, mosquitoes, and especially unfriendly savages made the trip a trying one. Some of the men were taken down with fever and once when a threatening band of Indians ap-

[7]

proached in canoes he had to make a show of numbers by putting the hats of the ill men, who were lying in the bottom, covered with tarpaulins, on the ends of sticks. Once, after several days of hard rowing, he had a full-fledged mutiny on his hands and had to make a speech, at once cajoling and threatening, to bring his gentlemen to their senses.

But he kept plugging up the bay, making notes for his map as he went along. He charted the marshy islands and the deep waters beyond them which lie off the lower eastern shore. To some of these islands he gave names, and one of them is still called Smith's Island after him. He noted also the wide and deep rivers on the western shore. He went up the Potomac as far as he dared and meticulously on his map he put a cross showing the extent of his own exploration. What is set down beyond that point, he explains, he got from Indians. He found the Patuxent and noted that it abounds in fish, as, indeed, it does to this day, to the enrichment of the people of Solomon's Island. Beyond he found the cliffs of Calvert which for some reason he decided to call "Richard's Clifts." He got a little confused when he reached what is now Talbot County on the Eastern Shore, and no wonder, for there isn't a more complex mingling of land and water this side of Holland. The present-day mariner had better not take this part of Smith's map for a guide. He missed, apparently, some of the western-shore rivers—West River, Rhodes River, South River, the Severn, and the Magothy are only vaguely suggested and with no indication that he guessed at their size, their variety, and their special qualities.

"Thirty leagues northward," says Smith in his journal accompanying the map, "is a river not inhabited yet navigable; for the red clay resembling bole Armoniac, we called it Bolus."

The contemporary traveler on the Patapsco River, for such is the present name of the River Bolus, is not likely to notice the red clay, unless by chance he come into the inner harbor of Baltimore on some spring morning after the winter's snows and rains have worked their will on Federal Hill and washed away the turf with which the city tries to keep it covered. Then he will see that it is, in fact, a great mass of red clay very like the substance of which the sharp-eyed captain was reminded. "Concurrent authorities," says Scharf, one of the several pedestrian chroniclers of Baltimore, "fix upon the Bolus and the Patapsco as one and the same river, either in words or by inference. Bozman says, 'The Patapsco is the Bolus River of Smith.'"

These are weighty authorities, and the burden of the evidence is with them. So we may perhaps assume that Captain John Smith, his gentlemen, and his sailors were the first white men to set foot on the site of what is now the city of Baltimore.

Leaving the Bolus, the captain and his men went up to the head of the bay, meeting the Indians and either fighting or befriending them, making their careful notes, working on their map, and finally reaching the unpleasant conclusion that here was no route to the Indies. Then back to Jamestown, its illnesses, uncertainties, and insurrections. One may suppose that there were other excursions after this first one, but the record doesn't show it. It was a long time before Jamestown passed out of the embryonic stage and became an organism sufficiently mature to grow and to move about.

[9]

Baltimore on the Chesapeake

One reason Jamestown didn't grow was that its colonists thought they had come there to search for metallic gold. It was years before it was borne in on them that an inscrutable Providence had employed a subterfuge and that their real function was to grow tobacco. Sir Walter Raleigh received his first tobacco pipe—a gift from Ralph Lane, first governor of the non-existent colony of Virginia—in 1586, though the Spaniards seem to have known of the weed nearly twenty years earlier. Its use was sporadic up to 1610 or perhaps even later. But the doctors of the time, having found a new drug, began acting as doctors always act under such circumstances and attributed all sorts of virtues to their new plaything. *Herba panacea* was one of the commonest of appellations for it. *Herba santa* indicated the grip it had got on their imaginations. Spenser called it "divine tobacco," showing that he was somehow in contact with the physicians of his time and, like poets today, believed what they told him. The habit thus took hold in the court and in upper society. Somebody saw an opportunity at last to make use of the colony of Virginia; plantings were essayed, and Virginia began to grow.

The early story of the development of Virginia is therefore the story of the growth of the tobacco habit and of Virginia's efforts to supply the market thus created. That story, in all its ramifications, is obviously too long for telling here. Tobacco grew best on the light soil of the Virginia tidewater, and once the demand was created it didn't take long for the capitalists and entrepreneurs of England to see the opportunity. What if it did "exhaust" the soil (of course it didn't really; it was, rather, the stupid cultivation which leached the soil), the Chesapeake was hundreds of miles long, and the rivers which bordered it added more hundreds. Every foot of it, as far as the adventurers could tell, could be made to produce tobacco in quantity. The rush to Virginia began. Men and women put themselves in pawn for years so as to be able to reach this El Dorado and partake, however belatedly, of the opportunities for wealth which it promised.

There were some complications, for not all the Indians were willing to give up their lands peaceably; they had to be driven off and kept in subjection. But this difficulty was mild compared to another the Virginians met. Charles, in a burst of generosity, had given a piece of Newfoundland to one of his favorites, a Catholic nobleman named George Calvert, the first Baron Baltimore. This tract, which Baltimore called Avalon, proved to be wholly impracticable, and so Charles grandly substituted another, that part of Virginia lying north of the Potomac and south of some rather vague line.

So the Virginians, moving up the bay, found their progress opposed and occasionally violently contested by the henchmen sent out, not by the first Baron Baltimore, but by Cecilius, his oldest son. This Baltimore, represented on the spot by his brother Leonard, fitted out two ships, the *Ark* and the *Dove*, loaded them with colonists rather carefully chosen, and sent them, late in 1633, to his new dominion. They landed in a little indentation on the north shore of the Potomac in the spring of 1634, acquired land for a town by a legitimate trade with the peaceable and, on the whole, industrious Indians they found there, and set up something very like an independent kingdom.

The settlement was not wholly a money-making adventure. The Calverts were Catholics, and in those days the lot of a Catholic in England was not a happy one. The

Calverts doubtless wanted to share in the money which Virginia seemed destined to produce. But they also wanted to provide something like a haven for their persecuted fellow religionists and perhaps, in the event of more serious trouble, a refuge for themselves. Religious toleration, at least for Christians, was a fact in the early days of this establishment, and, though it was subjected to attack and to occasional limitation as the political tides ebbed and flowed, the notion was never completely extirpated.

In any event, the Virginia Company and its settlers were destined to find their way blocked as they attempted to continue to move up the Chesapeake. One of their number, a Captain Thomas Claiborne, had established a trading post midway up the bay on the Eastern Shore. It must have been something of a shock to that gentleman, who was doing so thriving a business with the Indians that he had what amounted to a small village, to find a strange sail come into his little harbor one morning and to be told by the emissary who landed that he must move out forthwith. Of course he didn't. There were several pitched battles between his Virginians and Calvert's Marylanders before London intervened and settled the affair. Claiborne's influence was never completely obliterated from this part of Maryland. The Catholic caste which to this day is clearly marked in Southern Maryland (i.e., the lower western shore) does not extend to the Eastern Shore. Southern Maryland is Cavalier and Catholic. The Eastern Shore is Cavalier, in spots at least, and Protestant.

But these quarrels and their political repercussions remained secondary to the related primary businesses of the Chesapeake region. Those primary businesses were the sale of land and the growing of tobacco. Those who got grants of land in suitable locations—which meant, in the early days, almost anywhere along the littoral of the lower bay and its rivers, with the exception of the swamplands—were almost certain to get rich, provided they could command sufficient capital to employ the large number of hands necessary to produce and cure the crop.

Tobacco growing, by the standards which then prevailed in Virginia and which still prevail in Maryland, is a tedious process. The seed must be planted on the south side of a sheltered slope—a small clearing in a wood is excellent—as early as February. This nursery must be carefully watched during the spring and early summer. The seedlings will not stand transplanting until the soil is fully warmed up by the hot sun and until it has given up most of the moisture with which the spring rains impregnate it. Then the tender plants are set out in symmetrical rows by hand. If heavy rain falls immediately after transplanting they are often washed out and must be set again. After they have taken root they must be regularly cultivated to keep the weeds down. The suckers must be removed as fast as they come.

When, in late summer, the sweet-smelling flowers appear they must be cut off. All the strength of the roots must go into the leaves. Some growers think that they get a better average return if they remove the lower and coarser leaves. Others allow them all to mature and do their grading later.

When ripe—usually in late August or September—the plants are cut down; the leaves are stripped off one by one, bundled, wrapped, and "speared," which is to say, impaled on pointed sticks about four feet long. These sticks, with their burdens of weed, are hung in barns of a special type, where the crop is "cured." The barns differ from others not only in having racks from which the sticks are hung but also in having the alternate vertical planks on their sides hinged to permit the free passage of air when the weather is fair. The aroma arising from a curing barn on a warm day is surely one of the most intoxicating in the whole realm of perfumes.

Virginia now uses flue-curing in most of its successful tobacco-growing regions, but Maryland, a more conservative state, clings to the air-curing method just described. Its great disadvantage is the months taken to complete the process. Tobacco hung in September is not regarded as fully ready for the market until the following June at the earliest. When it is cured it must be packed (i.e., put by screw pressure into large hogsheads especially built for the purpose) and so, finally, sent to market.

The whole process—from February of one year until June or July of the next—takes about sixteen months. During that long period the farmer must support himself and must pay his numerous hands. Thus his working capital must be large. Small wonder that, in the early days, at least, tobacco growers regarded themselves as big businessmen. Small wonder also that they resorted to indentured servants and later to slave labor to solve their problem. Small wonder also that they became debtors to the British merchants who "financed" their crops and that when the Revolution came even the proudest and richest of them accepted the opportunity to emerge for a while from this galling relationship.

Tobacco was the money crop of the region. In the beginning it was more. It was the sole reason for the existence of Virginia and, if we leave out of account the idea of a religious haven which was in the back of the minds of the Catholics, Quakers, and other dissidents who flocked to Maryland, it was the sole excuse for that colony too. Of course it did not long remain so. People can't eat or drink tobacco, and Marylanders, like other Englishmen of the time, were conscious of the pleasures of the table and of alcohol in dilute aqueous solution. Fortunately—and the various promotion pamphlets issued by the realtors of the time did not overlook this aspect of things—the waters swarmed with sea food, including terrapin, oysters, and crabs; the land teemed with game and was magnificently adapted to the growing of those fruits which were regarded as luxuries in the old country.

These things did not cost money. They were at the disposal of everyone, from servant to master, who took the trouble to gather them. The Indians taught the cultivation and use of maize, just as they had earlier taught the New Englanders the same arts. They introduced the settlers to the sweet potato also. The edge of every woodland was—and is—a jungle of wild vines, many of them producing grapes which could be made into wine of a sort. The alluvial soil was so rich and so free of rock and the rainfall so abundant and usually so well timed that a mere scratching with hoe and rake ensured an overwhelming crop of vegetables. During most of the year poor people needed but few clothes. During eight months of the year fuel was unnecessary, save for cooking, and it was present in abundance at every man's door.

So in the early days when every plantation was a world in itself there was little need for money. When the crop was shipped and the planter found himself possessed of a credit in London he was under a temptation, to which he usually yielded, of using at least a part of that credit for the purchase of outright luxuries and adornments. It was a period when in London dandyism was at its height. Dandyism is contagious, and there are records which show that the planters of Maryland and Virginia caught the disease. It was the London credit also which accounted for the great masses of silver plate which the planters gradually collected for the libraries which a few of them built up, for the racing stables which they started, and for many of those evidences of aristocratic culture which have done so much to build up the myth of the old South. That there was a culture and that it was essentially a class culture no one can deny. That in the early days it was a culture which went much deeper than the surface may well be doubted. Some of the great lords of Maryland manors in those early days signed documents with a mark, while their servants frequently were able to write their names in a fair hand. The culture that existed was, I fear, more like that of a boom town in the West. It was a boughten culture shipped by the ton from London.

If we leave out of account the political struggles, with which we are not much concerned and which were, in any event, always secondary to the growing of tobacco, we shall be able to see that such a region was certain to be taken up quickly by men anxious to partake of the relatively secure and often luxurious life which it offered. The first settlement in Maryland, that at St. Marys City, on St. Marys River, a characteristic inlet from the broader Potomac, was founded in 1634. In less than ten years newcomers had taken up grants beyond the Patuxent, the next river to the north on the western shore of the Chesapeake. The settlers advanced up the bay in great leaps. They passed beyond Richard's Clifts, by now known as the Cliffs of Calvert, and swarmed into the lower and more hospitable creeks and rivers of what is now Anne Arundel County. Some of these patentees were Quakers who had fled from Virginia. Others were members of the same sect who had come straight from the old country. Anne Arundel County was relatively thickly settled—along the shores of the navigable streams, at least—by 1650.

Annapolis, first called Providence, was founded as a port of entry in 1649 by Puritan exiles from Virginia. Its name was changed thirty-five years later, and it was made the seat of the royal government which had by then displaced that of the Lords Baltimore. From then on it was the chief town of the colony. It seems to have taken on an urban character quite early in its history and delighted to call itself the Athens (or Paris) of America. There were but few towns in Maryland in those days, and, indeed, the only reason for any town at all was to provide a seat for the government. Nevertheless, the planters, many of whom had money to spend on luxuries, as we have seen, found here a place to display their wealth, and a number of them built elaborate houses in the town and by lavish display angled for the favor of the current royal governor and his entourage.

The settlement of the colony moved on apace. Men of various nationalities came down from the North—Germans from Pennsylvania and directly from their fatherland, Swedes from Delaware and New Jersey. At least one Bohemian, Augustine Hermann, was granted an extensive stretch on a river near the very head of the bay. It is still called Bohemia River in his honor.

CHAPTER III

Towns by the Dozen

TOBACCO is a money crop. It cannot be eaten or worn. Like all staples, it commands a varying price in the market. The rush to grow it for a long time kept barely abreast of spread of the habit of using it. So long as that was true the planters had a relatively easy time of it. They could live lavishly and even go into debt—as many of them did—because they knew that when their hogsheads were landed in England the next ship back would bring a cargo that would more than restore their credit. They neglected the purely subsistence aspect of agriculture, putting in just enough corn and wheat to supply their own needs. They learned very early that "tobacco exhausts the soil" but they didn't bother to try to save it, because back of their tidewater plantations there was a whole continent to be had almost for the asking. When one field gave signs of wearing out they cleared another piece of woodland and planted that. The cultivation of tobacco thus spread far inland up to the tidal limits of the rivers and even into the low hills of the piedmont. County after county was organized.

Towns by the Dozen

This was true of the western shore. It does not quite describe the course of events on the Eastern Shore. That is a long, narrow peninsula, its bay shore indented with dozens, even hundreds, of tidal rivers and creeks. The water area is almost as great as that of the land. Go inland only a few miles and you reach the low divide. On the other side of that the streams run toward the ocean. There is no hinterland on the Eastern Shore. The planters who took up grants there could move inland only a short distance before finding themselves back to back with others moving inland from the seacoast. Hence, out of sheer geographical necessity, the Eastern Shoremen began to have early doubts about the wisdom of putting all their eggs into the tobacco basket. It is hard to get dates which indicate the change in agricultural methods, but all the local historians of the Shore are agreed that cereal crops were substituted for tobacco on "worn-out" fields quite early in the history of the region. Long before the Revolution corn, wheat, oats, and rye were common produce there, while they were still relative novelties on the other side of the bay.

This enforced abandonment of tobacco as the staple crop had results which are apparent today even to the casual wayfarer. The farms of the Eastern Shore, taking them by and large, are better farms, making their owners more prosperous, than those on the lower western shore. For miles and miles in counties like Charles, St. Marys, Calvert, and Anne Arundel, the so-called "tobacco counties," the land looks poor. Much of it is simply abandoned to scrub pine. Bereft even of grass in many places, it leaches and washes into deep gullies. Many of the little creeks have filled up and become marshes. The inhabitants, some of whom still have the manners of great ladies and gentlemen, live at or near the subsistence level.

The Eastern Shore had earlier premonitions than the western of what dependence on tobacco might mean to the economy of the community. Released from that thralldom, it worked out relatively early a better-balanced way of life. Its planters grew tobacco on new lands and, rolling their hogsheads to their wharves or to one of their own ports, loaded them on ships bound for England, thus getting their credits in London. For the rest, they grew cereals and, later, magnificent fruits and vegetables, thereby living better themselves and becoming, gradually, the truckers for the towns when they finally began to put in their appearance.

The western shore, on the other hand, was so closely tied to tobacco and for a long time thought so exclusively in terms of tobacco that a failure of the crop or, what happened more frequently as time went on, a glut in the market brought them time after time close to ruin.

In the latter part of the seventeenth century many of the leading men of the time expressed their fears about the future of tobacco and wished that more of the planters would take to raising grain. At one time the assembly decreed that if a man who owned a mill site refused to utilize it any other citizen wishing to establish a mill there could seize the land and leave it to the courts to decide what was due the original owner. This was probably a bit of *ad hoc* legislation, but it does indicate both the fears and the hopes of the colonists.

Up nearly to the end of the seventeenth century—except for St. Marys and Providence (Annapolis)—there had been no towns in Maryland worthy the name. This lack

of urbanization was a trial to the successive Lords Baltimore, and they were constantly urging that towns be established. It is probable that they understood so little of
the economy and way of life of their tenants that they
thought it was purely stubbornness which prevented the
growth of towns. It was nothing of the sort. It was, rather,
because agriculture was the natural way of life of the people and they thought of no other. Every planter who came
out from England received a grant. Few were given more
than a thousand acres. Most of them received a hundred
or a hundred and fifty. If they wanted more they had to
acquire it from other owners by purchase or lease.

Moreover, a law of the colony held that every redemptioner, once he had served the time necessary to pay his
passage money, should receive a grant of fifty acres from
the proprietor as well as the usual gift of money (i.e., tobacco), clothes, and farming implements from his master.
A redemptioner might reasonably hope in a few years to
acquire more acres and to die, finally, a planter in his own
right, surrounded by sons, each of whom might acquire
lands.

Every plantation, in early Maryland as in the other tobacco-growing regions, was a little self-contained world.
It was either on or near navigable water. There were
canoes, pinnaces, and, later, sloops for visiting neighbors
and for carrying tobacco to the ship anchored in the roads.
Towns did not exist, because there was no need for them.

Still, in loyal obedience to the wishes of the proprietor
and of Queen Anne, efforts were made to give them what
they wanted. In 1683 the Assembly passed a law calling
for the establishment of towns, and a flood of charters was
granted. On South River, which is a singularly beautiful

estuary with a deep and relatively wide channel, some enterprising spirits laid out a town which they called, ambitiously, Londontown. It died early, and only a few signs remain today to mark its site. A more realistic effort was made on the Bush River, farther up the bay. This town also was laid out in 1683, but even the natives of the region are hard put to it to point it out. This town was called Baltimore after the proprietary, but its life was so short that ten years later another Baltimore, this one in Dorchester County, on the Eastern Shore, was boldly undertaken. I have been able to find no one to do more than suggest where it might have been.

As each county was organized it had to have a county seat, with a courthouse and, usually, a church. It had to have a general store and, because it was invariably built on the water in the early days, it had to have a wharf. It would also have roads or trails leading to the backlands. One such town was called Joppa. It was the first county seat of Baltimore County and it lay at the very place where the "falls" (i.e., that part of a river above the tide line) of the Little Gunpowder River meets its tidal estuary. It lay, that is, close to the junction of piedmont and coastal plain, about twenty miles northeast of the site of the town to which we are going to devote ourselves.

Joppa enjoyed a fair prosperity for almost fifty years. There is still a house or two on the site, and the expert eye can trace the outline of the church and the courthouse. But the Little Gunpowder is neither broad nor deep, and the swift flow of its falls brought down such increasing quantities of silt as the fields were cleared for tobacco that there was no hope in those early days of keeping its channels open. As long as Joppa could retain the courthouse it remained a place of some importance, as the persistence of such roads as the meandering Joppa Road and the Old Court Road testify. But after Baltimore got under way public opinion dictated that the larger town be the county seat, and the move was made. That was the end of Joppa.

The estuary of the Patapsco River is broader and deeper and reaches farther inland toward the hills than any of the streams selected for these earlier towns. It might be said that its tides lap at the very hills of the piedmont. It is fed, moreover, by a whole series of swiftly flowing streams, every one of which offered innumerable sites for mills, though it is hardly likely that these advantages were especially regarded by the planters hereabouts. The hills which border it and the streams which feed it are rich in iron ore, attractive to the landowners who found themselves possessed of it. Moreover, by the turn of the century a well-marked road had been worn through the forests from the northeast and meandered on toward the south. Another trail came in from the Pennsylvania Dutch country to the north. There was hardwood timber in abundance to the north and west; there were pines and other softwoods to the south. In the hills there was slate, granite, and even marble. All these things converged then, as they converge today, at the precise point where the tides of the Patapsco wash the foot of the hills, of which John Smith's Bolus is still the most striking.

As we have seen, the legislature had been chartering towns by the dozen—it "erected" forty-two of them at once in 1706—and when several gentlemen of Baltimore County petitioned for a town on the Patapsco the members probably thought that they were wasting their time and energies again. Still, they prepared to pass the bill.

[23]

Here, for a moment, we must be geographically precise. Several "falls," as I have said, feed the tidal estuary of the Patapsco. Each of them has scooped out a channel which the brackish water fills. From another point of view, it might be said that the tide rushed in to drown the valleys of several flowing streams. The main stream is, of course, the falls of the Patapsco River. Its tidal estuary is today called Middle Branch. Another stream, called Gwynns Falls, has an estuary called Spring Gardens, which is a branch, in its turn, of Middle Branch. This estuary, with pleasant hills around it, is deep and wide. Sizable ships of those days could sail almost to the point where its falls emptied into it. The high shore marking its southern side looked to the residents of the vicinity as a likely place for a town, and it was this shore which they decided to utilize for their venture.

This particular area, known as Moales Point, belonged to a gentleman named John Moale, recently come from Devonshire. Mr. Moale was a man of some substance and was called a merchant. He had bought the land because it contained a deposit of iron ore out of which he expected to make considerable money. English law forbade the colonists to use iron in manufactures but it did permit them to produce pig iron and later even bar iron. The English manufacturers even hoped for a time that this American iron would make them independent of the Swedish product. Shipping it from Maryland was no problem either. Tobacco was a light, bulky cargo, and the ships used the pig iron for ballast. Thus a planter who had a deposit of ore and could command the capital necessary for the erection of a "furnace" had an additional, though not impressive, source of money income.

Mr. Moale was a member of the legislature but was not in his seat when the bill was brought in setting up a town on his property. Word of the impending blow to his plans was brought to him, however, and, according to Scharf, he immediately "posted off" to Annapolis. There, taking his seat in the house, he protested so violently against the outrage that the bill was changed. The would-be incorporators had to be satisfied with a site on what was called Cole's Harbor.

Cole's Harbor was on still another branch of the tidal estuary of the Patapsco, called Northwest Branch. Here it was the valley of Jones Falls which the tide had invaded. Cole's Harbor was a small, shallow, swamp-bordered backwater lying to the west of the mouth of the falls. John Smith's hill of bole Armoniac marked the south side of it, but the other was marshy and generally uninviting. It was the best the developers could get, however, and so they accepted it.

The act called for the laying out of a town of sixty acres on the land belonging to Charles Carroll and Daniel Carroll, brothers, but occupied at that time by a tenant named John Fleming. The commissioners named for surveying the town and marking it out in lots were Major Thomas Tolley, William Hamilton, William Buckner, Dr. George Walker, Richard Gist (sometimes called Guest), Dr. George Buchanan, and Colonel William Hammond. They were all tobacco planters of some substance and owned land in the vicinity. The date of the passage of the bill was August 8, 1729.

CHAPTER IV

The Best-Laid Plans

SOME CHRONICLERS would have us believe that the incorporators of Baltimore Town were men of great vision and that they foresaw with miraculous intelligence the destiny which awaited the town which they founded. The evidence all points to the contrary view. The chances are that their own immediate convenience and necessities brought them to undertake the venture. The plantations were extending inland, which meant that the tobacco hogsheads had to be transported overland to deep water where they could be loaded on the waiting ships. This transportation usually involved fitting a sort of axle to the hogshead and a pole to the axle. A yoke of oxen provided the motive power. The rolling was over stony tracks through the forests. Such rough handling affected adversely the quality of the dry leaf within the hogshead. Hence it was important to the planter handicapped by lack of water front of his own that the loading point be as near at hand as possible. This probably accounts for the extraordinary number of "towns," so called, and the rush of charters for them. Baltimore was designed to be that sort of town.

There were other towns all around it, much nearer than Joppa. There was a landing place about five or six miles up the main stream of the river from Mr. Moale's point called Elk Ridge Landing. Here tobacco grown in the upper Patapsco Valley was loaded on barges or other light draft boats and floated downstream to the deep water off Moale's place. Big ships could anchor there and await cargo, which they couldn't do in Cole's Harbor. Mr. Moale took advantage of his situation to open a store and trade with the waiting captains and with the planters who came down to load their tobacco. Elk Ridge Landing and Moales Point were thus in direct competition with Baltimore Town.

There was another chartered town on Whetstone Point, where Middle Branch and Northwest Branch came together. This probably served only the plantations on the long neck of which Whetstone Point is the apex.

Mr. William Jones, who operated a store across Jones Falls from the site selected for Baltimore Town, got a charter for a town of ten acres the year after the venture of the Carroll brothers and their associates. Three years after the Baltimore charter another ten acres was set aside on the land "whereon Edward Fell keeps store," and the town of Fells Point was begun. This was a truly maritime undertaking, for Edward Fell's brother William was a ship carpenter and wanted a place where he could exercise his art. The water off Fells Point was deep enough for a shipyard, and the town on it thus had advantages which Baltimore could not offer.

Thus the territory on which the proposed Baltimore Town could draw for tobacco was very limited. But the incorporators went ahead with their plan nevertheless.

On the twelfth of December, 1730, the county surveyor, Mr. Philip Jones, came to oversee the commissioners in their laying out of the town. They drove their first stake at the edge of the marsh near what is now the northwest corner of Lombard and Light streets. Their line ran roughly northwestward toward what was then called the Great Eastern Road to a great gully which would be near the present Sharp Street. Then they turned toward the northeast, along what are now McClellan's Alley and Crooked Lane, and farther until they came to a sort of clay cliff which overhung Jones Falls, which then made a big loop or bend in that part of the region. They followed the meandering course of the stream to a point where it was bordered by a broad marsh just east of the present Gay Street. There being no point in going farther in that direction, they turned their line south until they hit the other marshland on the north side of the basin, following the low banks thence westward until they came to their starting point. Scharf says that the area thus enclosed was shaped like an ancient lyre. To most eyes it looks like an arrowhead pointing toward the west.

Through this area they ran three main streets. Long (later Market and now Baltimore) Street ran due east and west for approximately thirty-four hundred feet. Intersecting it at right angles were the present Calvert Street, which began at the Falls and ran south to the marsh bordering the river, and the present Charles, a little over four hundred feet to the west of Calvert but strictly paralleling it. In addition they marked off nine lanes or alleys. Then they subdivided the whole into sixty lots of about an acre each and opened an office for "takers-up."

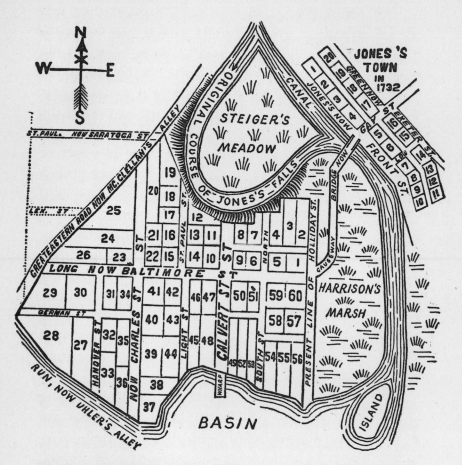

PLAN OF BALTIMORE TOWN, AS LAID OFF IN JANU-
ARY 1730, BY MR. PHILIP JONES, COUNTY SURVEYOR.
AFTER SCHARF.

Mr. Charles Carroll, one of the proprietors, took up the first lot, No. 49, on January 14. It lay on the east side of Calvert Street, nearest the river. The commissioners, or several of them, followed in succession. Under the terms of the sale each taker-up had to build a house with an area of four hundred square feet within a certain period. If he failed his land would be resold by the commissioners or revert to the proprietors. A number of those who made purchases found it inconvenient to build, and their land was disposed of to several speculators, one after the other, before being improved.

The sale of lots was discouragingly slow, and so, too, was the arrival of tobacco for shipment. In 1739—nine years after the founding of the town—Captain Michael Wilson, of the ship *Parad and Gally*, sailed as close to Baltimore as he dared and advertised in the *Maryland Gazette* of Annapolis (as the law bade him do) that he was prepared to load tobacco there. According to the accounts, he received exactly one hogshead, consigned by Avarila Day to Messrs. Delmitt and Heathwat of London. The freight rate in that year was seven pounds sterling per ton. Therefore, if the hogshead he took aboard weighed the customary five hundred pounds his total takings out of Baltimore on that voyage were less than two pounds sterling. The *Parad and Gally* is said by some historians to be the very first vessel to take on cargo in Baltimore, but this is difficult to believe, for the men responsible for the venture would almost certainly use the "facilities" of the port. Yet it does show that the town had no special attraction for the generality of the planters of the neighborhood and that Elk Ridge Landing, Fells Point, and Whetstone Point were quite capable of serving their needs. Even as late as

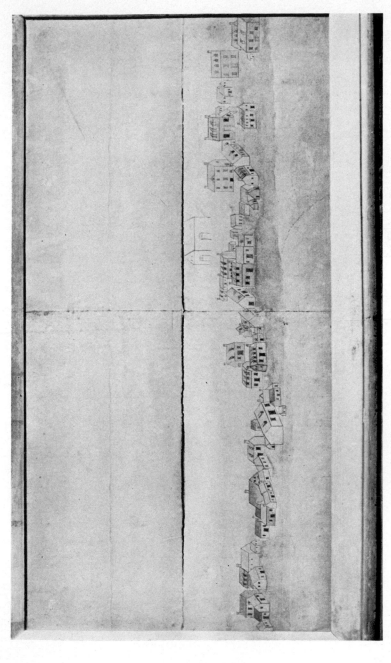

JOHN MOALE'S DRAWING OF BALTIMORE IN 1752

Moale, then a small boy, made this drawing of Baltimore twenty-three years after its beginning and before the grain trade had stimulated its first boom. The original, unaccountably preserved, is in the possession of the Maryland Historical Society. This drawing is the basis of the Currier print reproduced on the front end papers of this volume and of many other early pictures.

1748 only seven ships came into the Northwest Branch in the course of the year and advertised there for cargo.

There are notations in the record which show how feeble was the enterprise of the town and the poverty which was its lot. In 1745 an Indian scare ran through the colony. The dwellers in the region felt themselves very much on the frontier. The result was a vote by the commissioners to build a stockade around it. Thus Baltimore became perhaps the only walled village in the several colonies. Some say that the stockade was not really built to keep out Indians but, rather, to keep wandering hogs from making their wallows in the streets. In any event, it did not serve either purpose for very long. The ensuing winter was a cold one, and, bit by bit, the stockade disappeared. The needy inhabitants, seeking firewood, slipped out by night and carried away its palings one by one. By 1748 it was nearly gone, and a public subscription was taken up for rebuilding it. This time the terms of the subscription leave no doubt that it was raised, not against the depredations of Indians, but against those of hogs and geese.

There were other homely and irritating troubles. One of the first signs of enterprise in the community was the raising of a fund to build a bridge across Jones Falls, at the place where the Great Eastern Road crossed the stream, in order that there might be proper communication between Baltimore and Jones Town. It wasn't long before a freshet carried away the bridge, and it had to be rebuilt. A little later the Assembly, by petition, added Jones Town to Baltimore Town proper, thus eliminating the former as a legal entity but by no means extinguishing it from the public consciousness. The neighborhood across the falls, in the vicinity of Gay Street, remains Old Town to this day, with a special quality and a special civic pride of its own. The reasons for the alliance are obscure, but it seems likely that the compelling factor was to make Jones Town pay at least a share of the cost of keeping up the bridge.

In 1752 Mr. John Moale's son, then but a lad, was moved to make a drawing of the village. By some chance the original of that drawing survived and is reproduced herewith. Many of the early drawings and engravings of Baltimore are based upon it. It shows that after twenty-two years of chartered existence Baltimore Town consisted of but twenty-five houses, all of them small and insignificant.

The truth was, of course, that the commissioners and everyone else in the region had assumed that Baltimore Town was to be just another tobacco port. Thinking only in terms of tobacco, they had overlooked some rather important happenings to the north of them.

CHAPTER V

Romulus and Remus

IN 1745, OR THEREABOUTS, a ship came up the Delaware River and landed, among other passengers, two young Irishmen named Stevenson. They were both physicians, educated at Oxford and therefore presumably of good birth and not impecunious. The ship which had brought them over had come to get, not tobacco, but flour. That is why it sailed up the Delaware. There was but little tobacco grown in Pennsylvania, for tobacco was a difficult crop both to grow and to transport. Because of its dependence on slave and indentured labor it implied a form of social and economic organization as distasteful to the Quakers scattered along the Delaware as to the Germans who were filling up the country back of William Penn's early settlements. But the rolling lands of that region were especially suited to the growing of wheat, and the several streams provided sites for mills. There was a sort of wheat boom going on in Pennsylvania at this time. Not much of it was shipped to England. The Corn Laws, which put heavy imposts on imported wheat except in times of great scarcity, kept that market pretty well closed. But Ireland, and especially Northern Ireland, was a good market. There was a sale also in parts of Scotland. A market was developing in the West Indies, too, as we shall see a little later.

The two young doctors had been born in Londonderry. John, the elder, first saw the light of day in 1718. His brother Thomas was two or three years younger. They were not Quakers but Presbyterians. Maybe that is why, instead of taking up grants in Pennsylvania, they moved down to Maryland. It is possible that they thought they were still in Pennsylvania, for at that time William Penn was engaged in a boundary argument with the Calverts and was claiming land as far south almost as the present site of the District of Columbia. The good William wanted access to the Chesapeake Bay.

Thomas, younger of the two Stevensons, was an excellent practitioner. He acquired a piece of land just outside the limits of Baltimore Town, overlooking the trail coming down from York, and with the money he had brought from the other side built himself a fine house. It was by far the most imposing structure the community had yet seen. He called his place Parnassus, but the cynical townsfolk, dispirited because their town hadn't yet justified itself and filled their pockets with riches, nicknamed it "Stevenson's Folly."

Dr. Thomas, nevertheless, opened his surgery, laid out his remedies, cleaned his instruments, and began his ministrations. One of the things he knew about was applicable to an immediate problem. Smallpox was the scourge of the times. George Washington had contracted it at about this era and carried the scars for the rest of his life. But Dr. Henry Stevenson knew that a man inoculated deliberately with the mild disease called cowpox was thereafter immune to the more dangerous ailment it resembled. When, a year or so after he moved into his new house, there was a specially severe visitation of smallpox he persuaded a few of the townspeople to try his new method, using Parnassus as a hospital for them during the period of their infection. The results were so enheartening that his place in the community was established. Thereafter he was a pillar of society, and his name appears in nearly every list of prominent citizens. He was one of the organizers of the first medical society in Baltimore and in that limited sense might be called a progenitor of the Johns Hopkins Hospital and Medical School.

His life, however, was not uneventful, for, true to the tradition of the land from which he sprang, he gave his allegiance to the King of England during the Revolution and even served as a surgeon in the British army from 1776 to 1786. In the latter year he returned to Baltimore and to the general practice of medicine, continuing his useful work until he died in 1814, when the British were once again at war with their former colonies.

Dr. John, the older brother, may or may not have been a good physician. It may be that he did the calling while Dr. Thomas confined himself mostly to office and hospital practice. In any event, he was a great rover and soon, despite the evil quality of the few roads which existed, got to know the country round about much better than most of those who had lived there longer.

He did not fail to notice the multiplicity of problems which beset the tobacco growers. He lived through at least one period when the price which the stuff fetched in London hardly paid the freight and left little or nothing for the grower who had shipped it. He saw in how few years the fields which in the beginning grew superior tobacco deteriorated until the coarse weed which they produced brought but poor prices in even a good market. He remembered the thriving business in wheat and flour which was being carried on between Philadelphia and his native Londonderry. He saw the rolling hills so soon leached out when devoted to tobacco but so productive, despite the leaching, when sown in wheat and corn.

He lived with his brother on the mean little road winding down from York and he probably talked with the dispirited Germans who had been persuaded to settle along that road in the belief that they would make fortunes out of tobacco. We know he got as far west as Frederick, where tobacco planters were struggling with the almost impossible problem of getting their perishable product to tidewater. He walked along the many swift-flowing streams which ran down the hills into the muddy and inconsequential harbor of Baltimore Town and noted, as an alert man would, that the little mills for grinding their own flour which the planters erected alongside them would just as easily work twenty-four hours a day every day in the week and every week in the year as they would for the occasional few hours which their owners demanded of them.

Dr. John, in brief, saw the obvious, the thing to which their own addiction to tobacco and the manorial culture founded on tobacco had blinded the planters of the whole upper shores of the Chesapeake.

So Dr. John sat down and wrote a letter. It was addressed to a friend of his in Ireland. We do not know who that friend was, though it is likely that he did business in

Londonderry, Dr. John's native town. In due course a reply came. A ship was coming to Baltimore to load flour.

This news, which we may be sure Dr. John did not keep to himself, was perhaps the most significant piece of information ever bruited about in Baltimore, either before or since. To him it meant that he must go to work. He set about contracting for vast quantities of flour. The word "vast" is used relatively, for up to now the planters had grown wheat grudgingly and almost entirely for their own use. Dr. John may have had to go as far afield as southern Pennsylvania to command a sufficient supply to make a cargo. The planters, unaccustomed to dealing in such a commodity, may have accepted Dr. John's promises to pay with misgivings. Still, they had little to lose and everything to gain.

Almost certainly it was in 1750 that the ship finally arrived and discharged whatever cargo she had brought. It was probably mostly brick for ballast, for the credit of Maryland planters was not especially good at this period. In all probability she anchored off Fells Point, for the harbor of Baltimore Town had not sufficient depth for most vessels which made the trans-Atlantic journey. After a while, however, her cargo was on board, and she sailed out, probably with the tobacco fleet.

We may be sure that Dr. John was there to see her off. Perhaps some of those who had been infected with his hopes were there as well. But most of the townsfolk—the obscure shopkeepers and the tenants of the houses the purchasers had built on speculation—were not impressed.

The ship cleared and on her way, there was nothing for Dr. John to do but wait. It may be that he helped out Dr. Thomas with his rounds of visits to the sick. It is more probable that, with his sanguine temperament, he began to figure on the repaying of the planters who had entrusted their flour to him and on his own possible profits. It may be that he made tentative contracts for further cargoes should this venture be successful.

The venture was successful. Word came from his correspondent in Ireland that the flour had been sold at a good price and that further cargoes could likewise be disposed of. That settled it as far as Dr. John was concerned. Thenceforth he was a merchant. He built himself a considerable house right in the town on the south side of Long Street at Grant Alley. Behind the house, toward the marshes, he built a warehouse. We know this because the warehouse was still standing when the worthy doctor died. He redoubled his efforts to promote the growth and shipment of flour.

With this undertaking begins the real history of Baltimore Town. It is true that if Dr. John Stevenson hadn't conceived the idea some other man would almost certainly have stumbled upon it. But it was he who conceived it and he who put it into execution. From then on there was no doubt in the mind of any Baltimorean that his town had a future. Moreover, he knew exactly what was to be the economic foundation of that future. Baltimore was to be the port for the exportation of flour.

The title which heads this chapter is no invention for the purposes of this book. All Baltimore—all Maryland, in fact —regarded Dr. John Stevenson as the true founder of Baltimore Town. In 1771 Mr. William Eddis, then holding the office of Surveyor of the Port in Annapolis, wrote a letter to a friend in London. Eddis was a voluminous writer and he set down in detail all that he saw and heard. In this par-

ticular letter he describes the arrival in Maryland of the
new governor, Mr. Robert Eden, brother-in-law of the
Proprietor. Eden was a hospitable man, much given to
entertaining. One of his first distinguished guests was
General Sir William Draper, who was making a tour of all
the colonies, working his way up from Carolina. Eden says
that Sir William had heard of Baltimore and asked to be
taken to see it. Mr. Eden took him. Indeed, he himself was
paying his first visit to the place. They demanded to know
who was responsible for the growing town, its bustling
enterprise, its general air of knowing where it was going
and why. The townspeople brought forward Dr. John
Stevenson, whereupon Sir William, in a graceful and elegant speech, bestowed upon him the title of "the American
Romulus."

But Baltimore's Romulus remains, in spite of all search-
ing, a vague and misty individual. He was one of the
founders of the First Presbyterian Church in Baltimore. As
the Revolutionary War approached his sympathies seem to
have tended to the loyalist side, though, unlike his brother,
he played no active role. He served on at least two committees—he presided over one of them—to pass on the
propriety of the importation of certain goods while the
merchants were bound by the non-importation agreement.
In both cases he voted for the importation of the goods but
was overruled by his colleagues. In 1777, after the war was
well under way, he was living as far off as Frederick on a
farm he had acquired there. Here he must have done himself fairly well, for William Eddis, the correspondent
whom we have previously mentioned, visited him and ex-
claimed over his hospitality. But Eddis was an officer of
the crown and an outspoken loyalist, expecting every day

to be evicted from his post as Surveyor of the Port of Annapolis. It is therefore to be assumed that the worthy doctor had retired to this relatively remote spot to avoid the stresses and strains of a war for which he had little stomach. He spent his energies in the pursuit of agriculture, and we may be sure that it was the clearing of fields for the growing of more wheat to which he gave his greatest attention.

He returned to Baltimore after the war but did not long survive. The issue of the Maryland *Journal and Commercial Advertiser* of Friday, March 25, 1785, contained this notice:

On Wednesday afternoon departed this life, at his House in Market-Street, Dr. John Stevenson, aged Sixty-seven, a Native of Londonderry, in the Kingdom of Ireland, and of a very respectable Family. A grateful Remembrance of him will long survive in Baltimore, where he lived upwards of Forty Years, and was formerly one of the most eminent Merchants. . . . It may be remarked that he was the first Exporter of Wheat and Flour from this port, and consequently laid the foundation of its present commercial Consequence; and it was the delight of His Heart to promote and see the Increase and Prosperity of this Town in particular, and of the State in general.

As a Gentleman he was distinguished for a nervous and Manly understanding, sprightly Wit, steady Friendship, a high sense of Integrity and Honour, and an unbounded hospitality. . . . His Funeral Obsequies are to be solemnized at Four O'Clock this Afternoon, when, no doubt, the Inhabitants of this Town will pay the last Tribute of Respect to the Remains of a worthy Citizen, who has been of so Much Public Benefit.

Romulus and Remus

Stat sua cuique Dies; breve et irreparabile Tempus,
Omnibus est Vitae, sed Famam extendire Factis,
Hoc Virtutis Opus.

One may guess that the chief reason the worthy doctor is so little celebrated is that his memory was darkened by the overwhelming brilliance of the heroes of the Revolution. Until recently no Tory has been painted, by Americans, at least, as the possessor of any virtues whatever. One can imagine that the composer of the obituary notice in the journal just quoted thought of himself as an exceedingly noble fellow to speak so generously of a man whose sympathies were on the wrong side.

CHAPTER VI

The First Boom

WORD of Dr. John's successful venture spread all over the countryside and up and down the range of settlements. There was the smell of money-making in the air, and the winds of rumor carried it fast and far. The first influx came, naturally enough, along the York road which was passable all the way up into the rich farm lands of the lower tier of Pennsylvania counties. One begins to find German names in the list of subscribers to various causes. Two of these, Leonard and Daniel Barmetz, bought a vacant lot at the corner of Hanover and Baltimore streets, near the western limits of the town, and erected thereon a brewery, that eternal symbol of urbanization.

In the house which he had erected at the corner of Long Street and Grant, Dr. John was conducting a new kind of store, stocked with goods brought over by his ship on its return from that wonderful venture. The store became the gathering place of the excited newcomers, and they laid all sorts of grandiose plans. One of the first, naturally, was the erection of a public wharf. For this purpose Dr. John and some others embued with the new spirit organized a lottery to raise 450 pieces of eight. This wharf was to be built, not at Fells Point, where the deep water came close to the shore, but, instead, right out from Lombard Street over the marshes to Baltimore's own channel.

The harbor was a continuing problem, and the commissioners tried various dodges to prevent its further silting. One ordinance forbade anyone to dump any earth in the marshes in order to build up his fast land without first building a retaining wall of stone or "dovetailed log pens." The penalty for infraction was five pounds current money. At this time tobacco was legal tender at a penny a pound, so that the fine for the infraction of the ordinance would be twelve hundred pounds of tobacco or well over two average hogsheads.

It wasn't only from Pennsylvania that the new settlers came. Several came from Boston, men experienced in the ways of trade and perhaps possessed of a little capital as well. Moreover, the ship which carried that first cargo of wheat to Londonderry spread the news in Ireland, and there came many men from that country and especially from the northern parts thereof. Many of them took up land, as Dr. John had done, but even as landowners they kept an eye on the port. Some bought lots in the original town. Others felt it wiser to be nearer Fells Point where the deep water was. Some played safe and bought in both places.

There was another influx of inhabitants in the late 1750s from an unexpected source. The British expelled the Acadian French from Nova Scotia, and at least one shipload of them was sent to Baltimore. They were lodged at first in private houses but, in the boom that was in progress, they soon found ways by which to earn their keep and, a little later, to build small houses for themselves. They moved beyond the limits of the city proper to an area bordering the southwestern corner of the town's little harbor, an area which oldsters still call Frenchtown. Some of them, naturally, were accustomed to the ways of the sea and found berths on the ships now coming in numbers. A few of these graduated into the ship-owning class in later years, and their names are still found among those of Baltimore's leading families.

Some of the growth came from a less happy cause. This was the time of the French threat on the western borders of all the middle colonies. The Indian allies of the French were raiding the outlying farms and robbing and killing such families as they could catch unawares. Panic seized these pioneers, and they abandoned their lands in numbers and sought safety in the nearest settlements. Some of the settlements even were abandoned, and down the trails toward Baltimore the refugees came fleeing. They were welcomed in the crowded city because the boom was providing work on a scale not before known.

The Braddock expedition was organized and set forth full of high hopes. It came to unexpected grief, and still more refugees piled into the town, jostling in the muddy streets the newcomers from Ireland and the North and competing with them for the habitations available. Perhaps this is why we find records of the building of several inns and also a series of bills in the Assembly at Annapolis authorizing the town commissioners to take in new territory. Those who would ordinarily have gone into the back country to open up new lands found themselves compelled by circumstances to remain in the town. Fortunately there were jobs for them.

But Baltimore was not able to monopolize all this prosperity. In 1732, the same year in which Mr. William Jones and Mr. Edward Fell, storekeeper, procured their charter for Jones Town, across the Falls from Baltimore Town, Mr. Fell's brother William came over from Swarthmore, Lancashire, and bought a tract of land lying a mile or two to the southeast.

William Fell was a shipwright by trade and a canny fellow to boot. While he doubtless hoped to make a living out of the land, he still wanted an anchor to windward. Hence when he was seeking a site of his future agricultural operations he was careful to buy not inland nor yet along a swampy shore but, rather, at a waterside spot where, in case of desire or necessity, he could work at his trade. He selected, therefore, a tract called Copus Harbor. How it got that name the record does not say. But it is a fact that at that point the land rose into a low bluff which thrust itself like a fishhook into the widening river. The water at the foot of this bluff was deep and clear. The currents flowing back and forth with the tide kept it that way. The deepest part was close to the shore.

William Fell built his house on this hooked bluff. On the shore beneath he set up a shipyard and went to work. He called his place Fells Prospect, but the hooked point was soon known as Fells Point, which is its name today. The hook has gone, because the little indentation which it enclosed has long been filled in, save for one dock. But the houses built on the filled-in land are still said to be "on the hook." This area was for many years taken over largely by prostitutes. Those who practice that profession are frequently called "hookers" all over the English-speaking world. Baltimore may or may not be responsible for the spread of this appellation, but it is certain that in Baltimore there is a good reason for it.

How busy a shipbuilder William Fell was we know only by tradition. That tells us he constructed a number of small sloops. Perhaps the sloop shown in Mr. Moale's drawing of 1752 is one of them. It is just as likely that she was built lower down the bay, perhaps on the Eastern Shore. But Mr. Fell built "Chesapeake Bay Ketches" as well. "Ketch" is a broad word, having little definite significance except when applied to rigging. Some have said that Mr. Fell's ketches had lines very like those of the later Baltimore clippers. It is just as likely that the ketch rig which he seemed to favor was the forerunner of the rig common on the present-day bugeye, another product of the Chesapeake builders. Technical nautical knowledge is the property of but few historians and of almost none of those anonymous chroniclers who are summed up in the word "tradition."

But, whatever Mr. William Fell's contribution to naval architecture, it is a fact that as a realtor he had what is called "vision." Unfortunately he did not live long enough to reap the benefit of his foresight. The old gentleman gave up the ghost in 1746, leaving his land, with its pleasant house looking over the broad Patapsco and the shipyard at the foot of the bluff, to his son Edward. Edward continued the business of building sloops and ketches but he also had the wit to see that his land had a special value if ever trade should come to the port.

The advantage of the situation was relatively obvious. His neighbors to the west, in Baltimore Town, had chosen to build on a little snippet of land bounded on the north and west by high hills cut through with deep gullies and on

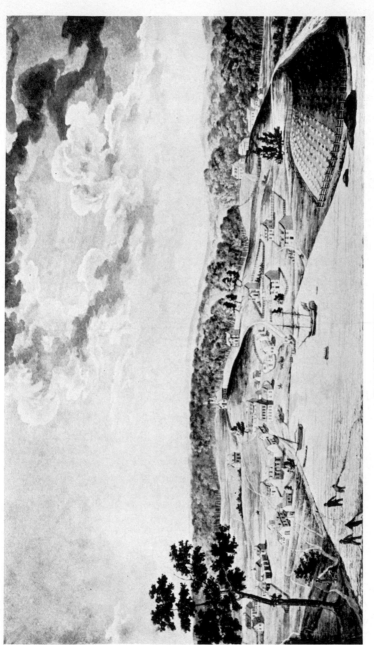

BALTIMORE IN 1752

This is from a Currier print, derived apparently from an emendation by Daniel Bowley of John Moale's original drawing. The stream to the right is Jones Falls. The field beside it is planted in tobacco. The church on the knoll in the background is the original St. Paul's. It stood, like its present-day successor, near the corner of Charles and Saratoga streets. The roadway in the center of the picture, terminating in a wharf, is the present Calvert Street. The Great Eastern Road, which was hardly more than a trail, is marked by the low bushes in the left center. Long, now Baltimore, Street can be traced from Jones Falls, the stream on the right, clear across to the group of houses farthest on the left.

the south by a series of mosquito-bearing marshes separating them by a good many hundred feet from water navigable even to small boats. On the east they were hemmed in by a stream which was given to bad flooding at every freshet above the tidal line and which was bordered below that line by swamps on which it was all but impossible to build roads. Fells Point, on the other hand, was high land with the pleasant water prospect we have spoken of. But in addition it lay on water deep enough to float any ship which might venture up the bay.

So it came about that when Dr. John Stevenson's dream came true and the ships actually came and the grain and flour came down to meet them it was off Fells Point they cast anchor. It was to Fells Point that their skippers brought their boats. It was Mr. Edward Fell who greeted them and entertained them and gave them their first pointers about what was what and who was who in the town.

By 1763 Edward was sufficiently sure of himself to lay out a regular town with streets and offer lots for sale. There was no lagging this time. Many of those who had already ventured in the original Baltimore Town found it wise to risk something on the Point as well. New settlers, coming in from England or Ireland, disembarked here and put their small capital in land offered for sale by Mr. Fell. As a matter of fact, there was a time when practically all of those whose names have come down through the years as great merchants owned houses in this neighborhood. In a little while they were striving each to outbuild the other. It was a period when prosperous people were highly conscious of architecture and wanted something rather fine for their money. Some of these ample houses are still standing, though, for the most part, they are bereft of the columns, the fanlights, the molded mantels, and all the fine detail which once made them delightful. Only a few of them still attest the wealth which once clustered around the Point.

All the historians agree that for a while there was great rivalry between Town and Point. One should not lay too much stress on this agreement, for the chroniclers of Baltimore have, for the most part, merely rewritten each the work of the other. But there are real evidences that the townsmen of Baltimore were worried for fear the Point would take from them the trade they had planned to get and reap the profits therefrom. We have already seen how, soon after his first venture, Dr. John Stevenson helped organize a lottery to provide for the building of a public wharf in Baltimore. That wharf had to be built out over about a thousand feet of swamp before it reached deep water. In the ensuing years there were a number of such ventures in the town proper, including one erected at his own expense by Mr. William Spear, who not only built a wharf all the way out to one of the marshy islets in the harbor but put a bakery at its extremity. One may imagine that he knew the extraordinary drawing powers of the smell of a baking loaf and hoped therewith to lure the ship captains, or at least their crews, to his place of business.

But the Point had a real advantage and one that brought its returns. Soon Mr. Fell's wasn't the only shipyard there. A man named Benjamin Nelson, who had been building boats in a small way at the head of the bay, came down and put a railway and stocks right close to those of the founder. Another man, George Wells by name, also ventured in a shipbuilding way in the neighborhood. He was to be famous in later years as the builder of the *Virginia* frigate, an ill-starred vessel of which we shall hear more later. By that time little Fells Point had become a bustling town of eight hundred souls, nearly every one of whom had something to do with ships or the cargoes thereof.

The Baltimore perambulator of the present day may wander for miles through the streets of the town and hardly be conscious of the fact that he is in one of the great ports of the world. But let him once cross the Falls and turn his steps to the southeast, and he soon finds himself in a truly maritime region. The bluff which was once the characteristic of the Point is gone. Broadway, a great wide street, leads down to the water. The last few blocks are given over to a market. But the ancient buildings which line it are the buildings of a seaport. They could be nothing else. Here are typical saloons for deep-water sailors. Here are flophouses of the sort which only sailors frequent. The same little narrow streets, with the names which Fell gave them, still lead off on cither side. There are Shakespeare Street, Lancaster Street, Fleet Street, Thames Street. The latter is pronounced as it is spelled. There is Bank Street, which bordered the bluff overlooking the little indentation of the hook. Between the larger houses are little ones which, in the days which admitted the fact of prostitution, were cribs where the sailors, home from their long voyages, met their girls and spent in a night the wages of months. Here and there one finds an old ship chandlery, though not many of these survive in these days of mechanical propulsion. But sailors still roam these streets and they still have the look of the sea about them. The skippers go uptown to visit their agents and pay their respects to the consuls. But the sailors know that Fells Point is their Limehouse and, for the most part, they stay there.

CHAPTER VII

Evolution of a Work of Art

THE ROMANTIC REPUTATION of Baltimore as a port is based almost entirely upon the phrase, "Baltimore clipper." The average Baltimorean, like the average American elsewhere, thinks that the Baltimore clipper was a clipper ship. But only a few Baltimore clippers were ships —that is, vessels with three masts all rigged with square sails. The typical Baltimore clipper of the golden age was not a ship but a schooner. For special purposes she might be rigged as a brig or a brigantine. But she came into being as a schooner, and for most of her uses the schooner rig was more useful.

Though the Baltimore clipper burst upon a surprised world about 1776 as an almost perfect thing, her evolution was a long, slow process. She was developed to meet a special need. Other vessels, almost equally able to meet that need, developed alongside her. Some of them had powers of adaptation under changing conditions which she did not possess. They have survived and even continued to evolve.

[50]

But, like a highly specialized organism, she could not adapt herself and so she passed from the picture almost a hundred years ago. Her collateral relations display some of her traits, but none of them has her beauty or her imaginative appeal.

When Baltimore was chartered there was but one real town on the Chesapeake above the mouth of the Potomac. That town, as we have seen, was Annapolis, which became the capital of the palatinate in 1695. It had an excellent small harbor—it still has—and, beyond a doubt, most of the vessels which came into the bay looking for cargoes of tobacco called there, recorded their entry, paid their respects to the governor, and sold their redemptioners. All the other towns were called so by courtesy only.

Going to town, therefore, meant going to Annapolis. For nine out of ten of the planters there was only one way to get to Annapolis, or even to a neighbor's place, for whatever reason, and that was by boat. The earliest settlers undoubtedly used the Indian canoe, a hollowed log, as their craft. The making of these cumbersome boats has been described many times. Fallen logs were placed on trestles and then by a combination of fire and stone tools were burned and scraped out until they would do duty as boats. The process was a laborious one, and for a long time the colonists entrusted it to the Indians. Groups of natives, usually hailing from the Eastern Shore, cruised up and down the shores of the bay and its rivers, taking orders for such canoes. As often as not they were made right on the foreshore of the planter placing the order. The Indian contractor and his workmen, if he had any, burned and scraped until the task was completed and then took their pay in the form usually of matchcoats (skins sewn together) or, in rarer cases, of axes or even of some sort of cheap guns.

Balancing such a canoe, let alone propelling it, was a considerable art in itself, and it is not likely that the planters were satisfied long with such products as the Indians could provide. As a matter of fact, the Chesapeake Bay log canoe has been in continual process of development ever since the first white man decided that the crude Indian product would not do.

The Indians had no way of fastening timbers together, hence all their canoes were made of a single log. The beam was hardly ever more than three feet, though the length might run to twenty or twenty-five. The white man, on the other hand, could fasten one or more logs together with pegs or spikes, hence he could increase the beam any convenient degree. With ax or adze, and according to his skill, he could hollow his logs to any desired thickness. By adding a center board he could turn his canoe into a sailboat. One of the most beautiful boats I ever saw was a canoe which was then said to be more than 150 years old. If it is still afloat it is more than 175 years old, which means that it was built around 1765. It was about eighteen feet long and about four feet beam. It was made of three logs doweled together. They had been together so long that it was almost impossible to see the joints. But the man who fashioned that boat had given it the delicacy and grace of the lightest skiff. Its sheer was perfect, and, equipped with the cloud of canvas which experts in canoe racing know how to pile on, it could outstep many a yacht on the wind and off it. In all probability it was on some such vessel such as this one that the early settlers depended for their personal transportation.

Evolution of a Work of Art

Log canoes with center boards developed along still another and more imposing line and produced another type of vessel indigenous to the Chesapeake. It occurred to some ship carpenter that if a sufficient number of shaped logs were bolted together to make a substantial hull below the water line the sides could be built up above it with mere planking and held in place with a minimum of frame. On the Chesapeake, where it is still one of the common small cargo carriers and widely used for oystering as well, such a boat is called a "bugeye." Some say, though by what authority it is hard to discover, that the proper spelling of the word is "buckeye."

Save for its greater relative beam, the bugeye, being sharp at both ends, looks and is very much like an overgrown log canoe. Nowadays, in order to produce the necessary beam for the davits for the tender, usually called the "yawl boat," a so-called patent stern is often built on. This is a mere extension of the deck and does not alter the hull. The characteristic rig of the bugeye is almost that of the modern ketch, but the masts of the former have an exaggerated rake. Both mainsail and mizzen are jib-headed, thus giving the vessel a yachty appearance. The bowsprit is short, and the headsails—usually a jib and staysail but often only a jib—get their size from the fact that the mainmast is stepped rather far aft. Bugeyes ordinarily run from about fifty to seventy feet in length. The curve of the sheer is deep, so that they have little freeboard amidships. Their decks are flush, and they can carry a considerable bulk of freight thereon. They are fast on the reach and fairly good on the wind. There are fewer bugeyes being built today because of the growing scarcity of timbers large enough for their peculiar bottoms.

Shipbuilding, as a specialized business, must have come to the colony rather early in its existence. Every tidewater planter had to have a boat, so he became a boatbuilder of sorts, especially on the Eastern Shore, where there was no hinterland to lure the settlers away from the sea. It is as true today as it was then that the average native Shoreman has built his several boats in his time. But the boats built on the beach below the manor house were necessarily small affairs, turned out in the intervals of cultivatng tobacco and corn.

New settlers were constantly coming into the country, and many of them, especially the redemptioners, were skilled craftsmen. Among the latter we find an occasional shipwright. A planter lucky enough to purchase such an expert would almost certainly seek to utilize his services to the best advantage. Hence we find little shipyards on the rivers and creeks from very early days. When William Fell set up his yard at the foot of his bluff overlooking Copus Harbor he was following a pattern entirely familiar to the other colonists.

This is easier to say than it is to establish by documentary evidence. Yet there is a record that as early as 1735 shipbuilding was well established on both the Choptank and Nanticoke rivers. The record of vessels in the Maryland archives relates that registry was granted to William Edmondson, of Maryland, a merchant, "being of the people called Quakers, for Schooner *Charming Betty* of Maryland, John Coward Master, square sterned vessel, burthen ab't thirty tons, built at Choptank river, in the year 1735 by Henry Trippe, John Anderson and the said Wm. Edmondson, owners thereof."

In the same year we find "register granted in common

form unto Adam Muir of Maryland, Merchant, for the Brigantine *Sea Nymph* of Maryland Law, Draper, Master, Burthen about fifty tons, square sterned, built in Dorchester County in the year 1735 for the said Adam Muir, owner thereof." In 1739 register was granted to James Billings, merchant, for the ship *Rider* of eighty tons, built on the Nanticoke River in the preceding year. Billings was her master as well as her owner. Eighty tons is the burden of a vessel of considerable size. The fact that the *Rider* was rigged as a ship suggests that she was intended for use not in the bay alone but even in tobacco trade to England.

From this time forward the building of ships was a major industry on the whole Eastern Shore, probably ranking next to agriculture. The records of most of the small towns, including those as far up the river as, for instance, Federalsburg, which lies at the head of navigation on the Nanticoke, contain references to shipyards. Lumber, especially white oak—the largest-known oak in the country still stands at Wye Mills in Talbot County—was plentiful, and the demand for ships was a persistent one.

We know, from present-day survivals, that competition between the shipbuilders and shipowners of the various rivers of the bay has always been keen and that designers and sailors, even in the smallest of fishing communities, have developed characteristic types and styles. An experienced bay waterman, with an eye for such things, can tell almost at a glance whether a given bugeye was built at Crisfield or at Oxford. The skipjacks used for oyster dredging have subtle differences which indicate whether they originated on Hooper Island or on Deal. The same thing is true even of the tiny crabbing skiffs. But the designers adopt, and have always adopted, the successful

ideas of their rivals, so that their products, however differ-
entiated, always have the look of the bay about them.

So at the very time the shipwrights were painfully turning the hollow log into a thing of beauty and developing it,
along different lines, into the artful sailing canoe and
finally into the sinister bugeye, they were also trying out
new and better notions on their larger vessels, such as Captain Coward's *Charming Betty* and Captain Draper's *Sea
Nymph*.

We cannot follow this development historically, because the records are not in existence. We do know that
when the clipper finally emerged she was something different from anything in the way of a sailing vessel that had
ever existed before. She was a smallish schooner, usually
between seventy-five and a hundred feet long, with two
very tall, slender masts, sharply raked and very lightly
stayed. Her foresail was ordinarily loose-footed and was
carried back so that it overlapped the main. She had a
square topsail on her foremast. Occasionally she had one
on the mainmast too. In that case she was called a "double-
topsail" schooner. She had a reasonably long bowsprit and
usually a staysail and a jib or two. Now and then a large
square lug was hung from the yard which normally spread
her fore-topsail. Her skippers were adept at bending
strange canvas wherever there was something to bend it to.

What, then, were the characteristics which gave her her
overwhelming reputation for speed? All the experts agree
that the answer to this question is that she had a hull which
surpassed any other of her time for slipping through the
water. Doubtless some of the modern yacht designers have
improved on her lines, but up to the time of her passing she
was incomparable. Perhaps it is not quite correct to talk of

her as extinct, for even today, if secondhand observation is to be trusted, there are shipbuilders on the south shore of Cuba who build schooners with hulls much like those their ancestors learned to build when the privateers, slavers, and pirates from the United States operated in the Caribbean. They built such schooners in Grand Cayman too. As recently as 1926 a schooner for all the world like a Baltimore clipper was wrecked in the Florida Keys, and not long ago a so-called "pungy," hauled up in the shipyard in Oxford, Maryland, displayed lines which looked like all the pictures of Baltimore clippers ever seen.

It is not easy to describe the special qualities of the clipper hull in non-technical language. It is easier to understand her by making a comparison with other vessels of her era. Those were the days of the bluff-bowed sailing vessel whose beam was great until close to the bow, when the frame curved sharply in toward the stem. Moreover, the average vessel of those days had sides like a wall. They came down almost perpendicularly to a point just above the keel, then curved sharply in, so that the actual bottom was almost flat, save for the projection of the keel.

In those days also, when men were thinking more about safety at sea than about speed, ships were built of great heavy timbers and with equally heavy planking. Designers tried to keep their ships steady and dry by giving them as much depth as possible and by building them as high out of the water as possible. They trusted neither their spars nor their rigging, so that the normal work vessel, however safe, was overweight and undercanvased and hence slow and unwieldy.

The Baltimore clipper was lightly built and heavily canvased and, though seaworthy, she was wet in a heavy sea, partly because of her low freeboard. Because of her lightness above, in a very strong blow she was likely to lose rigging and even a mast. She was an excellent vessel in the comparatively mild winds and weathers of the Atlantic in the lower latitudes and the Caribbean. She was not nearly so good in the north Atlantic in the winter, when many of her virtues became shortcomings. She was an inferior vessel for the passage round the Horn, although, given favorable wind and weather, she could outstep the best of them even there.

Not as much research on the origin of the Baltimore clipper as a type has been done as one would think. The one really original work is that of Mr. Howard Irving Chapelle, the distinguished New England yacht designer. His book, *The Baltimore Clipper, Its Origin and Development*, was published by the Marine Research Society, of Salem, Mass., in 1930. It is a scholarly and informative work, written *con amore* by a man who appreciates better than anyone else the true place of the Baltimore clipper in the history of sail and who has, as well, an authentic historian's sense of the causal relationship between climate, geography, ships, and men.

The Baltimore clipper was a perfect thing, suited to her purpose in that time and clime, and Mr. Chapelle has the wit to see that no perfect thing springs full-blown into the world but must evolve slowly and painfully from something that went before. The Baltimore clipper followed this general rule. It may have evolved, as Mr. Chapelle suggests, from the French lugger. It may have evolved from the Bermuda sloop, of which it is certainly a close relative. Bermuda sloops were frequent visitors to the bay. It may owe something to those vessels which the Swedes built on the Delaware. Yet it must be apparent that the shipbuilders of Baltimore and the Chesapeake were forced by local conditions and local traditions to alter and adapt their borrowings.

The Baltimore clipper was not a log boat like the canoe but she may have owed something to this indigenous craft —her sharp bow and her clean forefoot, perhaps her comparatively great length in proportion to her beam, her sharp dead rise, and her unusually low freeboard, as well as her beautiful sheer and her general meticulous fairing.

It was as a "Virginia-built" schooner that the type first attracted outside attention during the Revolutionary War. The name is significant. It means that here was a type evolved to meet the special conditions of the Virginia— i.e., the Chesapeake—tidewater. What were those special conditions? The bay with its tributaries was the highway system, as we have seen. In the early days everything brought to the plantation and everything taken from it was moved by water. Some plantations had wharves, and some did not, but all of them had access to the deep tidal waters of the bay system. Most of the estuaries had fairly deep channels offshore but innumerable points and bars which made navigation a matter of intimate and ever-changing knowledge, as it is today. Wharves, where they existed at all, were small flimsy affairs built low to the water. Larger vessels approaching them were constantly running aground and having to be shoved off. Where there were no wharves the vessel itself had to be run ashore or within wading distance, lest the labor of loading and unloading be doubled.

It followed, therefore, that the most useful vessel would be sharp in the bow, so that when her nose was run onshore by accident or design it would be easy to push her off again.* It would follow also that her bow be shallower than her stern and rake if possible. It would follow, further, that, instead of having a flat or nearly flat bottom, she would serve better if she had a lot of dead rise. Since sharp dead rise cuts down capacity, it would follow, further, that her decks would have to be comparatively free for taking deckloads. It would follow, as a moment's thought will show, that her freeboard, amidships at least, would be low, to allow easy loading from the low wharves and from the shore.

Why was she a schooner? The first sizable vessels built on the Chesapeake were almost certainly sloops or cutters. But vessels of this type have large mainsails with long, heavy booms. Such a rig is difficult to handle, especially if the gaff is long and heavy. "Pinkies" from New England came frequently into the Chesapeake for tobacco. The New Englanders had learned early that the pinky rig was a more convenient one for their undermanned vessels, and it is probable, or, at least, possible, that the Maryland builders learned a lesson from them and divided their sail area and so made it easier to handle. But two masts demand or at least will accept greater length in proportion to beam, so the builders could add to the length of their vessels without altering the cutaway lines of the bow. It is highly likely that when the Chesapeake builders lengthened their sloops and cutters and made them into schooners the long run aft which they gave the new type produced spontaneously the greatest of all the virtues of the Baltimore clipper —her ability to sail close to the wind.

*Mr. Chapelle does not regard this point as a sound one. He thinks the shallow bow made for ease in going about.

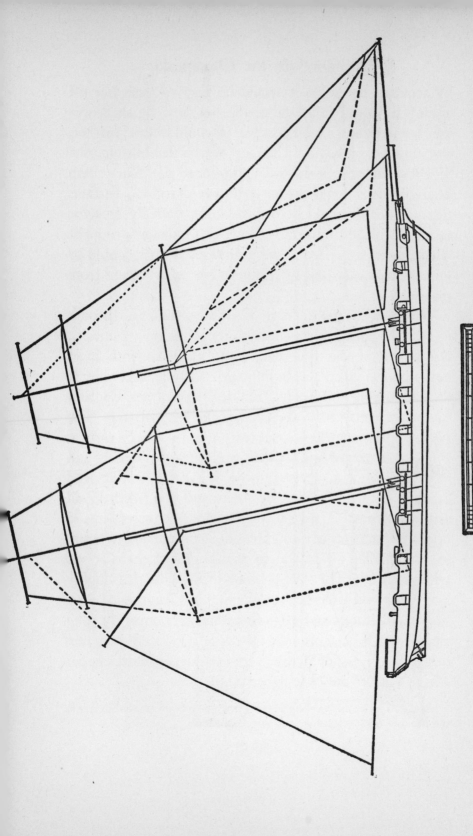

From *The Baltimore Clipper*, by Howard I. Chapelle

TYPICAL MAST AND SAIL PLAN OF A BALTIMORE CLIPPER-TYPE SCHOONER, IN THIS CASE THE *GRECIAN*.

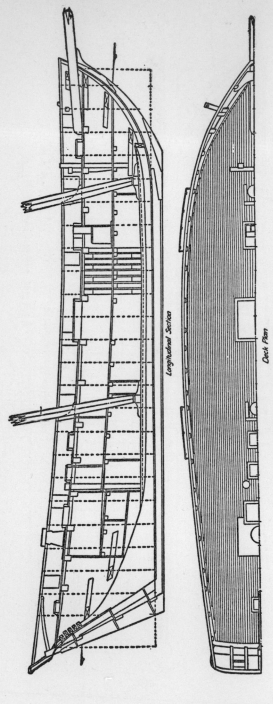

Longitudinal Section

Deck Plan

Longitudinal Section and Deck Plan of His Majesty's Schooner, "Musquidobit,"
as taken off at Portsmouth Yard, May, 1816

From *The Baltimore Clipper*, by Howard I. Chapelle

LONGITUDINAL SECTION AND DECK PLAN OF ONE OF THE MOST
CHARACTERISTIC OF BALTIMORE CLIPPERS, THE LETTER-OF-
MARQUE SCHOONER *LYNX*, CAPTURED BY THE BRITISH IN 1814
AND RENAMED H.M.S. *MUSQUIDOBIT*.

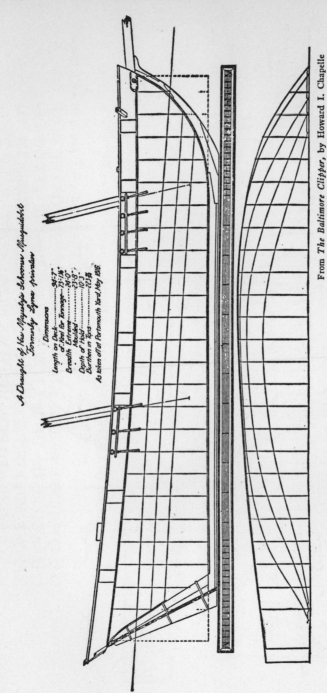

A Draught of His Majestys Schooner Musquidobit
Formerly Lynx a privateer

Dimensions

Length on Deck.............94·7
of Keel for Tonnage...73·1¼
Breadth Extreme............24·0"
Moulded............23·8"
Depth of Hold.................10·3"
Burthen in Tons.............225¾

As taken off at Portsmouth Yard, May 1816

From *The Baltimore Clipper*, by Howard I. Chapelle

A DRAUGHT OF THE *MUSQUIDOBIT* (*LYNX*) TAKEN OFF AT
PORTSMOUTH, ENGLAND, AFTER HER CAPTURE.

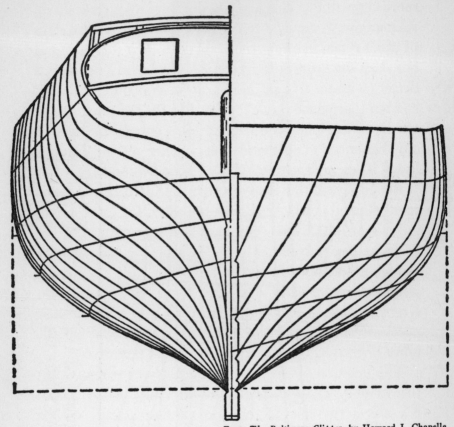

THE LINES OF THE *MUSQUIDOBIT* (*LYNX*)
AS TAKEN OFF IN PORTSMOUTH, ENGLAND.

Evolution of a Work of Art

But when we have listed these characteristics we have listed all those which gave its special quality to the hull of the Virginia-built schooner, which is to say, of the Baltimore clipper. The characteristics of her hull were a sharp, raking bow, as opposed to the bluff bow and vertical stem of other types, her long run aft, her shallow forefoot, and her deep drag, her low freeboard, her broad uncluttered decks (with no fo'c'sle and hardly ever a quarter-deck), and her sharp dead rise, as opposed to the rounded, almost flat bottoms of her contemporaries. Look at the lines of any Baltimore clipper and you will see all the features listed. They *are* the lines of the Baltimore clipper.

But to say all this is to say that the speed of the Baltimore clipper and her remarkable ability, for her time, to sail close to the wind were accidental by-products of her other necessary qualities. That is probably largely true, though it does not follow that the builders of the type did not know from early days that their vessels were fast. Knowing that, they were almost certain to build to their necessary specifications with at least one eye on the possibility of turning out something swift and beautiful.

The question of rigging is more complex perhaps than that of hull. The typical Baltimore clipper of the golden era was a two-masted schooner, almost always with a square topsail on the foremast and frequently with such topsails on both masts. We have guessed at the reason for the schooner rig. The masts were very sharply raked. Why?

One thing we should notice first of all is that the raking mast is characteristic of the Chesapeake Bay. All the indigenous craft are built that way—the sailing canoe, the bugeye, and even the skipjack. The little skiffs which the boys build for themselves all have raking masts, sometimes with no stays save that for the jib. Hence we might say that the raking mast was the custom of the country and let it go at that.

But there are other considerations which may have played their part. On the Chesapeake, especially in the summertime, there is often an air stirring above when little is moving close to the surface of the water. Hence there was manifest an early tendency to build masts higher than was the custom elsewhere in order to catch those upper airs. In addition, since the Chesapeake boats had relatively little below the water, it was necessary for them to be lightly rigged above so as to be as stiff as possible under the circumstances. The tall mast could be stayed lightly without having the whole rail taken up with standing rigging if the masts were sharply raked. The effect was that of a tripod.

Another and perhaps more immediately practical reason for the prevalence of the raking mast on the vessels indigenous to the Chesapeake has been suggested by Mr. Chapelle in a letter printed in the *Sun* of Baltimore early in the current year (1941). He wrote:

The rake of the masts in the skipjack was brought about by many factors. Fashion had something to do with it, but the position of the mast at deck, which was desirable in order to get sufficient room to work the (oyster) dredging gear, was probably the chief cause. This position having been fixed, it was an easy matter to balance the sail against the hull by raking the mast. As long as the leg-of-mutton sail was used in these boats the scheme worked very well, and, as it brought the masthead and mainsail halyard over the main hatch, the halyard could be used for hoisting out oysters or cargoes.

Evolution of a Work of Art

When there were few wharf facilities this was of great importance. It is worth observing that the gaff-rigged sloops had little or no rake to their masts, as the gaff could be used as a cargo boom. The use of the rake of the mast to obtain cargo-handling advantages was not confined to the bay; the old New York sailing lighters employed a raking mast for the same purpose.

Thus a method of stepping the mast which had originally a purely utilitarian motive became fixed by fashion. But the fashion, in its turn, served a useful end in that it promoted speed when the vessel was working to windward. For, as Mr. Chapelle pointed out in another paragraph in the letter just quoted, the rake made it possible "to increase the 'entering edge' of the sail without increasing the height of the masthead from the water line. The value of the entering edge is aerodynamic; the shape of the modern airplane wings will illustrate; the forward edge rakes aft, or away from the direction of movement."

If these considerations account for the raking mast, they do not entirely account for the continued prevalence of the fore-and-aft rig. But this need cause us little difficulty. Sailing the narrow channels of the tidal rivers of the bay region, vessels had to be highly maneuverable; they had to be able to come about quickly without loss of way. The fore-and-aft rig is the best rig for a vessel that must spend much of its life in narrow waters.

But fore-and-aft sailors are a special breed, from skipper down. All the sailors on the Chesapeake were trained in fore-and-aft sailing, and so it is likely that as the size of the vessels increased it was easier to procure competent crews for them if they were rigged in the traditional fashion. Another consideration perhaps is the fact that labor was both scarce and dear in the early days. It takes fewer men to handle a schooner of a given tonnage than to handle a square-rigged vessel of the same size. Later on, when Baltimore's reputation as a port attracted seafarers and her ships went on longer and more profitable voyages, the governing conditions changed also. When ships were armed, either for privateering or for self-defense, larger crews were called for. If the crew must be large, then there is no reason for sticking to the fore-and-aft rig. Hence the coming of the square topsail, on one or both masts, the brigantine, the brig, and even the full-rigged ship. But these developments were later and, as we have suggested, they helped bring about the disappearance of the Baltimore clipper.

CHAPTER VIII

The Two Civilizations

THE PERIOD immediately preceding the Revolutionary War found two civilizations in Maryland. There was first, and most important, the tobacco civilization. This was a civilization based on great plantations, indentured servants, slaves, and debt. Thanks to the Navigation Acts and especially to the system of "enumeration," it was wholly dependent on Great Britain and British merchants.

The second civilization was fundamentally different. Its basis was wheat. The growers were mostly pioneers of small means. They were not only Englishmen; they were also Germans, Irishmen, Swedes, Bohemians, and a few Frenchmen. To aid in the filling up of the lands to the West, the colonial governments were especially hospitable to such non-conforming people. But wheat growing did not depend on slave labor. It did not depend on the capital supplied by British merchants. Wheat was not "enumerated." Outside of England it could be sold wherever a market could be found. This civilization came to a head in Baltimore.

[69]

One might say also that a third civilization was coming into being. This civilization had no special focus, though it found most of its recruits on the Eastern Shore. It was a maritime civilization and it originated wherever the combination of water and timber made shipbuilding possible and it roved wherever cargocs offered and *force majeure* did not interfere.

These three civilizations had something in common but at certain points they warred rather violently each against the other. One might say, in the effort to simplify the problem, that the Maryland struggle in the decade before the Revolution was between Annapolis and Baltimore and that the prize they fought for was the domination of the maritime interests of the colony.

We already know the special advantages and disadvantages under which the tobacco grower operated during the first hundred or so years of the colony. We have not yet watched the development of the tobacco trade nor examined the special problems which arose from the sometimes rather shortsighted views of the British merchants who handled it and of the British government committed to the impossible mercantilist policy of trying to maintain a balanced economy at home while at the same time allowing the planters to prosper enough to buy British manufactures.

Under the law growing out of this effort the Maryland tobacco planter had only one market, England. The importer brought it to London or Bristol or some other port south of the Tweed and there resold it as well as he could.

For a number of reasons Maryland tobacco wasn't popular in England in the later years of the eighteenth century. The chief markets for it were Holland, Germany, and

France, where it was favored by the peasants. But in those countries it was in constant competition with the tobacco the peasants had learned to grow for themselves. If the price went up, even a fraction, they were inclined to use their own product.

The prevailing prices were thus low and tended to get lower. Freight rates were high, and of course the English importer had to have his profit. Thus after a year or fifteen months of effort the planter sometimes found that the money due him hardly paid the freight on the crop and he would be in debt to his merchant in England. More than a few planters went bankrupt in that unlucky decade, and some of them actually pulled up stakes and moved to the new lands of Ohio and Kentucky. The remainder probably thought more than once that if they could trade directly with their continental consumers they would do much better. Thus they were dissatisfied and, having little to lose, protested vigorously against the Stamp Act and the duties which were afterward imposed. They resented to the point of open rebellion even the symbolic tax on tea.

Some careful historians have said that, although New England had a definite economic reason for seeking independence of England, the Chesapeake colonies—that is, Maryland and Virginia—were prosperous and contented at this period and hence had only political reasons for joining the war. It is hard not to conclude that such writers were thinking of the great tobacco days before the French and Indian wars. They may have overlooked the upsetting fact, known to all tobacco planters of the time, that the fields of Maryland produced their best tobacco for only a few years after they had been cleared. After the soil had been leached by a few summers of hard rains the tobacco grown on it became coarse and harsh to the tongue of all save the toughest smoker.

So long as there was plenty of land this was no problem. But as the colony filled up it became a major issue, not uncomplicated by the fact that transporting hogsheads weighing five hundred pounds from the back country was a laborious process and one which, in itself, lowered the quality of the weed. A few farsighted planters whose land was thus exhausted or whose transportation problems were costly were turning when they could to the growing of wheat. In 1763 three sons of a Quaker family by the name of Ellicott moved to Baltimore from Buck's County, Pennsylvania, and brought a whole set of milling machinery along with them. Casting about for a site, they found a little meadow on the upper reaches of the Patapsco, not far from where Charles Carroll, of Carrollton—later to be a signer of the Declaration of Independence—had acquired an inland farm of ten thousand acres. Carroll was having trouble getting his tobacco to a landing—he used Elk Ridge, from whence barges floated the crop to Moales Point—and was dissatisfied with the prevailing prices. He therefore took kindly to the Ellicotts' suggestion that he go in for the growing of wheat for them to mill. So hundreds of the vast acres of Doughoregan Manor were thereafter devoted to the new and more promising crop, and, to one more influential planter, an outlet for wheat as well as tobacco became a major necessity.

Carroll, as everyone knows, was an Irishman and a Catholic. He therefore had religious and political reasons for being less than 100 per cent devoted to Britain. But he had also an economic reason for being dissatisfied with the status of tobacco and the strongest possible reason for wanting a wide market for flour. His American patriotism thus was soundly founded on three strong bases.

When Mr. Carroll gave up his allegiance to tobacco and cast his lot in with the wheat civilization he performed a symbolic act. His was one of the most important families in the state. He was the third generation in that family. It had always maintained its main residence in Annapolis and, despite its fervent Catholicism, it had had continuing relations with the royal governors who had succeeded the proprietary representatives. But to shift from tobacco to wheat meant shifting the family's center of gravity from Annapolis to Baltimore. This perhaps made it more certain that when the final break came the loyalty of the family would be given to the American cause.

The development of a market for Maryland wheat, usually shipped in the form of flour, did not proceed without difficulties. The first shipments went to Ireland, as we know, and there was steady demand in that island for the Maryland product. But the Irish market was a small one, and even that of Scotland was not too demanding. Besides, it wasn't only Baltimore which had flour to sell; Philadelphia and even New York had taken to shipping grain and flour on a large scale.

The factor which provided a new and greater market was, interestingly enough, the sudden development, all over Western Europe, of the sweet tooth. This taste was created by the early cargoes of sugar and molasses which the ships of England, France, and Spain carried to their homelands from their island possessions in the West Indies. For ages anything sweet had been a luxury in all Europe. But when the taste for sugar was once created it grew by leaps and bounds, much faster and more demanding even than the craving for tobacco. Sugar plantations spread over all the islands, ousting not only tobacco but even the food crops on which the inhabitants depended for their sustenance. This gave them an unbalanced economy which persists to this day. The demand for labor in the sugar fields had as much to do also with the development of the slave trade as did the similar demand for labor in the tobacco fields of Maryland and Virginia and (later) in the cotton fields of the South.

The American colonies thus acquired a special role in the West Indian trade. From their middle region they could supply the flour for food and from the North the staves for the barrels in which the sugar was shipped to the continent. Maryland was fortunate in that it could supply both. The traders took in exchange sugar and molasses and also bills of exchange on London for the manufactures they sorely needed. Baltimore, as the southernmost port of the grain area, had an economic advantage in this trade from the very first days. Its grain came from its back door, and it was nearly two hundred miles closer to the islands.

The same advantage was held, of course, by any other point on the Chesapeake Bay. Gould thinks that the first shiploads of grain and flour to the Islands went, not from Baltimore, but, instead, from one of the other little towns on the bay. If this is true Chestertown was probably the one, for it was the port for the new wheatlands of the upper Eastern Shore.

How the flour was carried, whether in English-built ships or those built on the bay and sold or chartered to British merchants or whether, as some accounts seem to suggest, it was begun by New Englanders venturing into the bay in search of cargo, it is difficult to say for certain.

It is more than a good guess—it is almost a certainty—that the schooners of the Chesapeake ventured into the trade under the stimulus of war and that their undertakings were considerably less than legal and therefore dangerous. The Seven Years' War broke out in 1756, not long after the grain and flour trade of the northern Chesapeake in general and Baltimore in particular was well established. Britain was busy with her naval warfare with the French, and most of the French islands were under siege of a sort. Commerce between the colonies and those islands was theoretically stopped, and the British frigates were there to see that the theory was an actuality.

But the Frenchmen needed food badly and were willing to pay for it. Unable, on account of the stupidity of their own government, plus the activity of the British fleet, to get rid of their own accumulating supplies of sugar and molasses, they were looking for buyers.

The activities of the bay skippers of this period are difficult to trace, because, being extra-legal, they are not recorded. It is only by indirection that we can learn of their existence. But the record does show several developments which indicate the way in which the wind was blowing. There is the fact, for instance, that the French and Indian War, as this struggle is called in our history books, never engaged the wholehearted cooperation of the Marylanders.

There were several reasons why the dwellers on the upper Chesapeake and its environs did not look on the war for the possession of the Western country as one which affected their interests very profoundly. In the first place, their own Western lands did not stretch off to infinity as did those of Virginia, Pennsylvania, and New York. They could have, under the circumstances, no great dreams of empire.

A second reason, not compelling but still carrying some weight, was Maryland's large proportion of Catholics, some of whom were men of influence and wealth. These people had fared badly under the royal rule. The toleration which had marked the regime of the Calverts had almost disappeared as far as they were concerned. They could not vote or hold office and for a while they paid double taxes.

France, the enemy of England in the wars, was a Catholic country. Therefore the threat of French subjugation did not appear as appalling to the Catholics of Maryland as it did to the Protestants in this and the other colonies. There is plenty of evidence that the citizens of Pennsylvania were convinced that Maryland's backwardness in supporting the British cause was due to the Catholic influence. There were many Protestant Marylanders who regarded the Catholics among them as little better than traitors during this period.

But it would be unwarranted to assume, from this consideration, that it was disloyalty which promoted the illegal trade with the Dutch and French islands. All the maritime colonies engaged in it. The Puritans of Massachusetts and Connecticut vied with the Quakers of Pennsylvania in supplying the enemies of Britain both in the Islands and in Canada. If Maryland Catholics engaged in it as well, it can be said for them that they had less reason for being loyal to His Majesty's cause than had the people of the Northern colonies.

The British government was conscious of the situation and kept reminding its colonial governors of the necessity of putting down the trade. The governors all did what they could. Governor Sharpe, of Maryland, twice assured London that there were no such illegal goings on in the colony under his control. But that they existed there can be no doubt.

At first most of this illegal trade was based on the little Dutch island called St. Eustatius. The Dutch didn't have much of an empire in the Caribbean but in this islet, which has an area of something less than eight square miles, they had something rather special. St. Eustatius lies about twelve miles to the northwest of St. Kitts, which is to say it is in a central situation with reference to the whole system of the Leeward Isles. Its harbor isn't good, consisting of a rather shallow indentation on which lies the little town of Orangetown. But the virtue of this indentation is that it lies on the western side of the island and hence is sheltered against the prevailing trade winds.

For the two years from 1754 to 1756 this roadstead must have been one of the busiest ports in the whole world. It was here that the little American ships came, bringing their cargoes of wheat, flour, corn, salt fish, staves, and other useful stuffs. From the French islands scattered about, the Dutch brought cargoes of sugar and molasses. The Americans venturing there on this business were just barely within the letter of the law, if that. It is certain that they had to do all sorts of slick sophisticating of their papers. But it was business, and the canny Dutch took full advantage of their position. We know that some Chesapeake vessels engaged in this trade but we cannot be certain how many. After all, the total tonnage in Maryland, even as late as 1761, was only thirteen hundred. Finally the British could stand it no longer and began to seize the Dutch ships in the inter-island trade and forced them to abandon it. Thereafter trade with St. Eustatius was extremely hazardous.

But the special qualities of the Chesapeake schooner were such that a voyage whose perils would be overwhelming to a New England pinky or a New York brig was much less dangerous to her. She was faster than they off the wind and could outrun all but the best frigates. But on the wind she had no peer. She was not only fast but she could point into the very eye of the trades. If a Chesapeake schooner could get to the windward of a pursuer she was safe.

Hence, the very effectiveness of the British navy, which kept the French in their harbors, which forced the Dutch to abandon a lucrative business, and which kept even the daring seamen of New England from taking any save an occasional chance, provided the Chesapeake adventurers at last with a virtual monopoly of an illegal and hazardous trade. Most of the histories say that the Baltimore clipper emerged (as the Virginia schooner) during the Revolutionary War. It is a much more certain speculation that its skippers learned the art of blockade running and lawbreaking while carrying flour and barrel staves to the enemy and his agents during the long struggle between the French and the English during the fifties and sixties of the eighteenth century.

During all this period the tobacco growers continued, as before, to ship to England and by precisely the means they had always used. English command of the seas made the trade perfectly safe. Thus a whole new economy was growing up in which they had no part. New trade routes were opened, and vessels capable of handling that trade under difficult circumstances were developed. Thus there came into being a partnership between the new merchants of Baltimore and the shipbuilders and sailors of the bay. Together they were to determine the future course of the colony, against the protest of the conservative if dissatisfied men who had no escape from the thralldom which tobacco imposed upon them.

CHAPTER IX

Merchants' Choice

IN THE 1770s one of the busiest as well as one of the most prosperous of the new merchant class of Baltimore was Mr. William Lux, who owned a ropewalk on the edge of the town. He took part in nearly every civic activity of the time and was a leader in the various schemes for draining the marshes, bridging Jones Falls, deepening the harbor, and extending the roads to the North and West which utilized the surplus time and energies of the bustling little place.

His father, Darby Lux, was a sea captain. Born in Devonshire, he took naturally to the sea and commanded a ship trading in the Islands and the Chesapeake as early as 1733. In 1743 he bought two lots close to the marsh on the lane between Charles and Calvert streets. This lane was then given the dignity of a street and named Light Street in honor of the man who had raised its estate. The house he built is one of those shown in the Moale drawing. When the flour trade began Captain Lux was one of the first to see its possible future and brought up his two sons, William and Darby, Jr., to be merchants. William, the elder, who was born about 1723 on a farm his father owned in Anne Arundel County, took both business and politics seriously. In 1765 he was a prominent member of the Sons of Liberty, an organization strong enough to force the hurried departure from the colony of Zachariah Blood, who had been appointed stamp distributor. William married a daughter of Dr. George Walker, one of the original commissioners of Baltimore Town, and thus became possessed of a countryseat—not more than a mile from Charles and Baltimore streets—called Chatsworth. Here, after the flour trade was established, he lived on a lavish scale.

In 1773 William Lux was one of those who helped persuade William Goddard, a Philadelphia editor, and his sister, Miss Mary Goddard, to move to Baltimore and establish a weekly journal. On August 20 of that year there appeared on the muddy streets of Baltimore the first issue of the *Baltimore Journal and Commercial Advertiser.* George Washington was one of the advertisers in that initial issue, appealing, in language which present-day realtors would not find uninspired, for settlers on the new lands on the Ohio and Kanawha which he had just acquired. "A reasonable number of years rent free," "excellent meadows . . . almost fit for the scythe," "most valuable lands in the (proposed) new government" are some of the familiar sales phrases.

Goddard was a rover by temperament and two months after his journal was launched he left for a trip through the Northern colonies, leaving his sister to act as editor. He made such trips frequently, and the result was the establishment of the first truly American postal service. By August 1774 his system covered all the colonies from Maine to Georgia.

Mr. Lux's activity in such affairs gave him a reputation throughout the colonies, and so when Samuel Adams was appointed by the people of Boston to communicate to the other colonies the news of the non-importation agreement reached at the Faneuil Hall meeting it was to William Lux that he sent his formal communication to the people of Baltimore. Mr. Lux called together "a number of merchants and respectable mechanics" (we quote Mr. Goddard's *Journal*), and the whole subject of non-importation was discussed at length.

It wasn't an easy problem. The proposal was the cessation of all purchases from Great Britain and her West Indian colonies. But Maryland, as a whole, was dependent upon the tobacco trade with England, and Baltimore had a special concern with the West Indies. But, as we have seen, the tobacco trade was producing debt almost as regularly as it was producing profit, while the late experience during the war with France had shown that the Chesapeake schooners were not necessarily bound by the activities of the British navy.

Thus of the eight resolutions proposed five were unanimously adopted and three were passed with only small objections. The merchants bound themselves not to import goods from Great Britain or her colonies and to cease intercourse with those colonies which failed to follow a similar course. They voted also to send delegates to Annapolis to a general meeting representing the counties of the colony and, if the occasion demanded, to appoint men to attend a general congress representing all the colonies. The necessary committees to look after the various matters were selected.

The letter the committee on correspondence sent to

Merchants' Choice

Boston recounting the action taken at the meeting is a model of patriotic fervor disciplined by practical considerations. Here is the final paragraph:

Permit us, as friends truly anxious for the preservation of your and our common liberties, to recommend firmness and moderation under this severe trial of your patience, trusting that the Supreme Disposer of all events will terminate the same in a happy confirmation of American freedom.
We are, with much sincerity;
Your truly sympathizing friends,
SAMUEL PURVIANCE, Chairman
WILLIAM BUCHANAN, in behalf of the committee

Every one of the recommendations was immediately carried into effect. The meeting at Annapolis was speedily arranged; the concurring resolutions were adopted by representatives of the whole colony. Mr. Lux was a member of the final Baltimore committee, though not chairman, for he seems to have been the sort of man who preferred to pull strings rather than appear in the lead. A special subcommittee was set up to report the arrival of all vessels in the port and to see that no goods were discharged.

The support which the Marylanders had voted to Boston did not find expression in words alone. The Baltimore meeting was held on May 25. In early July a vessel sailed from the Eastern Shore (Chestertown?) loaded with foodstuffs for Boston. On August 29 a journal of that town contained the following item:

Yesterday arrived at Marblehead, Captain Perkins, from Baltimore, with three thousand bushels of Indian corn, twenty barrels of rye, and twenty-one barrels of bread, sent by the inhabitants of that place for the benefit of the poor of Boston, together with one thousand bushels of corn from Annapolis, sent in the same vessel and for the same benevolent purpose.

News of the support which Baltimore had offered the beleaguered Bostonians reached that city on July 16, and the committee there acknowledged the prompt action in a letter which is worth quoting:

The part taken by the province of Maryland must henceforth stop the mouths of those blasphemers of humanity who have affected to question the existence of public virtue. So bright an example as you have set cannot fail to animate and encourage even the lukewarm and indifferent; more especially, such honest men as wish to be assured of support before they engaged in so weighty an enterprise. The noble sacrifice you stand ready to make of the staple commodity of your province, so materially affecting the revenue of Great Britain, and your generous interposition in our favor have our warmest acknowledgments.

Just how much the people of Boston knew of the current state of Maryland economy we can only guess. It is true that the planters of Maryland stood to lose the direct tobacco trade with England under the non-importation agreement. But, in so far as Baltimore Town itself was concerned, the tobacco trade was a minor factor. The citizens' chief interest was in wheat and flour and they had reason to believe that, war or peace, they would be able to dispose of it. The fact that they so quickly loaded a vessel with foodstuffs and dispatched it to the port nearest to Boston indicates that, however altruistic their motives, their benevolent activities took a form natural to enterprising merchants accustomed to looking for a wider market. Mr. William Lux surely had that kind of mind.

Having made the decision to follow the political lead of Boston, the merchants of Baltimore Town began to cast about for a definite course of action. Their chief need, of course, was to keep the channels of commerce open. This meant not only ships to carry their goods but also a navy to protect those ships. The Continental Congress, which held its first meeting in September 1774, didn't do much about naval matters, leaving the problem to the individual colonies.

Although the British kept ships in the bay, for quite a while they did not attempt seriously to interfere with trade. They wanted the tobacco if they could get it. The interference was on the other side. The people of Baltimore built a fort on Whetstone Point, which commanded the entrance to the Northwest Branch, on which lay both Baltimore and Fells Point. From Whetstone Point to the opposite shore—now called Lazaretto, because it was the site of the first quarantine station—they stretched three massive chains kept afloat by wooden blocks. The only opening was on the side close to the fort. This meant that any ship coming in would have to stop for examination or else pass close under the guns of the water battery. This barrier, so like the present anti-submarine nets, was the work of the committee especially charged with keeping tabs on incoming vessels. There wasn't much chance of breaking the non-importation agreement under such circumstances.

The export trade, however, continued. The harbor of Baltimore was crowded with small vessels which had little or no difficulty getting crews. The stifling of the tobacco-export business with England threw many out of work and provided a reservoir of men who had grown up with some knowledge, at least, of seamanship. Since the royal governors and their staffs had given up almost all attempts to exercise their authority and had yielded place to the citizens' committees, a ship outward bound was under no obligation to pay any heed to the Navigation Acts with their "enumerations" and other elaborate devices which the British government had set up to make the colonies wholly dependent upon their English overlords.

The Dutch immediately reopened the almost abandoned warehouses on St. Eustatius, called Orangetown a free port, and invited the colonists to make use of it. Thus an outlet was provided for wheat, corn, wheat flour, and barrel staves from the Chesapeake and for fish and other necessities from the Northern ports. In a little while, indeed, the tobacco trade was established by this route after a fashion, and for the first time in their long history the planters of Maryland had direct connection with the merchants of the country which consumed and distributed their product on the European continent. This connection was to prove of great value to Baltimore in the ensuing century.

When Congress reassembled in May 1775 hostilities had begun. The battles of Lexington and Concord had been fought, and all Americans knew that a long and bitter struggle was ahead. The British fleet changed its patrol into an attempted blockade. Since the maintenance of trade was essential, the Congress addressed itself almost immediately to maritime measures.

By October the Congress got to the point of authorizing the purchase of ships suitable for naval use. There were two vessels in the harbor of Baltimore at that time which appeared to the patriots to be able enough for naval duty. They were the sloop *Hornet*, owned by Captain William Stone, like his vessel, a product of Bermuda, and the schooner *Wasp*, a Chesapeake-built vessel, William Hallock, of Baltimore, master. Both were hired under the Congressional authorization.

Also in Baltimore at this time was Joshua Barney, one of those incredible beings who happens along now and then. Barney, who was born in 1759, had just returned from a voyage in which he started out as a sort of apprentice under his brother-in-law and came back in full command. His brother-in-law, having sailed without a mate, had, himself, died on the way out. Barney, the only person aboard who knew navigation, thus became a responsible skipper at the age of fifteen and a half. He had a cargo of wheat for Nice and, despite the active opposition of God and man, he managed to deliver his cargo, collect for it, and bring his vessel back in safety.

On his way up the bay the British sloop of war, *Kingfisher*, stopped him, searched him, and took off his arms. This was the first he knew of hostilities between England and the colonies. He arrived in a town seething with revolutionary activity. Volunteers were drilling in the surrounding fields in new uniforms, and men were talking about the young navy. Barney was thrilled, offered his services, and was given the post of second lieutenant on the *Hornet*, under Captain Stone. He was told off to raise a crew and so, carrying with his own hands the first Continental banner to be raised in Baltimore, he paraded the streets calling for recruits. His crew was signed in jig time, as was that of the *Wasp*.

The merchant vessels gathered in the harbor, waiting for an escort down the bay past the *Kingfisher*, were duly convoyed beyond the capes by these, the first vessels in the American navy to go to sea.

There wasn't much glory in this particular expedition for the ambitious and perhaps conceited young second lieutenant. The order required the *Hornet* to foregather with a squadron being assembled off the Delaware capes to patrol the Southern coast, under Captain Esek Hopkins, commander-in-chief of the new navy.

The latter decided to attack New Providence, in the Bahamas, and ordered his skippers to accompany him thither. But off the coast of South Carolina the *Fly* tender fouled the *Hornet* and pretty well wrecked her rigging. She put into a harbor for repairs but was driven out to sea by a sudden storm, leaving some of her crew ashore.

Thus tossed about and almost beyond control, she finally made the Delaware capes again, to be confronted by the British frigate *Roebuck*. Seeking to escape this danger, the *Hornet* crossed to the other side of the bay, to find herself in the path of the tender *Maria*.

Barney, always impetuous, was for giving battle and ran out a gun. But Stone, the master, ordered him not to fire, as he "had no inclination for shedding blood." This so incensed Barney that he threw the burning matchstick at his commander, to the horror of that gentleman and the scandal of the crew.

Immediately thereafter the *Hornet* ran aground, breaking her rudder in the process, and lay helpless for several days. Her captain, according to Barney, remained in his cabin singing psalms and praying during the whole period. Barney managed to get the little vessel up the river to

Philadelphia, whereupon Stone rushed ashore and was never seen on a ship again. A fine beginning for the young officer, and hardly a boost for Baltimore's maritime reputation!

The *Wasp* also returned to Philadelphia in a damaged condition, having got in trouble in the attack on New Providence. Barney was transferred to the second of the Baltimore boats and helped refit her.

He did his share in the ensuing effort to defend the shipping in the Delaware Bay against the depredations of the *Roebuck* and a second frigate, the *Liverpool*, which joined in the blockade.

His activity and his bravery were proved in the famous effort to land powder from the brigantine *Nancy*, which had been chased ashore by the British. As a result he received, from the hands of Robert Morris, fiscal agent of the Continental Congress, a lieutenant's commission in the American navy. He was the thirteenth of his rating and was still only seventeen years old.

In December 1775, while Barney was thus earning his stripes, Congress authorized the building of thirteen real ships of war, and the contract for one of these, the frigate *Virginia*, twenty-eight guns, was landed by Mr. Wells, one of the shipwrights who had followed the example of William Fell and set up a yard on the deep water off the Point.

The industrial effects of the town's second war boom thus began to be felt, and patriotism mounted accordingly. The poor, busy with the struggle to make a living, and the dull, whose energies had been sapped and mental processes slowed by years of indentured slavery in the fields, could not perhaps understand the fine words about fiscal policy which were current in the counting houses and taverns but they knew the meaning of a job and at high wages.

There was need of such a boom. The shift from tobacco to wheat in Baltimore County, though highly profitable and advantageous to the landowners and to the merchants of the town, had the effect of ousting from their customary employment on the plantations a good many of the laboring class. In 1773, under an enabling act passed by the assembly, the county—including the town—had purchased an outlying tract of 350 acres from Mr. William Lux and erected thereon an almshouse, divided into two sections. The first section was for the worthy poor; the second for the vagrants, beggars, vagabonds, and other offenders who were caught up and committed. In 1776 half the almshouse burned down, and there was such a dearth of occupants that the business of re-erecting it was indefinitely postponed.

Baltimore's enthusiasm for war was not entirely shared in Annapolis, where the royal governor, Sir Robert Eden (he was a connection of the Calverts and, incidentally, a forebear of Anthony Eden, at this writing foreign secretary in the Churchill cabinet), had behaved with meticulous propriety. He was a cultured, gracious man, gave agreeable parties, and was on intimate terms with many of the leading families who had their residences in Annapolis.

When Mr. William Lux received his letter from Samuel Adams telling of the blockade of Boston he had duly dispatched a copy of it to the capital, and a general meeting of representatives of all the counties had been called. The vote was for the non-importation agreement but it was by no means unanimous. the lower counties, tied entirely to tobacco, being especially loath to go to extremes. There may have been also some feeling that it was not fitting that the lead in such weighty matters should be taken by the upstart town on the Patapsco, whose interests *and* manners were so different from the standards set in the capital. Annapolis had some trade, and a few merchants were settled there, but the main basis of its life was official.

In October 1774 this conflict came to a head. Mr. Andrew Stewart owned the brigantine *Peggy Stewart*, which was engaged by Thomas C. Williams and Company, merchants, of London and Annapolis, to take out tobacco and bring back supplies. Mr. Williams himself had taken a voyage in the vessel and had purchased in London twenty-nine cases of tea which were loaded with the other cargo.

When the ship cast anchor in Annapolis harbor Mr. Stewart looked over her manifest and found the tea listed there. He had subscribed to the non-importation agreement and he was naturally perturbed. Still he took the manifest to the customhouse and asked that the cargo be admitted without the tea. But the royalist official on duty ruled that the cargo would have to be entered in its entirety, or else the ship would be subject to libel. With this ruling to guide him, Mr. Stewart paid duty on the entire cargo.

The local Committee of Observation got news of the affair and called a meeting. It was expressive of their own lack of definite convictions that they took no action but preferred instead to see how public opinion would move. Accordingly they had handbills printed for distribution outlining the circumstances. The news was passed along by word of mouth as well, and, as Mr. Matthew Page Andrews, the distinguished Maryland historian, suggests, it lost nothing in the telling. Mr. Stewart, like many of his fellow townsmen, was committed to the colonial cause but made no effort to keep his patriotism at white heat. By the time the tale had spread around he was an out-and-out Tory in the minds of those of the opposite persuasion.

Sensing the drift of affairs, Mr. Stewart, along with Mr. Williams, the consignee, and his brother, offered to appear before a public meeting, apologize for their action, and submit to any penalty which might be imposed. The meeting was called; the accused made their explanation—Mr. Williams taking his share of the blame—and left it to the citizens to decide.

To the great majority it seemed that the apology had been so handsome that the burning of the tea would be a sufficient punishment. But it wasn't only the mild Annapolitans, with their tendency toward loyalty to the royal government, who had come to the meeting. Also present was a group of "gentlemen from Elk Ridge and Baltimore Town." These were the true hotheads. They wanted to make an example and they made it clear that if the gathering didn't act more vigorously they would take matters in their own hands. There were rumors that a gallows had been erected before Mr. Stewart's door and that it might be put to use if the meeting was halfhearted.

Mr. Stewart's partner, Mr. James Dick, who was also his father-in-law, was a mild man, eager for peace. He took his son-in-law aside and reminded him that Mrs. Stewart had just given birth to a baby girl. He spoke of the dangers with which not only the father but also the mother and child were threatened. Mr. Stewart weakened and finally stated to the meeting that not only the tea but also the rest of the cargo and even the vessel itself should be burned.

Then, in broad daylight, accompanied by Mr. Williams, the consignee, and his brother, he got into a small boat, was rowed alongside the *Peggy Stewart*, and set fire to her with his own hands. She was burned to the water's edge while the crowds on the shore looked on.

This was probably the first time in the history of Maryland that proud Annapolis was made to see that in Baltimore and its merchants and artisans it had to deal with a new and perhaps dominating political force.

Annapolis and most of Maryland outside of Baltimore was exceedingly slow to take fire, and the various committees and assemblies which met in the capital were always careful to put themselves on record as hoping for a happy settlement of the difficulties with the government of George III. But Baltimore went its own persistent way, and circumstances favored its course. Maryland's delegates to the Continental Congress—one of them was Charles Carroll of Carrollton, whose special point of view we have already examined—voted along with the others for the resolution declaring the independence of the colonies. The news of the vote did not reach Annapolis as soon as it had been expected. On July 6, therefore, two days after the Congress had acted, the men assembled passed the following:

DECLARATION OF THE DELEGATES OF MARYLAND

To be exempt from parliamentary taxation, and to regulate their internal government and polity, the people of this colony have ever considered as their inherent and inalienable right. Without the former, they can have no property; without the latter, they can have no security for their lives and liberties.

The Parliament of Great Britain has, of late, claimed an

uncontrollable right of binding these colonies in all cases whatsoever. To force an unconditional submission to this claim, the legislative and executive powers of that state have invariably pursued, for these ten years past, a studied system of oppression, by passing many impolitic, severe and cruel acts, for raising revenue from the colonists by depriving them, in many cases, of the trial by jury; by altering the chartered constitution of one colony, and the entire stoppage of the trade of its capital; by cutting off all intercourse between the colonies; by restraining them from fishing on their own coasts; by extending the limits of, and erecting an arbitrary government in the province of Quebec; by confiscating the property of the colonists taken on the seas, and compelling the crews of their vessels, under the pain of death, to act against their native country and dearest friends; by declaring all seizures, detention, or destruction of the persons, or property of the colonists, to be legal and just. A war unjustly commenced, has been prosecuted against the United Colonies with cruelty, outrageous violence, and perfidy; slaves, savages, and foreign mercenaries have been meanly hired to rob a people of their property, liberties, and lives, a people guilty of no other crime than deeming the last of no estimation without the secure enjoyment of the former. Their humble and dutiful petitions for peace, liberty, and safety, have been rejected with scorn. Secure of, and relying on foreign aid, not on his national forces, the unrelenting monarch of Britain hath at length avowed, by his answer to the City of London, his determined and inexorable resolution of reducing these colonies to abject slavery.

Compelled by dire necessity, either to surrender our properties, liberties, and lives, into the hands of a British King and parliament, or to use such means as will most probably secure to us and our posterity those invaluable blessings:

We, the Delegates of Maryland, in convention assembled,

do declare, that the king of Great Britain has violated his compact with this people, and that they owe no allegiance to him, We have, therefore, thought it just and necessary, to empower our deputies in Congress, to join with a majority of the United Colonies, in declaring them free and independent States, in framing such further confederation between them, in making foreign alliances, and in adopting such other measures as shall be judged necessary for the preservation of their liberties, provided the sole and exclusive right of regulating the internal polity and government of this colony be reserved to the people thereof. We have also thought proper to call a new convention, for the purpose of establishing a government in this colony. No ambitious views, no desire of independence, induced the people of Maryland to form a union with the other colonies. To procure an exemption from parliamentary taxation, and to continue to the legislatures of these colonies the sole and exclusive right of regulating their internal policy, was our original and only motive. To maintain inviolate our liberties and transmit them unimpaired was our duty and first wish; our next to continue connected with, and dependent upon Great Britain. For the truth of these assertions, we appeal to that Almighty Being who is emphatically styled the searcher of hearts, and from whose omniscience nothing is concealed. Relying on his Divine protection and assistance, and trusting to the justice of our cause, we exhort and conjure every virtuous citizen to join cordially in defense of our common rights, and in maintenance of the freedom of this and her sister colonies.

There is strength and forthrightness in this declaration, though obviously it lacks something of the finality of its great prototype. The reader who knows something of present-day Maryland will recognize in it not only its reiterated concern for property rights, the natural preoccupation of an agricultural community, but also, and more especially, its insistence upon the fact that the powers delegated to the Continental Congress would be sharply limited. There is not in all the union a state more articulate on the subject of home rule than Maryland.

CHAPTER X

Wealth by Stealth

THE *Hornet* and the *Wasp* were contributions to the national cause. Having gone immediately to sea, they did not solve the problem of protecting shipping in the bay. H.M.S. *Kingfisher* was operating there, accompanied by a tender and several barges. She was being supplied, moreover, by a number of loyalists on both sides of the bay; some of the latter, in their own boats, were cooperating with her, attacking the little local vessels of the patriots as they moved on their various errands. Occasionally they became bold enough to act on their own, self-appointed privateers, taking prizes when they could and burning and wrecking when prize-taking was not feasible. The lower part of the bay, south of the Patuxent, was soon given over to general lawlessness not far from piracy.

The merchants of Baltimore were thus hampered in their efforts to serve the national cause by carrying on their trade with the West Indies and with the other colonies. Also, they were not making as much money as they had hoped. Accordingly they procured from the delegates at Annapolis the right to acquire and operate at their own expense a regularly commissioned ship of war operating under Maryland colors. Messrs. William Lux (of course) and Daniel Bowley were appointed agents for the undertaking.

The accounts of the agents are still extant. They show that the vessel, called *Defence*, was seventy-six feet long on the keel and eighty-five feet over all. Her extreme draft, when fully loaded, with provisions for four months for 180 men, was twelve feet, six inches. From the fact that she was provisioned for four months it can be deduced that she was not expected to confine her endeavors to inland waters alone.

She had a full suit of sails when purchased, but they were only "tolerable good," so a new suit was bought, together with a vast amount of new cordage, doubtless manufactured in the ropewalk of Mr. Lux. The bill for rope alone was £740–18–3. Messrs. S. and R. Purviance sold her £285–9–8 worth of canvas.

Her armament was heavy, taking her size into consideration. Twenty-two six pounders were bought, of which twenty cost £1500. The agents bought 1600 round shot, 100 grape with ten 9-ounce balls in each, and 72 double-headed shot, useful in cutting the rigging of an opponent. There were 200 hand grenades, 60 pole axes, 60 half-pikes (for boarding and for resisting boarders), 30 iron crows, and 40 hand spikes. There were muskets, bayonets, cutlasses, and two blunderbusses with brass barrels. Probably not many ships were so lovingly furnished. Nearly every merchant in the town seems to have sold her something.

The hull cost £1350. James Nicholson, chosen commander, received an advance of £500. The carpenters, joiners, riggers, etc., who worked on her fitting out got

£1817. The total outlay, with some small bills still outstanding, was £11,272-18-8, which is no small sum in a
town whose first census, taken in 1775, showed a total
population of 5934. Probably the Point helped in the
undertaking. That settlement, in an enumeration at the
same time, contained about 800 persons.

By March 1776 the *Kingfisher* had been succeeded as
the principal British vessel in the bay by the sloop-of-war
Otter. Hearing of the unusual maritime activity in Baltimore, her captain moved up that way, taking on his way a
New England schooner which had come down in the hope
of picking up a cargo of flour. The Yankee tried to hide in
the Patuxent, but the *Otter* sent a tender up the river after
him, taking on the way several smaller vessels.

On March 7 she sailed past the Severn with her tenders
and their prizes and was observed from Annapolis by,
among others, William Eddis, the royalist officcholder
who was still in the colony hoping for an opportunity to
get back to England. Not he, of course, but some of the
patriots sent word to Baltimore of the impending danger,
and Captain Nicholson summoned his crew, weighed
anchor, and dropped down to meet her and give battle.

The *Otter* spied the *Defence* somewhere off Seven Foot
Knoll, which marks the entrance to the Patapsco, and for
some reason turned tail and sailed off down the bay, leaving her prizes, which were thus retaken by the *Defence*.
Captain Nicholson's reputation was made by this sortie,
and he was regarded locally as a naval hero from that time
forth. So much was this so that he could pursue courses
which would have shaken the reputations of other commanders, as we shall see.

Though the *Defence* was Baltimore's special pride, she

was not the only vessel fitted out by Maryland and commissioned as part of the state's navy. The brigs *Friendship* and *Amelia*, the sloop-of-war *Hebe Johnson*, the galleys *Johnson, Independence, Baltimore, Conqueror, Chester,* and *Molly*, the barges *Revenge, Terrible, Intrepid, Protector, Experiment, Venus, Defence, Reformation, Dolphin, Fearnaught,* and several others were armed, manned, and commissioned and did their part in keeping the bay channels open. In all, Maryland commissioned twenty-five vessels by the end of 1776.

The observant reader will have noticed that there are no schooners among those commissioned. The reason is not far to seek. The merchants of Baltimore and the other towns on the bay had better and more profitable use for their fast boats. Early in the war the Annapolis Council of Safety began issuing licenses to privateers. A few took advantage of this privilege, but when in March 1776 the Congress authorized such practices there was a rush to the new Admiralty Court for letters of marque.

It hadn't been easy to get the necessary legislation passed by the Congress. Many of the members were of the opinion that privateering, however profitable to the owners, officers, and crew of the vessel concerned, was not the best way to meet the threat of the British fleet. They felt that, on the whole, it would be better to trust to a regular navy. That view prevailed when they passed the first bill calling for the establishment of Esek Hopkins' squadron and it was still prevailing when the thirteen frigates were authorized.

But the Hopkins adventure at New Providence was none too successful, and there were many delays both in the building and the manning of the frigates. Meanwhile hundreds of small vessels lay in harbor, their owners straining for a chance to cover themselves with glory and make fortunes as well. The states, naturally enough, were the first to give way, and after that it was easy enough for the Congress to follow suit. The shipowners thus formed perhaps the first pressure group in our national history.

Massachusetts had the largest merchant marine and hence provided the most privateers. During the course of the war that state issued about a thousand letters of marque, while 626 commissions were issued by the Continental authorities to Massachusetts vessels. It has been estimated that, taking duplicates into account, some seven hundred different Massachusetts privateers were at sea during the seven years after serious fighting began.

Maryland's official list of privateers, which dates from April 1, 1777, contains the names of 248 vessels. One famous historian has written that four out of five of the privateers engaged in the attack on British commerce during the Revolution were from Massachusetts. The above figures indicate that Maryland's share, at least, is not accurately represented in such a statement.

The operations of the regular navy enriched the general store of goods. The operations of privateers also increased the national resources, but it was the owners, officers, and crews of privateers who were enriched if the voyages were successful. There was much debate over this point. The case against privateering was well stated by William Whipple, writing to Josiah Bartlet from Portsmouth, N. H., on July 12, 1778. He says:

I agree with you that the privateers have much distressed the trade of our enemies, but, had there been no privateers, is it not probable there would have been a much larger number of Public Ships than has been fitted out, which might have distressed the Enemy nearly as much & furnished these States with necessaries on much better terms than they have been supplied by privateers? . . . No kind of business can so effectually introduce Luxury, Extravagance, and every kind of Dissipation, that tend to destruction of the morals of people. Those who are actually engaged in it soon lose every Idea of right and wrong, and for want of an opportunity of gratifying their insatiable avarice with the property of the Enemies of their Country, will without the least compunction seize that of her Friends. . . . There is at this time five Privateers fitting out here, which I suppose will take 400 men. These must be by far the greater part Countrymen, for the Seamen are chiefly gone, and most of them in Halifax Gaol. Besides all this, you may depend no public ship will ever be manned while there is a privateer fitting out. The reason is plain: Those people who have the most influence with Seamen think it their interest to discourage the Public service, because by that they promote their own interest, viz., Privateering.

A more favorable opinion of privateering is found in a letter of John Adams to the President of Congress, dated Amsterdam, September 16, 1780. Speaking of commerce destroying, he says: "This is a short, easy, and infallible method of humbling the English and bringing the war to a conclusion. In this policy I hope our countrymen will join [the French and Spanish] with utmost alacrity. Privateering is as well understood by them as any people whatsoever, and it is by cutting off supplies and by attacks, sieges, or assaults that I expect deliverance from enemies."

In the course of Baltimore's revolutionary privateering

we can see both of these points of view well illustrated. Congress authorized the building of the frigate *Virginia*, twenty-eight guns, in Mr. Well's shipyard on the Point, in December 1775. She was ready for sea early in 1777. James Nicholson, who had made his reputation in the *Defence*, had been appointed as her commander as early as June 6, 1776, receiving on that date a commission which ranked him immediately after Esek Hopkins, commander-in-chief.

In April Nicholson was ordered to proceed to sea. But Dunmore's fleet was then blockading the bay, and he felt it better not to risk his ship. As a sailor he remained inactive in port throughout the rest of the year, though he found some other not so savory activities to use up his time. His crew, perhaps more impatient than he, was continually drifting away from him. To make up the lack he tried impressment and was immediately made to feel the community's objection to that sort of thing. Sailors were needed to man the privateers, and taking them by force for the regular navy was not cricket. Governor Johnson, representing the new government of the state, protested so violently that Nicholson was suspended from his command. He had to apologize to the state of Maryland before he was reinstated. But this didn't supply the men he lacked.

About this time the Marine Committee of the Congress assigned Joshua Barney, the turbulent and headstrong, to the *Virginia*. Barney was for action. Acting under orders from Nicholson, he proceeded to York, where Congress was sitting. There he got the ear of the Marine Committee and won from them permission to take from Bordentown (where the remnants of the fleet which had been driven from Philadelphia were stationed) fifty or sixty men for the *Virginia*, plus ten each for two vessels loaded with tobacco which were waiting in the Chesapeake for a convoy.

Barney got his men and marched them overland, stopping on his way at Valley Forge to pay his respects to General Washington, then in the midst of that painful winter. He arrived in Baltimore with his party before the end of December. Soon after January 1 the *Virginia* was under way, and the Marine Committee wrote from York to Samuel and Robert Purviance, their Baltimore agents, that they "rejoice(d) to hear that Captain Nicholson is off your hands."

Their rejoicing was premature. Nicholson got almost to the capes when he was sighted by the British frigate *Emerald*, which chased him all the way back to Baltimore.

The committee then sent twenty more seamen down from Bordentown, and Nicholson was ordered to try again. This time he sent Barney ahead in the pilot-schooner *Dolphin*, a clipper, to spy out the enemy. Barney found a British cruiser, unnamed, in Tangier Sound but escaped her with ease. While she was still in sight he came up with a little Baltimore sloop he knew, discovered that she had been captured and manned by the enemy, and retook her after a sharp fight. Barney always found action. But when Nicholson heard Barney's tale he turned back once more. Barney was sent to York to carry his commander's report of this new failure.

Here is the committee's reply:

Your letters of the 25th and 26th ult. per Lieut. Barney are before us. We are concerned to find your last attempt in getting the frigate *Virginia* to sea has been fruitless, but, as your letters inform us, such is the fondness your officers and seamen retain for the ship, that you think they will cheerfully make another trial. This has induced the committee to resolve that another trial be made as soon as possible, and to expedite the same they have this day requested Governor Johnson to continue to you the use of the tender, as well as to furnish you with a skillful pilot. By information from Lieut. Barney we have reason to apprehend our late agents will not supply the ship unless more money is put in their hands. This we are restrained from doing until the large sums already placed there is accounted for, and lest this should throw embarrassment in your way, the committee have this day appointed Stephen Howard Esqr., of West River, their agent for supplying the *Virginia* and have put money into his hands. . . .

We assure you that we retain a tender regard for your character and hope you will by this successful attempt be enabled to wipe off any malicious reflections (if any there be, for we know of none) on your character. . . .

Thus encouraged, Nicholson made another attempt to get to sea toward the end of March. He had procured a brig, commanded by a man supposed to be a good pilot, to lead the way. The wind was fair and strong. It was arranged that he should take his vessel through the capes at night. But either he lost his brig or else the pilot was not as competent as had been supposed, for the *Virginia* struck on the famous Middle Ground. With the wind astern, she pounded violently and before she was clear had lost her rudder. There was nothing for Nicholson to do but anchor.

When morning broke, the unlucky commander saw two British frigates lying within two gunshots of him. Whereupon he hoisted out his barge and with ten men and the ship's papers made for shore. Barney refused to desert the ship and tried to persuade the other officers to allow him to cut the cable so that she might drift ashore and be destroyed. But he was overruled, and the crew, seeing nothing ahead but captivity, broke open the stores and got roaring drunk.

The British came aboard at ten o'clock and took the whole lot prisoners. Barney was put on the *Emerald* and given a berth in the captain's cabin. The next day he suffered the mortification of seeing his late commander come aboard under a flag of truce and ask for his clothes. This so outraged Barney that he proceeded to tell Nicholson precisely what he thought of him.

Thus ended the ill-starred *Virginia*. She was the bitter fruit of divided counsels. She was commanded by a man better at political maneuvering than at leadership. But her chief trouble was the lack of a seasoned and stable crew. How could a sailor be enthusiastic in the regular navy, under political officers, when by the easy device of slipping over the side he could find a berth on a romantic privateer? Why should he accept the harsh discipline and the low and uncertain pay of the navy when, on a privateer, he could take life easy, see plenty of action, and perhaps make a fortune?

The sailors argued this way, and owners and captains saw things in much the same light. By this time maritime Baltimore, both Lombard Street and the Point, had only one immediate aim, and that was to take advantage of the golden opportunity to make money and make it quickly. The cause in which they were engaged now had the blessing—belated perhaps but sincere—of the older landowning aristocracy. The survival of the new nation depended upon the ability of the ships to outwit the British blockade and continue the export trade. The supplies upon which both the civilian population and the army depended must be acquired and brought in. The quickest, most profitable, most exciting, and perhaps most productive way of procuring such supplies was to take them from the enemy. Privateering was the natural answer, and it was supported by the public morality.

The watchful Mr. Eddis, writing from Annapolis on January 1, 1777, was perturbed over the situation:

It has been a matter of surprise to many that the capes of Virginia have, in great measure, been left open since the departure of Lord Dunmore and his fleet from the Chesapeake. (Dunmore was the last royal governor of Virginia and he tried vigorously to maintain his prerogatives and put down the rebellion until the weight of opinion forced him to quit). In consequence of this remissness, on the part of the British cruisers, a considerable commerce is carried on, with very little interruption, between Virginia and Maryland, and the French and Dutch islands, and even with several ports on the continent of Europe. Those who continue attached to the interest of Britain, behold, with infinite concern, many valuable prizes continually brought into American harbors by privateers so inconsiderable in appearance, that they might readily be mistaken for boats belonging to the vessels they were triumphantly conducting. Almost all the ships which have hitherto been taken, had not the least apprehension of danger, consequently were not prepared for resistance; and if a certain judgment may be formed from the success which has attended the adventurers from this, and the adjacent colony, Great Britain must sensibly experience the loss she has already sustained, by the rapid and spirited exertions which have been so unexpectedly directed against commerce.

The privateers he watched sailing triumphantly up the bay were the little Chesapeake schooners. The ships they were conducting were, nine times out of ten, merchant-men they had picked up in the islands. If bound out from England the prizes were usually loaded with the very commodities the colonists needed—linens, cottons, and woolens, cutlery and utensils of all sorts, even arms and ammunitions intended for the fleet.

The relative freedom of commerce of which Eddis complained was not destined long to endure. In August of 1777 Lord Howe's fleet came into the bay. His sails were estimated, extravagantly perhaps, to number 260. He had on board most of the army organized to make the attack on Philadelphia. On the twentieth he passed Annapolis, and word was carried to Baltimore, almost completely unprepared for any sort of attack.

On the twenty-first the whole fleet entered the Patapsco and anchored just inside Bodkin Point. The town was in something very like a panic. The militia was called out and word sent out to the counties for help. From faraway York, in the center of the wheat country of lower Pennsylvania, came word that their militia was prepared to fight if needed.

Howe's maneuver was just a feint, or perhaps he was uncertain of the channel. In any event, the next day he hauled up anchor and moved on up to the head of the bay. His only landing was in the Gunpowder River, where he put off a small body of troops for an attack on little Joppa. The militia of Harford County assembled, built a series of earthworks armed with four-pounders, and prepared for the defense of the declining town. Howe had other matters to attend to and so ordered a withdrawal. Having disembarked his troops at the Elk River, he sailed down the bay again, leaving only two considerable vessels to maintain the blockade. With the rest of his fleet he proceeded up the coast to the Delaware, where he cooperated with the army in the attack on Philadelphia.

The blockade was severe enough to bring a shortage of many essential materials, and the inhabitants of the town, to fulfill their own needs and to meet the constantly increasing calls upon them being made by the Continental Congress, established manufacturing plants on a scale that they had hitherto not attempted.

The growing of flax was well established in York County, Pa., and the raw material and the seed were more and more being brought to Baltimore for shipment. A Mr. McFadon therefore established a linen factory, and a Mr. Riddle a bleachyard. Mr. Goddard, editor and publisher, set up a paper mill. Mr. Charles Carroll, a far-seeing as well as a wealthy man, built a plant for spinning and weaving both linen and wool. The supernumerary factories were undertaken by other individuals. There was even a dyeing plant. Two nail factories were built by Messrs. Matthews and Stewart, respectively. Baltimore thus began to have industrial as well as commercial importance.

During this year, 1777, twenty-one privateers were commissioned under continental letters of marque, of which eleven were schooners, which is to say clippers. There was one ship, one brig, and one brigantine. The remainder were sloops. The brigantine *Buckskin Hero* carried one hundred men to serve her sixteen guns. The little schooner *Beggars Permission* had six guns but admitted to a crew of only six. Doubtless she picked up more on the way down the bay, for another schooner, the *Adventure*, with one gun and two swivels, had seven men aboard.

Such vessels were built or purchased, equipped, and

manned by the established merchants of the town. Mr. William Lux had a share in at least two of them. The Purviance brothers, Samuel and Robert, who were agents for the Marine Committee of the Congress, ventured in two and perhaps three. Daniel Bowley, Mr. Lux's father-in-law and occasional business associate, was in at least three ventures. So was William Hammond.

It should here be noted that this is the last time Mr. William Lux's name appears in the annals of Baltimore Town. He had been working like a Trojan in his own interests and those of the community ever since the days of the Sons of Liberty. There was almost no public undertaking in which he didn't have a leading part.

When in the autumn of 1776 the British moved on Philadelphia and Congress had to flee he was instrumental in persuading the members to make Baltimore their new headquarters. Rooms were found for them in a new three-story-and-attic tavern which Mr. Jacob Fite had just built on the corner of Sharp and Baltimore streets at the very westernmost edge of the town. It was probably the largest building in Baltimore. It stood until after the Civil War and was always known as Congress Hall to the townspeople.

The members didn't like the looks of the place to which they had been enveigled. There had been a scheme to pave the streets, but the outbreak of the war caused a postponement of this improvement. There were no sidewalks, and the burgers, unrestrained by a building code, had built their houses in higgledy-piggledy fashion, at all angles. Their porches sometimes extended over the place where the sidewalks should have been. The pedestrian was thus forced to pick his way between the ruts made by the wagons and carriages which plowed through the muddy streets.

But the well-to-do put themselves out to give the members of Congress the best entertainment possible. John Adams, who arrived after the sessions began, kept a diary of the visit. On his very first evening he attended a dinner at Mr. William Lux's place, Chatsworth, about half a mile from Congress Hall. Here he met the Lux brothers and their wives and William's son George. Samuel Adams, William Lux's old friend, was there and several other notables. John Adams was impressed:

. . . an elegant [seat] it is [he wrote]; has a large yard, enclosed with stone in lime, and before the yard, two fine rows of cherry trees, which lead out to the public road; there is a fine prospect about it. Mr. Lux and his son are sensible gentlemen. I had much conversation with George about the new form of government adopted in Maryland. . . . The whole family profess great zeal in the American cause. Mr. Lux lives like a Prince.

Mr. Adams went to a number of other dinners. He met Charles Carroll, the barrister, a cousin of Charles Carroll of Carrollton and wrote an enthusiastic description of the latter's seat (which is still standing, in part of its original park, and well merits praise). He talked with the merchants about a plan they were then considering for removing the rocky obstructions in the Susquehanna River so that it might carry barges down to Baltimore from Pennsylvania. He had "a good deal of free conversation with Mr. R. Purviance. He seems to me to have a perfect understanding of the affairs of this state. Men and things are very well known to him."

Yet after all this he could find it in his heart to put down in his secret diary:

The object of the men of property here, the planters &c., is universally wealth. Every way in the world is sought to get and save money. Landjobbers, speculators in land; little generosity to the public, little public spirit.

We need not take this judgment too seriously. In the first place, John Adams was unusually endowed with public spirit, so that few could hope to meet his standards in this regard. In the second place, he was a New Englander, and urban life was second nature to him. The people with whom he found himself thrown into close contact were newly urbanized. Their standards, social and economic, were still set by the feudal life which had been established before trade became a preoccupation. Their ideal was still, in spite of everything, the self-contained manor to whose support their business ventures were supposed merely to contribute. That ideal still obtains among the successful families of Baltimore. The city is the place where men make the money with which they support the country places to which they retire at every opportunity.

In any event, Mr. Adams didn't have to endure this disturbing society for very long. The Congress adjourned its Baltimore session on February 27, 1777, and was back in Philadelphia—for a very short stay—early in March.

Less than three months later, on May 10, Mr. William Lux was dead. Chatsworth passed to his son George. But George had no head for business, and the ropewalk was bequeathed to Daniel Bowley, a nephew. Darby, the younger brother, continued to carry on much of the business of the trading firm and survived until 1795. He had interests in

Barbados and was associated with that island in the public mind.

The records of the successes and failures of the privateering venture of 1777 are not available, but we know that they were sufficiently profitable to stimulate a great increase in the business in 1778.

In that year the licenses issued number thirty-seven, of which fourteen were schooners. The largest crew on any of this year's crop was fifty on the *Burling* brig. A similar number was found on the *Fly* sloop. This last named is important because it was owned by William Patterson, a native of Donegal, who had come to Baltimore from Philadelphia only the year before. Patterson was destined to become a very rich and important man in Baltimore, but his chief claim to fame will always be that he was the father of Elizabeth Patterson, known as Betsy, who married Jerome Bonaparte, the brother of Napoleon.

The winter of '79–'80, like that of '78–'79, was a hard one all through the colonies. It was particularly bad in Baltimore, where the harbor was completely frozen up for weeks on end. Such a persistent handicap was unknown to the oldest inhabitant. Ships were kept in idleness; trade dwindled, and specie disappeared. The people had plenty of opportunity for gloomy thoughts and gloomy expression. The extremists were dissatisfied with the conduct of the war and blamed the Congress and even Washington. The loyalists, long forced to keep silent, found in the growing unrest an opportunity for stirring up trouble.

There were several unpleasant incidents. Perhaps the most striking and most characteristic was that which involved William Goddard, the publisher. He was disgruntled himself, for he had hoped, on Franklin's retirement, to be made postmaster general of the country. He thought that his achievement of a private postal system covering the seaboard from Maine to Georgia made his claim irresistible. The job went, however, to Richard Bache, Franklin's son-in-law.

One of Goddard's most intimate friends was General Charles Lee, of Virginia, whose troubles with Washington are well known. At Lee's instigation Goddard printed in his journal a series of "Queries, Political and Military," the purpose of which was to undermine public confidence in the commander-in-chief.

The publication caused considerable excitement. Everyone immediately recalled an incident of the previous year when Goddard's journal had published an anonymous and indirect plea for the acceptance of General Howe's peace terms. On this first occasion the editor had been called to account by a volunteer association of overardent patriots who called themselves the Whig Club. Their chairman was our old friend Captain James Nicholson. This group had threatened Goddard, in the hope of forcing from him the name of the author. Failing this, they had ordered him to leave town. But he was resourceful and laid a complaint against the club in the legislature. That body, remembering the strong declaration for a free press in the new constitution, instructed the governor to order the immediate dissolution of the Whigs and the full protection of Mr. Goddard's person by all officers of the law. This round was clearly Mr. Goddard's.

But the attack on General Washington in the next year was taken more seriously by the whole community. Mr. Goddard had in the meantime enlisted a partner, one Eleazar Oswald, who was a fire-eating follower of the code *duello*. Goddard, having bluffed off a mob led by several Continental officers, appealed once more to the governor at Annapolis. But Oswald wanted physical revenge. He wrote a letter to Colonel Smith, one of Baltimore's outstanding military figures, filled it with insults and aspersions, and demanded satisfaction. The letter, carried to Smith by messenger, brought only an evasive reply, whereupon Oswald published the correspondence, with sardonic comments of his own on Smith's military and personal character.

This bold stand by his partner steeled Goddard to stick fast and in the same issue of the paper he, too, trumpeted his righteousness, his patriotism, and, especially, his unwillingness to retract. There was no certain outcome of this incident, but it showed the temper of the times. Baltimore was harassed by material losses, physical hardship, and, what was probably worse than anything else, uncertainty about the cause to which it had devoted itself.

With such a mood pressing upon the merchants and with signs of want all around, trade became no mere adventure for profit but a hard necessity. Privateering as a source of income was more incumbent upon the town than before. All during the winter the ships were preparing for the spring exit. In March ten newly commissioned privateers slipped past the capes to join those already harrying the trade routes. By the end of the year the new commissions amounted to forty-seven, of which fifteen were schooners.

It is impossible to give any idea of the value of their takings, just as it is impossible to tell which returned safely and which did not. Captured vessels were not often brought back to Baltimore but sent instead to the nearest

American port, where their cases were disposed of to the local Court of Admiralty. Such records as the owners kept were destroyed, to a tragic degree, by the Baltimore fire of 1904.

In the late spring of '79 Baltimore had another scare from the sea. The command of British forces in American waters was given to General Sir George Collier. One of his first concerns was to clean out the "nest of pirates" in the Chesapeake. He had two large ships, three sloops-of-war (one of them was the *Otter*), and a number of galleys, as well as transports carrying two thousand troops under General Matthews. The fleet came into the bay on April 10 and proceeded to attack Portsmouth, on the Elizabeth River. The troops razed a fort which had been built there and burned a lot of timber being seasoned for shipbuilding. The two large ships and the troops on their transports then sailed out to sea, but the sloops, headed by the *Otter*, moved up the bay, capturing no less than 130 American vessels on the way and landing at various points and destroying tobacco warehouses and private property. They were accompanied by four smaller "private vessels" (i.e., privateers on the English side) which the Americans described as "Goodrich's pirates."

Baltimore took fire at this news, called out the militia again, sent word to Annapolis for help from the counties, and received once again from York a spontaneous promise of assistance. But for once the Marine Committee of Congress was on the job. The *Deane* and the *Boston* were off the Delaware and they were ordered to clear the Chesapeake. The British sloops and privateers were speedily driven out to sea or captured and destroyed.

The records are incomplete, but Richard Henry Lee

wrote a letter of thanks to the Marine Committee in which he notes that two "vessels of war" had been captured.

This was probably one of the most useful of American naval actions during the war. It made it possible for all the trade which centered in the Chesapeake to operate with comparative safety, in its home waters, at least, until 1781.

CHAPTER XI

Darkness and Dawn

THE YEAR 1780 was a grim one. Despite French help the states, as a federation and as individual entities, had a hard time keeping afloat. The paper money issued on the say-so of the Continental Congress was depreciating rapidly. Taxes levied by the state governments were unproductive. For a while there was a race between military advantage and economic chaos, with the latter making some terrifying gains.

The General Assembly of Maryland issued a loan and called for subscriptions in paper money, tobacco, or specie. The members of the Assembly themselves started off the list. They gave generously of both paper money and tobacco—Daniel of St. Thomas Jenifer headed the list with two thousand dollars of paper and five hogsheads—but the total amount of specie subscribed was three dollars from one member and 3 pounds sterling from another.

The harassed legislators found another source of income, one which other states had used earlier but which Maryland had been loath to tap. They decided that the time had come to confiscate the property of the loyalists.

In Baltimore Town this meant that all the land which had been held by the departed loyalists—some of it was improved with good buildings—was put up at auction. Because the states agreed to accept notes and be reimbursed in installments there was no lack of buyers, and the public treasury was enriched by many thousands of pounds from these transactions. Poor Dr. Henry Stevenson (Remus to Dr. John's Romulus) was one of those whose holdings went under the hammer at this time.

By such devices the state was kept going.

Under such uncertainties internal trade was difficult and barter became a general method of transfer. Export, however, was the life of the region and it had to be carried on. Baltimore's fleet, augmented by that of the other towns on the bay, was carrying not only flour to the West Indies (usually to St. Eustatius) but tobacco as well. Some of the larger vessels were going to France direct, and a few were hawking cargoes of both wheat and flour in the Mediterranean parts. In a little while there were direct sales of tobacco to Holland.

These transactions developed so rapidly and were so prosperous that the General Assembly decided to see if it could procure a loan from the Dutch buyers with the tobacco business as security. Matthew Ridley, of the firm of Ridley and Pringle, which was active in the news business, was deputized to carry on the negotiations. He made a deal of a sort and brought back (1782) a credit of £40,500. The Assembly, however, regarded the terms as disadvantageous and turned down the whole transaction. The ensuing lawsuits were not settled for many years.

Privateering continued to engage a large portion of the time and energies of the merchants. The bay was relatively clear of English war vessels, both naval and private, for a large part of the year. Moreover, the privateers had learned to travel in company and hence were usually more than a match for the smaller of the armed vessels they encountered.

Fifty-six of these reckless fellows started out during the year, and of this number no less than thirty-six were schooners. One notices for the first time a few French names both among the merchants owning the vessels and among the skippers commanding them. At this time also one begins to find the names of Philadelphians, including the great Robert Morris himself, among the owners and at least one Portuguese firm, Verdue, Karlognew, Pagan & Co. Baltimoreans were on their way toward a knowledge of Madeira wine!

Late in the fall the British made another attempt to break up the trade. A naval force with one large ship of forty-four guns, a frigate, and some smaller vessels, including one manned by the ubiquitous Goodrich's retainers, came into the bay, bringing General Leslie and about three thousand men. They seized Portsmouth once more and used it as a base for their blockade and for a number of marauding expeditions.

In January (1781) Benedict Arnold joined Leslie with several more frigates and fifteen hundred men. Arnold was a wrecker. He raided up the James River as far as Richmond and destroyed much property. Virginia's navy opposed him strenuously. It received the aid of a French sixty-four and two frigates. It was a hot campaign while it lasted, but the British were too strong for the Virginians and finally nearly destroyed the navy in which they were beginning to have so much pride.

Darkness and Dawn

From this period until Cornwallis' surrender at York-town the merchants of Baltimore, whether their operations were those of legitimate traders or of privateers, must have felt like feathers being blown about in a battle royal of puffing giants. Much greater things were at stake than the tobacco and wheatlands of Maryland and the little vessels which were struggling so hard to dispose of their products.

One of the first blows came in February 1781. The Americans didn't know that England had declared war on Holland and that one of the chief reasons for this move was to break up the trade which centered in St. Eustatius. The little roadstead of Orangetown was crowded with shipping, much of it from the Chesapeake. Rodney sailed in with his fleet and simply took over the island, the town with its stuffed warehouses, and every American, Dutch, and French vessel in the harbor. Worse than that, he kept the Dutch flag flying over the fort and thereby lured in more dozens of unsuspecting vessels.

Rodney crowed loudly over this achievement. "I may speak within bounds when I say," he wrote to Germain, "that since taking this island upwards of two hundred thousand pounds in value of tobacco has fell into our hands."

In one respect he was premature, for the thirty-four ships in which he loaded his spoils for dispatch to England were intercepted by the French in the Channel, and most of them were captured. St. Eustatius, however, remained in British hands for most of the year, and as a result the Americans and the French were deprived of the use of what had been a valuable *entrepôt*.

Late in March De Grasse, with a powerful fleet, sailed from Brest for the islands. Rodney was so busy counting

[121]

up his spoils that he would neither go out to meet the French himself nor permit Admiral Hood, with his smaller squadron, to do so. But De Grasse wasn't particularly avid for action, either, and spent much of the summer mopping up here and there around Martinique. In July he was anchored off Cap François.

Back in Baltimore the people knew that something tremendous was impending. Washington was calling upon them for troops and supplies. Lafayette set out for Virginia in February under the general's orders. When he reached the Head of Elk with twelve hundred men he sent word to Baltimore asking for transportation down to Annapolis. This was supplied by barges, the expedition being convoyed by Captain James Nicholson with the privateer *Nesbit* and several smaller vessels. When he arrived in Annapolis Lafayette learned that his information was inaccurate and that the French fleet had not yet got into the Chesapeake, so he asked and received transportation back to the Head of Elk, which was, of course, a more favorable location in the event the expected battle should take place in the Delaware.

But the British continued, nevertheless, to concentrate their forces near the mouth of the Chesapeake, with Portsmouth as their chief base. Cornwallis, working up through the Carolinas, was to take command of all the forces in the lower Chesapeake region and, according to a plan which Baltimore thought it knew all about, he was to sail up the bay, reduce the town, and then set up headquarters on the other side of the Susquehanna, near the present Perry Point. Here he was to be joined by all the loyalists of the region and so was to break the backbone of the rebellion.

Baltimore, and, indeed, the whole of Maryland, was in a

state. At a meeting held in the courthouse on April 5 a committee was set up and given practically dictatorial powers to attend to the security of the community. Governor Lee wrote a moving appeal to Lafayette to detach part of his force for the business of defending Baltimore.

Lafayette complied but, being a Frenchman with a certain sense of the realities, he took advantage of the joy which his arrival occasioned by suggesting to the merchants that they advance him, on his own note, ten thousand pounds for the conciliation of his troops and the supplying of their wants. The merchants were in no mood to bargain. The ten thousand was immediately forthcoming, and the names of all the leading citizens of the town, including that of William Patterson, who was now second to none, are in the list.

The transaction concluded, the occasion was celebrated by a ball in the general's honor. Here, too, he took practical advantage of the prevailing enthusiasm. One of the ladies present railed him about his sad countenance. "I cannot enjoy the gayety of the scene," he explained, "while so many of my poor soldiers are in want of clothes."

The next day the ballroom was turned into a workshop, and the ladies who had danced so lightly the evening before turned to with needle and thread to fashion into clothes for the soldiers the materials which their fathers and husbands had provided.

This whole summer was the occasion of a series of alarums, but it didn't take the minds of the business community entirely off its reason for being. Things were a little more difficult with the lower bay in British hands, but privateering was still possible and profitable. Besides, it was necessary to recoup as far as possible the blow which the capture of St. Eustatius had given to trade. Some of the best of the schooners had been lost, but it was still feasible to fit out and dispatch twenty-three armed vessels, of which eleven were of the characteristic type.

Lafayette and his little army remained on the outskirts of the town all summer, waiting for word of the movements of Cornwallis and, more especially, for some news about De Grasse's fleet. During the waiting period Washington called for more help so that he could move promptly south when the word came. Powers of impressment of all vessels, wagons, and trams capable of transporting troops and material were given his local quartermaster, and he made full use of them.

On September 4 the French cutter *Serpent*, Captain Amie de la Lanne, sailed into the harbor and announced that De Grasse had successfully entered the bay with twenty-eight ships of the line. Word was sent to Washington, and he began his southern movement, stopping off in Baltimore long enough to attend a banquet in Lindley's coffeehouse and spend the night in the Fountain Inn. Immediately following him came Rochambeau, who rested with his troops for five days in Howard's Park, on the northern edge of the town.

After the rumble of the last of his carts and wagons died away there was suspended animation for more than a month. But finally, on October 20, the awaited news came from Yorktown, and Baltimore was enabled to come out of its coma and once more take stock of its losses and consider its future.

CHAPTER XII

Dreams of Empire

IT WAS JUST AS WELL for the merchants of Baltimore that during the years immediately after the Revolution they kept their minds on trade rather than on politics. There probably has never been a period in the history of the country when public affairs, domestic and foreign, were more confused. A man could spend his lifetime trying to figure out what was wrong inside the country while it was carrying on under the Articles of Confederation. He could spend another life, if it were given him, trying to figure out the role of the United States in the vast struggle which was still being waged, after Yorktown, between England on the one hand and the French-Spanish-Dutch combination on the other.

Baltimore's problem was affected, of course, by all these considerations. But there was little that its people could do about them, save through the small influence of their own legislature at Annapolis. Besides, their minds didn't work that way. What they wanted was trade. That meant, in the first place, bringing together in their harbor the agri-

[125]

cultural products of their own hinterland and the ships which were to carry those products to the rest of the world. It meant, in the second place, doing business in a town made more convenient and, if possible, more comely than the muddy little village with which they had so far had to content themselves.

While facing these major problems they had to carry on as well as possible under the conditions as they existed. The surrender of Cornwallis did not end the war. It had a full two years to run before the peace was finally signed. During a year and a half of that time privateering, the business they did best, was still legally possible. Thus we find that during 1782 Mr. Robert Morris, by that time virtual dictator of maritime and naval affairs, permitted the licensing of fifty-one private vessels from Baltimore to prey on the commerce of Great Britain. Of this number twenty-one were Chesapeake schooners. Several merchants from Mr. Morris' home town, Philadelphia, owned shares in these ventures, but for the first time in years he himself did not take a chance in any of them. It may be that the financial difficulties which were soon to overwhelm him had diverted his mind.

While their vessels were thus cruising the merchants at home had an opportunity to look about them and see what manner of community it was that had grown so quickly out of the straggling village of the sixties into a town important enough to be the meeting place of the Continental Congress and to entertain, with increasing frequency and increasing extravagance, such distinguished personages as General Washington, General Lafayette, Count de Rochambeau, and others.

It wasn't much to look at. They had to admit that there

was more than a little justice in the condescending comments made *sotto voce* by their guests and repeated from mouth to mouth all along the seaboard. Word was brought to them from several sources that many thoughtful men regarded the place as a mere boom town certain to decline to insignificance after the war was over.

This they were determined not to allow. For all its shortcomings, Baltimore was their own handiwork. If they didn't like its looks, at least they liked the livelihood it had provided. They liked the opportunity it gave them to acquire countryseats and to live in the fashion of the manorial squires who had established the tone of the region. Even the newcomers among them—e.g., the Pattersons and the Gilmors—had taken on the manners and habits of aristocrats. Men who have acquired such a status do not give it up without a struggle.

The first thing they did was to arrange to have the main streets paved, to provide for sidewalks, and to insist that householders who had encroached on the public way lop off their porches, cellar doors, and other excrescences which made the lot of the pedestrian so precarious. The laying of cobblestones in Market Street (now Baltimore) was begun in the spring of 1782 and was finished before the end of the year. Considering the fact that the country was insolvent, the state probably so, while the merchants themselves had debts on a scale they could only guess at, this was a remarkable undertaking.

But they went even further, for they arranged to have the streets lit at night and even provided for a permanent police force. Three constables were hired to patrol the town during the daylight hours and fourteen after sunset. There is a suggestion here that some of the returning soldiers and beached sailors may have been a little less than law-abiding.

That was about the best they could do at the moment in the way of giving the town a metropolitan air. They had more fundamental problems to meet. One of these was to better their communications to the North and West so as to insure a steady flow of wheat for their mills and ships. The second was to improve their harbor, which had an unpleasant way of silting up every spring and keeping vessels from the wharves in the basin.

Messrs. John and Andrew Ellicott, of the same family which had established the big flour mills and persuaded Charles Carroll of Carrollton to shift from tobacco to wheat, gave them a notion on the latter problem. The Ellicotts owned a lot at the foot of Light Street, with riparian rights, and decided to build a wharf there. But instead of building a long structure out over the marsh and hauling fill from the uplands they walled up a much shorter pier. Then by an elaborate arrangement of scoops, ropes, and pulleys they dredged mud from the bottom of the river and filled in their causeway. Thus they got a wharf and a channel with one operation and at very much less cost.

This achievement impressed all the merchants, and by petition to the legislature they acquired the right to impose a levy of one penny a ton on all vessels entering the port. The impost was soon after raised to twopence. The funds thus received were entrusted to a committee called the Wardens of the Port with authority to maintain and improve the channels. This committee took its work seriously, began the dredging of the basin and the filling up of the bordering marshes.

It wasn't all accomplished in a year or even five, but the steady income did enable them to make progress as steady. At the western end of the basin the dredged mud was used as fill until finally the whole swamp there was relatively fast land. Light Street was extended, and for the first time there was a water-front highway. The land thus made was sold off as fast as it was available. By a similar process the marsh on the north side was gradually filled in, and a new street, called Pratt, skirted the water's edge there. To the east most of the little shallow bay inside of Fells Point was likewise filled up, and the area known as the Hook was thrown open to the developers.

Jones Falls and the marshes which bordered it were more difficult problems. At first causeways were built across the flats, with wooden or stone bridges across the stream proper. Then after a time the big bend of the Falls was filled in, a cutoff canal was dug and the stream kept from overflowing its banks in all save the worst freshets by a series of stone walls. With the waters thus under control, it was possible to think about draining Steiger's Meadow, and by degrees this, too, was accomplished. By such means the merchants made their town more useful as a place of business, if not noticeably more beautiful.

The problem of extending communications with the North and West was much more complicated and long-drawn-out. Here for the first time they had to consider seriously their real chances for future growth. Already they had found themselves in competition with Philadelphia for the products of the farm lands of the southern Pennsylvania counties. Now they had to think of possible competition from little Georgetown, a Maryland community which had grown up at the head of tidewater on the Potomac and was beginning to cherish delusions of grandeur.

Georgetown was only a few miles from Mount Vernon. George Washington knew it well. He always had one eye on the Western country and had extensive ventures of his own on the Ohio. He and many others wanted to find an easy way to get the potential products of this region to the seaboard. The Potomac seemed the natural route and Georgetown the inevitable port. Many Marylanders agreed with him. Hence it was not difficult to get subscribers to a plan to make the river navigable. On paper it sounded simple, quick, and cheap.

Baltimore protested in vain against the granting of the charter. Her merchants argued that it would divert some of their trade, to which the former commander-in-chief blandly replied that their fears were "perhaps not without cause." The scheme, being undertaken, wasted the money of many investors, including George himself. The promoters estimated that it could be done for twelve thousand pounds sterling. Twelve millions would have been a more conservative figure.

Years later the Chesapeake and Ohio Canal was actually dug. It runs—or ran, for it was abandoned only a few years ago—from Cumberland, Md., down to Washington, which had swallowed Georgetown in the interim. A lot of good money was poured into it, but it never really amounted to much, save for local traffic. The railroads choked it off as they choked off many similar undertakings.

The Baltimoreans had notions of their own about canals. A canal along the Susquehanna, which was impracticable for upstream navigation and uncertain, save for very shallow barges on the down course, was constantly under discussion. But the soundest of Baltimore's canal ideas was for the one connecting Chesapeake and Delaware bays. The Maryland money was available for many years before either Pennsylvania or Delaware could be persuaded of its importance. Today, after successive widenings and deepenings, it is a broad sea-level waterway of great value to every port from New York to Norfolk.

The major energies of the community at this period went mainly into road building. There had been roads of a sort through this region for a long time. The Great Eastern Road, as it was called, skirted the northwest boundary of the town when it was first laid out. One may follow the course of part of that road today by turning into the first alley west of Charles Street, on the south side of Lexington. It winds through to Fayette Street and jumps across to the west side of Hanover, just south of Fayette. The first part is called Crooked Lane and the second McClellan's Alley. In the Northern colonies this road was rather important. It was less important in Maryland, because most travelers, having reached the head of the Chesapeake on their way South, took to boats by preference.

There was another road leading almost straight north to York. The Indians were responsible for this in the first place. The warlike Susquehannocks had made a trail to the Chesapeake in the very early days before the coming of the white man. Over this trail they carried their furs and traded or fought with the more peaceable Indians of the bay region. One of its southern prongs ended at a place on the bay now called Gibson Island, now a smart summer resort. Here the Indians would come to gorge themselves on oysters after their trading was finished. Some of the handsome houses on the island are built on the shell piles produced by these perennial feasts. Mixed in with the shells the careful searcher can find bits of pottery. Few of the residents know that they are living on the midden of an ancient culture.

Another Indian trail came in from the West and met this main one a few miles north of Baltimore. Since it was down this Western trail that the French and Indian marauders would have come had they ever made an attack on Baltimore, it had long been defended by a little fort. The site of this fort, still called Garrison, lies to the north-west of the city at a distance of about ten miles. The settlers used the eastern end of this trail from the West in their travels to and from the little settlement at Joppa while that was the county seat of Baltimore County. Its route has been changed somewhat, but the old line is still fairly clear.

The development of the wheatlands made it necessary constantly to improve and extend these roads and to build new ones. By the outbreak of the revolution Baltimore had overland connections with the mouth of the Susquehanna on the northeast, via the Great Eastern Road, with York to the north, on the trail which had by now been developed to the point where it would take a Conestoga wagon, with four or eight horses, with Frederick on the west by means of a cutoff on the road which originally led from Annapolis to Frederick. This cutoff first went via Elk Ridge Landing, the tobacco port, then followed the valley of the upper Patapsco to Ellicott's Mills. A little later it led directly over the hills from Ellicott's Mills to Baltimore, thereby cutting off Elk Ridge.

This was the system which it was proposed to develop. In one year, 1787, turnpike companies were chartered to collect tolls and improve and extend the York and Frederick roads and build a new road to the northwest as far as Reisterstown, about twenty miles out. Another company was started the next year to build a road through the whole length of Jones Falls Valley, giving the many mills on that stream an improved access to the town. This road was on a scale never before thought of, for the charter provided that its right of way must be forty feet wide. Several years later, after the District of Columbia was established, a turnpike to the new capital was authorized. It took off from Elk Ridge. In 1797 the legislature authorized the extension of the Frederick road to Hagerstown, then called Elizabeth Town.

These undertakings, bunched together in so few years, made it fairly obvious that the merchants of Baltimore did not share the fears as to their future which were held in some quarters. Every one of them was designed to feed the port and not only to insure the continuance of its existing trade but also to seize as much as possible of the new business which was sure to come with the opening up of the Western country.

So many expensive projects could not be undertaken in such short order without setbacks. Everything, after all, depended upon the business of the port and moved up and down in strict consonance with that business.

To the peoples of Western Europe, Maryland was merely part of the Chesapeake and the Chesapeake was tobacco country. As soon as the war was over the British merchants who had previously handled the tobacco trade rushed over their men and ships in the hope of re-establishing the trade they had formerly monopolized. Among their representatives were a good many of the loyalists who had left during the Revolution, including the correct and likable Robert Eden, the former governor. They set up as factors at various points on the bay where the trade had hitherto centered and began to bid for tobacco. In contrast, Dutch, later German, merchants sent their representatives to Baltimore Town, for it was the merchants of that place whom they had got to know through the West Indian business.

Sharp competition between these rival groups bid up the price of tobacco out of all relation to its value. But the British labored under several handicaps. The first was the obvious one that they themselves did not consume Maryland tobacco but instead acted as middlemen, having to resell it to the merchants of the Continent, with most of which their country was at war. A second handicap was that of entrusting their business largely to the still unpopular loyalists. A third was that these same men, while buying tobacco, were also maneuvering to get back their confiscated property or at least to persuade the legislature to compensate them for it.

The Baltimore merchants recognized their advantage. They built a big tobacco warehouse and acted as go-betweens for the Dutch and German merchants. They were not averse to making the presence of the loyalists a political issue. The old Whig Club of Baltimore, the same which had played so violent a role in the affair of William Goddard, got up a public meeting in which all returning loyalists were roundly denounced. The quick result was the fading out of the effort of the English to re-establish themselves and, for the first time, the centering of the trade in Baltimore. England has had no appreciable share in Maryland's tobacco business since that time.

There was one result of the short, sharp encounter

which was less than happy. It was not unconnected with the general economic uncertainty of the time but it was particularly manifest in Baltimore and its trading area. The ships which came over from England, Holland, and Germany to buy tobacco brought with them all sorts of manufactured articles, including many that might be classed as luxuries, such as silks, velvets, fine cottons, and so on. In their competitive bidding for tobacco, the buyers pushed up the price of that commodity and pushed down the price of their own goods. The result was that the countryside was flooded with luxury goods, and a taste was established for niceties which had hitherto been beyond the means of any save the rich. This taste served to drain the countryside, after the tobacco war was over, of its cash money and caused country-versus-town frictions in an aggravated form. The influx of goods in foreign bottoms had the further effect in the town of depressing local industry, especially shipbuilding. Thus arose, in Baltimore as in other towns, the demand for a mercantilist system not unlike that of England.

It was this sort of thing also which made Baltimore extremely Federalist during the debates which followed the Constitutional Convention. When the Assembly met in April 1788 to decide whether or not to accept the draft constitution the town watched the debates with growing concern. When the vote was taken and the document was ratified the whole community expressed its gratification and relief with ceremonials more imposing than any they had previously concocted.

The chief feature of the celebration was, of course, a procession. Every trade, every profession, every business interest in the community was represented in it. The march began on Philpot's Hill, overlooking Fells Point, moved east on Market Street to Charles, south through Frenchtown, and then east again to John Smith's Hill, on the south side of the basin. This hill was thereafter called by its present name, Federal Hill.

In the parade there was a float on which was placed a miniature full-rigged ship called *The Federalist*, the gift of Baltimore's shipwrights for the great occasion. The famous Joshua Barney, the town's chief naval hero, was her captain. Poor Barney, covered with glory after the famous battle between the *General Monk* and his little *Hyder Ally*, an engagement which Fenimore Cooper called "one of the most brilliant that ever occurred under the American flag," was now on the beach, like many another valiant seaman. The excitement of the parade was well suited to his love of the dramatic and made him forget for a while the drabness of his life.

He "sailed" his *Federalist* to the top of the hill and ate and drank and sang with the three thousand celebrants who attended. After a while most of them went home. But Barney longed for a command and so in the early-morning hours he called together a crowd of men and boys to help him slide the little ship carefully down the hillside into the water. Then, getting aboard, he sailed majestically down the harbor and out into the broad river, giving Annapolis as his destination.

Word of his exploit preceded him, and off the mouth of the Severn he was hailed by a vessel carrying an invitation from the governor, General Smallwood. He spent three days in the capital as the guest of the governor, being feasted and made much over. Taking to sea again, he went clear down the bay to the Potomac and then sailed up that broad river to Mount Vernon, where he presented his vessel to General Washington as a gift from the merchants of Baltimore Town. Washington acknowledged the gift in a correctly phrased letter but in his diary he notes the visit without comment. He could understand the bravery and patriotism of a man like Barney but he could hardly understand the melodramatic flair which accompanied it.

When the Congress was called to order under the new constitution on March 3, 1789, the first two petitions presented for its attention were requests for the establishment in the new nation of a mercantilist system like that of England, with navigation acts, tariffs, and all. One of these petitions came from the "shipwrights, etc., inhabitants of Baltimore Town," the men who had built Barney's little *Federalist*.

CHAPTER XIII

Growth Unparalleled

THE CENSUS OF 1790, the first Federal count ever taken, showed that Baltimore had a population of 13,503, of whom only 1255 were slaves. Most of the Negroes were used as house and body servants. The census also showed that Baltimore owned a fleet of twenty-seven ships, thirty-one brigs, thirty-four schooners, nine sloops, and a scow. The increasing proportion of ships and brigs shows that longer voyages were being undertaken, even in north Atlantic and Pacific waters where the light upper works of the characteristic schooners were too fragile for strong winds. The statistics as a whole indicate the extent to which the enterprising town of millers and traders had constructed its own economy, divorced in basic interest from the manorial system into which it had insinuated itself.

The basis of its trade was the flour made from the hard wheat of its own back country and ground in the mills on its own streams. Its chief market was the West Indies, though there were developing outlets in Spain, Portugal, and the Mediterranean. More and more, too, the tobacco growers tended to use its shipping and credit facilities. Sales of tobacco in Holland and Germany provided the basis for a new import trade from the continent, though much of this was carried in the bottoms of the countries which produced it.

The situation in the West Indies was difficult. The French were blockading as far as they could the English islands. The English were almost completely blockading the French. Spain and Portugal still maintained their restrictive policies and tried to keep the trade of their own colonies as nearly monopolistic as possible. There were ways of circumventing such restrictions, for blockade running was an old game to the Baltimore skippers, and Surinam was a convenient *entrepôt* for Venezuela and Brazil. To ensure themselves against occasional losses the merchants formed associations to share the risks. These associations developed naturally into marine insurance companies, the first of which was chartered in 1795.

The typical West Indian schooner leaving Baltimore at this period carried a cargo of flour, barrel staves, dried fish (mostly herring and shad), Indian corn (which was now being brought to Baltimore from the Eastern Shore, where its cultivation had vastly increased), and dry goods imported previously from Germany. The cargo would be sold in Martinique, say, and the vessel would bring back raw sugar, molasses, coffee (usually picked up in Haiti), and perhaps lemons and other citrus fruit.

On its arrival in Baltimore, the whole return cargo would be offered at auction. The influx was so large that only part of it could be consumed locally. There was such a piling up of molasses and raw sugar, for instance, that at about this time Baltimore capital found it profitable to invest in a sugar refinery, the first of a long series. There was a distillery for rum also, but this drink was never an important item in the Baltimore list. The taste for corn whisky and later for that made from the native rye was too well established.

Much of the sugar and molasses was bought up either by the Germans and Dutch established in the town or else by the local merchants for continental account. In both cases the products were re-exported. More and more this re-export business became a prime factor in the economy of the port. The statistics on it are difficult to come at, but the extent to which the trade developed is indicated by the figures of the fiscal year 1805–06, when it was at its height. In that year Maryland exported $3,661,000 of her own produce and re-exported $10,919,000 of foreign produce. Nearly all of this went from Baltimore.

This trade was exceedingly profitable. But more stimulating perhaps than the immediate profits was the fact that by Federal action the men engaged in it suddenly found themselves possessed of vast aggregations of capital, much greater than they had ever dared hope to command. The adoption of the Constitution and the assumption of the debt had altered the credit structure of the whole country. The debt incurred during the Revolution was widely held, but the bonds had been quoted at a fifth or less of their face value. With assumption they reacted almost immediately to par and even went beyond it. Thus every holder suddenly found himself possessed of five times the capital he had had before. All the Eastern cities profited by this sudden increase, but Baltimore, because it was recognized as the most bustling and enterprising community with the greatest opportunity for immediate use of money, got far more than its share.

Organizing these riches for the use of business resulted in Baltimore's first banks. Efforts by the merchants to establish such institutions had been made as early as 1784, but the necessary capital could not be raised. By 1790 things were different. In November of that year the legislature granted a perpetual charter to the Bank of Maryland, and a group of citizens was authorized to receive subscriptions up to $300,000. In two weeks the requisite two thirds was paid in. The incorporators held their first meeting and elected William Patterson, a man with whose activities we are already familiar, to be president. By March, in 1791, the whole $300,000 was subscribed and the organization was completed. The first directors were Archibald Campbell, Richard Caton, James Clarke, Henry Nichols, Robert Oliver, Nicholas Sluby, and Jeremiah Yellott.

Caton was the English son-in-law of Charles Carroll of Carrollton and represented the interest of that rich man in the bank. But he was more famous as the father of the three "Baltimore Graces" who were later to make such an impression in London. Elizabeth married Baron Stafford. Louisa captured first Sir Felton Bathurst Hervey and after his death the Marquis of Carmarthen. Mary, after making a deep impression on the Duke of Wellington on her visit to London as the wife of William Patterson's son Robert, returned a little later as a widow to wed the Marquess of Wellesley and to become a lady in waiting to Queen Adelaide.

The Bank of the United States opened for business in Philadelphia in 1791 and in November of that year resolved to open branches in Boston, New York, Baltimore, and Charleston. The Baltimore office opened in February 1792, with a group of directors interlocking those of the Bank of Maryland. George Gale was the president of the branch.

Three years later, with the boom in full swing, the Bank of Baltimore was chartered with an authorized capital of $1,200,000. The subscriptions so far exceeded this that it was necessary to apportion the shares among the applicants. George Salmon was the first president, and there is no evidence in the board of directors of either the Carroll or the Patterson influence. What is notable about the board is that at least one Jew, Solomon Etting, was among its members.

The natural result of this organization of credit was enterprise on a vaster and more daring scale. The shipyards were enlarged, and the Point hummed with activity. Mr. Stodder, whose yard was in Harris Creek, got an order from a syndicate for a ship of six hundred tons, by far the largest yet constructed in Maryland waters. The vessel, called the *Goliath,* was destined for the East India trade. I have found no record of her performance, but a smaller vessel, the *Chesapeake,* built in one of the smaller yards down the bay, did, in fact, make India and flew the first American flag ever seen in the Ganges.

Foreign influences also stimulated enterprise. The French were using Mauritius, in the Indian Ocean, as a base for their attacks on British shipping in that remote region. At least two Baltimore vessels made the long voyage via the Cape of Good Hope and carried to the French the wherewithal to keep the garrison and the ships supplied with food. The whole journey was made through seas infested with British sea forces, but the goods were delivered, and the two little ships returned safely.

Baltimore's activity in the West Indian trade had one by-product which shows how closely the city was knit to the islands at that early date. Inspired by the American and later by the French example, Toussaint L'Ouverture, the great Haitian Negro, had organized a revolt against the French masters. The white men in the island fell into a panic, as they naturally would, considering how greatly they were outnumbered. The harbors of the island were crowded with shipping, most of it from Baltimore. The terrified Frenchmen piled aboard these vessels, carrying their gold, their families, their loyal slaves, and their household goods, begging the captains to carry them to safety. During the year, sometimes in squadrons of as many as ten at a time, fifty-three vessels loaded with these unexpected immigrants and their belongings sailed into the harbor. They numbered in all about one thousand whites and five hundred slaves.

A few of them were destitute, and the merchants raised twelve thousand dollars for their relief. But most of them were sufficiently well supplied with goods to be able to look after themselves. Some entered the mercantile life of the town. Others, being agricultural in habit, bought tracts of land in the surrounding country and went into the cultivation of produce for the local market. They introduced Baltimore to a new range of green vegetables and thereby permanently improved the diet of the community. More so than those earlier French immigrants, the Acadians, they colored the life of the town and enriched its blood.

The next year Baltimore had its first serious visitation

of what was to be a recurring plague. There was no proper quarantine for the vessels coming in from the islands, and one of them brought in yellow fever. It ravaged the town, particularly in the poorer quarters. A hospital was hastily built in order to segregate the sufferers. The outbreak had an interesting social effect. It convinced the merchants who had recently come to town and built themselves houses in its limits that it was no proper place for a residence, in the summertime at least. So more of them followed earlier examples and bought themselves country places in the surrounding hills. They may have wanted to be convinced, but the result, nevertheless, was an increase in the group of those who, though their money was made in trade, lived socially precisely like country gentry.

But it is not fair to say that they took no pride whatever in the town. In 1795, under the pressure of the clergy, they put up enough money to organize what was called the Library Company, thus making their first obeisance to the life of the spirit. There is no record as to what books were bought. But the Library had vitality, of a sort, and its collection formed the nucleus of what eventually became the Maryland Historical Society, always a useful institution and now a vigorous one.

They began at this time also to be proud of the statistics of the port. Down on North Point, which marks the entrance to the Patapsco on the northern side, an elderly gentleman known as Judge Jones had a house from which he could see every vessel which entered the river. During the whole of the year 1796 Judge Jones sat with his telescope glued to his eye. He may have been a paid observer for the Wardens of the Port. In any event, during that year he counted 109 ships, 162 brigs, 350 schooners and sloops, and 5464 bay craft of all kind moving in toward the harbor. The latter total indicates the extent to which Baltimore now dominated the bay and had made it tributary to her mercantile growth.

Judge Jones's figures were published at intervals during the year, and as they mounted a new ambition seized upon the people of the town. They laid their plans and got from the legislature, on the very last day of the year, the thing they wanted. On December 31, 1796, Baltimore became a legally incorporated city, with all the rights and privileges thereunto appertaining, including especially the right to lay taxes and spend them within its own borders without reference to the county government.

The old familiar cognomen of Baltimore Town, written on so many thousands upon thousands of business documents, was laid aside forever, and every merchant thereafter dated his communications Baltimore City or, more simply, Baltimore.

All of this activity went on under the constant annoying threats and outright hostility of both the English and the French. But for a long time the Federal government refused to allow itself to be pushed into retaliatory measures. It was the occasional exactions of the Barbary pirates which finally gave the advocates of a navy an opportunity to put real pressure on Congress. In 1795 the members voted, very reluctantly, to authorize the construction of six frigates and the enrollment of the necessary officers and men.

One of those selected to command in the new navy was Lieutenant Joshua Barney. Due to some quirk of conceit, he refused the rating offered him, his expressed reason being that he was made junior to a man whom he thought he should rank. It is more likely that the possibility of being ordered to act against the French, whom he loved, rather than against the British, whom he still hated, was a factor in his decision. Another factor may have been that his old and despised commander, James Nicholson, of the ill-fated *Virginia*, was also given a place ahead of him. In any event, in the stirring events that were brewing Barney played no official part. This didn't prevent him, of course, from occasionally stealing the limelight as the commander of a more or less peaceful trader. But these adventures of his are set down in other books and need not detain us here.

There was sharp competition for the honor and profit of building the new ships. Mr. Stodder, who had constructed the giant *Goliath* and who had a reputation for highly competent work, got the contract for a frigate to be called the *Constellation*. Captain Thomas Truxtun, her commander-to-be, was told off to supervise her construction. He personally examined every piece of timber which went into her and was so meticulous that her launching was delayed until September 7, 1797. But, though smaller than the *Constitution*, her famous contemporary, she was a proud vessel. The fact that after more than a hundred years she is still in active commission in the navy, though, of course, as a museum piece, is evidence of the endurance which her builders wrought into her.*

Hardly was she ready for sea when the Congress, emboldened by the possession of a navy, decided that French insolence at sea was even more unbearable than that of the English and authorized all American commanders to take all French cruisers, public or private, with which they

*The *Constellation* is stationed at New London, Conn., and there she remains despite constant efforts on the part of Baltimore groups to have her brought home.

might come up. This was the famous undeclared war with France.

To enable private vessels also to act against the French, the Congress authorized the issuance of letters of marque. As far as real privateering was concerned, this was a mere gesture, for the English navy had pretty well driven French merchant ships off the sea. The authorization was intended mainly to permit American merchantmen to arm for their own protection.

The terminology used in this form of warfare can be confusing. Two forms of commissions were issued for private armed vessels. The first was given to a privately owned vessel of war. Under its terms the captain was ordered to capture or sink any vessel of the enemy he could find. The second form of commission was given to a merchant ship armed primarily for its own protection. This commission permitted the ship which carried it to capture only those enemy vessels which it might encounter in the course of a lawful trading errand.

Both types of commission were called by the same name, "Letters of Marque and Reprisal." But the private ship with the unlimited commission was normally called a "privateer," whereas the armed trader with the limited commission was called a "letter of marque." It is the latter circumstance which ordinarily causes the confusion. The distinction is made clearer if we remember that the privateer was always said to be "on a cruise," while the letter of marque went "on a voyage" to a given destination just like any peaceful trader. Both, of course, saw sharp fighting.

The primary function of the *Constellation* and the other frigates built at this time was to convoy merchantmen and letters of marque to and from the West Indies and protect them from the several French frigates which were constantly cruising in the neighborhood. On February 9, 1799, Captain Truxtun was on his prescribed station about ten miles or so southwest of Nevis when he saw a large vessel leeward about five miles. She ran up American colors but failed to respond to private signals. Truxtun guessed she was French, and so she turned out to be, for when he ran down toward her she waited under easy sail. When he was almost within hailing distance the stranger fired a challenging gun and hoisted French colors.

This was the first time since the close of the Revolution that an American ship had had a chance to engage an enemy, and there was great eagerness among Truxtun's men, for they wanted to try out their quality in fairly equal combat. The captain therefore moved to come abreast of his antagonist while still keeping his windward berth. He sailed past her, giving her a full broadside as he did so.

She replied with spirit, her shot tearing the *Constellation's* rigging badly. One lucky shot from the Frenchman went through the fore-topmast, nearly severing it. The strain of the sails would have taken it off and probably rendered the vessel unmanageable had not young David Porter, the midshipman in command of the foretop, taken upon himself the responsibility, without orders, of cutting the stoppers and lowering the yard. This saved the foremast and perhaps the battle, for the *Insurgente*—for such the Frenchman turned out to be—had suffered badly from the broadside and was certain to yield if the *Constellation* remained maneuverable.

For nearly an hour the two ships hammered at each other, until finally Truxtun, feeling victory within reach, wore around, came up astern of the *Insurgente*, and placed himself in position to rake her with every gun. Seeing his imminent danger, the French captain struck his colors.

This victory was undoubtedly a brilliant one. The *Insurgente* was known as one of the fastest sailers of her class in the world. She carried more guns and hence more men than the *Constellation*. The latter, however, had twenty-four pounders to the *Insurgente's* French twelves. The *Constellation*, it might be said, was overarmed for her size, and the Frenchman underarmed. But the Frenchman had asked for the fight and had behaved gallantly throughout its duration. It was the heavier metal of the *Constellation* in his hull which wore him down.

This victory thrilled all of the United States when it became known, but nowhere was it more gladly heard than in Baltimore. The ill luck of Nicholson's *Virginia* had been much on the local conscience ever since the Revolution, and it was invigorating to have this proof that a Baltimore-built war vessel was as good for her purposes as a Baltimore-built schooner was for hers. Baltimore's happiness would have been perfect had the commander of the ship been a local man—say, Joshua Barney. But another Nicholson, on the *Constitution*, was to make up for that a little later.

The census of 1800 showed the town, now officially a city, to have a population of 31,514, an increase of almost 18,000, or 125 per cent, in ten years.

CHAPTER XIV

Mutterings Within and Without

THE PEACE OF AMIENS, in 1801, was a blow to all American shipping and especially to that of Baltimore. It meant that the merchant vessels of both England and France were free once more to carry the products of their respective empires without danger of molestation. Baltimore would have felt the sudden loss of the profits of her hazardous enterprises much more severely had not Northern Europe suffered a partial failure of its wheat crop at this very juncture. The Maryland staple thus commanded a good price, and money was brought into the town in sufficient quantity to make it possible to forget the idle sailors who thronged the water front and rioted on the causeway between town and Point.

The well-to-do, though suffering some temporary embarrassment, still had money to spend. They constructed a new race track on Whetstone Point, just adjoining the place where the water battery had been put up during the Revolution. A more imposing fortification was under construction here now. It was to be called Fort McHenry.

Mutterings Within and Without

The shipyards were fairly busy, too, for there were two sloops-of-war being built on the Point. One of these was the *Maryland*, the other the *Chesapeake*, a vessel soon to be involved in an incident of great import. These gave occasional employment to a class the wealthier citizens were beginning to regard as somewhat turbulent.

More and more the recurring epidemics of yellow fever put the town under expense and difficulty. In the first year of the peace a quarantine station was established on the little Point opposite the new fort. Here it gave protection to both town and Point. The next year a free dispensary was established for the poor.

Just before the turn of the century a company had been formed to provide a place for public dances and had purchased the old market house which the town had outgrown. In its upper story a large hall was elegantly furnished and a series of assemblies was held, with the price of admission set high enough to keep out the rabble. With dances and racing to attend and a new theater in the making, there was no lack of entertainment.

The great game of politics was being played rather assiduously in Maryland, with a new and complicated cleavage arising between Federalists and Republicans. In the Federalist ranks were found the remnants of the old Tories, (who were pro-British, of course), the more conservative of the old tobacco-planting families, the kind of people who were anti-urban by nature and especially resented the growing dominance of Baltimore in the state's affairs. It gathered support also from many of the merchants whose social ambitions sometimes blinded them to their own interests.

On the other side were the Jeffersonians, plus those who

[151]

still clung to their ancient anti-British animosities and found plenty of fuel to keep alive their suspicions, plus the workingmen of the city who were all imbued with the revolutionary notions spread abroad by the French Revolution, plus the idle sailors who wanted both excitement and jobs but especially the former. In addition to all these there were politicians, of whatever origin, who plied their trade to their own advantage. Also, there was a whole group of honest merchants, many of them Quakers, to whose simple and ascetic souls the extravagances of the more flamboyant spenders and show-offs made no appeal. These men loved the town for its own sake, and their names are found in all lists of subscribers to benevolent undertakings.

Yet even the Quakers must have been excited when word came that Jerome Bonaparte, the playboy brother of the First Consul, had arrived in Washington. Joshua Barney, who had served in the French navy during the dull days after the Revolution, posted over to see his friend and invited him to Baltimore. There was a fluttering among the young ladies of the town, and fathers were pressed to entertain the distinguished visitor should he arrive.

Neither the French minister in Washington not yet Jerome's own staff was anxious to have the brother of the great leader listen to the blandishments of Barney, whose swashbuckling reputation was sometimes painted in lurid colors. But Jerome saw good hunting in the offing and refused to be deterred. It was either at the race track or else at a ball given by Judge Samuel Chase that he first met Baltimore's current glamour girl, Elizabeth Patterson, known as Betsy. She was the daughter of that William Patterson who had come to Baltimore from Donegal during the Revolution. He had meantime become a very rich man, one of the richest in the state if not in the whole country.

There is a story which says that at the Chase ball Betsy's necklace caught in the button of Jerome's uniform. Everyone regarded this enchainment as symbolic. Jerome certainly did. Despite all the warning from his brother's minister, despite everything, he determined to marry her. Mr. Patterson, a cautious man in family matters, albeit a great gambler in shipping, was hard to win over. But finally, with all the solemnity which the harum-scarum nature of the principals allowed, the marriage took place. It was solemnized by no less a person that the Right Reverend John Carroll, Bishop of Baltimore and Primate of the Roman Catholic Church in the United States. All the dignitaries of the town were present. Never was a wedding more legal, more correct.

But Napoleon, as everyone knows, would have none of it. The Pope boldly refused his demands, but a complaisant bishop was found, and Betsy, an infant Jerome on her knee, had to learn that the wedding was annulled and that her loving, if somewhat inconstant, husband had been sentenced to the throne of Westphalia. She cut quite a swath in London before returning but back in this country she decided it was better to make the best of the situation, and the Assembly of Maryland was easily persuaded in 1812 to grant her a divorce.

She remained a grand lady long after her errant husband was an exile, almost an outcast. The tale tells that once, strolling in Florence, she saw Jerome passing with his dumpy queen. She made no overt sign of recognition but casually opened her cloak that he might see how well she had kept her figure.

That figure was well known in Baltimore for many a day, for Betsy lived to be a very old and rather queer beldame. There were those recently alive who remembered her as she visited the tenants of the properties she owned and collected the rents due her. The young Jerome became a substantial citizen and in due course begat a son, Charles J., who was attorney general and afterwards Secretary of the Navy in the cabinet of Theodore Roosevelt.

There were other incidents less glamorous but fully as typical of the high life of the town at this gaudy period. There was, for instance, the problem of building a new courthouse in keeping with the dignity of an incorporated city. The old courthouse had been erected on a high clay bank overlooking Jones Falls in what is now the bed of Calvert Street. When the bank was cut down so that the street could be extended the building was shored up, rather spectacularly, on four legs of masonry which made it look all too much like a gigantic stool. It was precisely the sort of traffic hazard which Temple Bar was in London. It was got rid of as soon as the new building was finished.

Razing it left an open plaza in the very center of the town. The well-to-do saw this as a possible social center —the Assembly rooms were only a short block away—and rushed to build houses facing upon it. These new houses were fine brick structures, much more imposing even than the showy houses which had been built on the Point.

Then it was proposed that the plaza be adorned by a monument to George Washington, lately deceased, and this project came mighty near to going through. But when the burgers saw the design and realized that a shaft taller than any they had dreamed of was to be erected they protested violently. It might attract lightning, they argued. It might even fall down. And, anyway, the times were not propitious for such a gigantic undertaking. The whole thing had better be postponed. So postponed it was.

Underneath, conditions were not so healthy. In 1804 a company was formed to supply water to the town. It offered its stock at public subscription. There was plenty of idle money—too much of it, in fact—and the subscribers rushed in. The total offered was $250,000, but the demand was so great that the first purchasers proceeded to turn over their shares, at increased prices, to the late-comers. But these found still other purchasers and made a pretty profit in turn. For nearly a week this went on until the shares were selling at nine times and more of their par value. A smash followed in short order.

More profoundly significant perhaps was the effort, made in 1805, to persuade the Assembly to increase Baltimore's representation in its membership. The city had two delegates. It wanted four. The Assembly listened impatiently and then, after only the second reading, voted the bill down by sixty to two. The two were, of course, the delegates from Baltimore. Here was country against town with a vengeance.

But trade went on after a fashion. The ship *Palas* (Palestine?) which was owned by Mr. John O'Donnell, had made a successful voyage to Canton in 1785 and brought back to Baltimore the first cargo from the Orient. The goods sold well, and Mr. O'Donnell used part of his profit of £70,000 to buy a tract of land lying to the east of the Point. He called his estate Canton, from the town which had so enriched him, and planted at least part of it with an orchard of a kind of peaches especially suited for making peach brandy, of which he was very fond.

Mr. O'Donnell died in 1805, but his example lived on. Moreover, all the Baltimore merchants knew that New England was getting rich out of the China trade. So a group of them decided to go into this line of business. They dispatched two ships, and the venture was highly successful. But the first voyages ended during the embargo, and the company found it wise to dissolve.

The truth was that carrying on the kind of seafaring business which Baltimoreans knew most about was getting to be almost impossible. The British, their men deserting them in such numbers that they had a hard time manning their warships, let alone their merchantmen, were getting harsher and harsher in their treatment of American vessels. Two frigates hovered outside of New York harbor continually and on one occasion even came into the Hudson River and stopped vessels and searched them. Mr. Jefferson clung to his notion that moral suasion was a sufficient answer to this sort of thing and refused to build up a navy. One of the two small sloops-of-war lately built in Baltimore had been a gift from the merchants thereof who hoped by this example to stimulate Washington to action.

The *Chesapeake*, second of these sloops, was ready for sea in 1807 and dropped down to Norfolk to pick up part of her crew and put aboard some of her stores. Her decks still cluttered with her new gear, she sailed toward the capes on June 22. The British frigate *Leopard*, 52 guns, was hovering in the channel. As the *Chesapeake* moved out the *Leopard* moved with her. At about ten miles out the Britisher hailed the American and by a ruse persuaded him to heave to. A messenger came aboard and brought a message from the *Leopard's* captain. His orders, it appeared, were to search the *Chesapeake* for deserters from the British navy. There were three such deserters on the *Chesapeake*, but they were Americans who had been impressed and they had seized the first opportunity to quit the harsh British service. Barron, commander of the *Chesapeake*, therefore replied that he had no such men as described and refused to muster his crew. Barron didn't know that he had a real deserter on board, a Britisher named Jenkin Ratford who had shipped under the name of Wilson, but the commander of the *Leopard* knew it and acted accordingly.

Lying not more than two hundred feet from his victim, he shouted a brusque command that the crew be mustered. Barron pretended not to hear. The other warned him once more and then fired a shot across the *Chesapeake's* bow. With her decks cluttered with gear, her guns not fitted to their carriages, the *Chesapeake* was helpless. She received a full broadside. Her only reply was from one gun which, being loaded, was fired by young Lieutenant Allen with a live coal he had brought from the galley in his fingers. There was nothing for Barron to do but to strike his colors.

The British came aboard, picked out the three alleged deserters, and after a search located the rascal Ratford. Thus accomplishing their purpose, they left the *Chesapeake* with her riddled hull and her torn rigging to limp back into Hampton Roads with her story.

CHAPTER XV

Baltimore's Own War

IT IS one of the contradictions of Baltimore's history that, riven by complex internal conflicts, she yet managed to play a major role in the War of 1812. Indeed, in one sense, that war was Baltimore's own. Her privateers were brilliantly employed during the whole of the contest and, though some of their activities had in them a touch of the comic, still, they and the numerous letters of marque which put out from the port did carry on, after a fashion, the national commerce. It was Baltimore and her trade which the British most sought to destroy. It was Baltimore, almost unaided, which turned back the British army which captured and burned Washington. It was Baltimore which, at this same juncture, supplied the nation with the song which was to become the national anthem. This record was made despite the fact that during the war and especially in the early part of it the town had to fight out, in its own streets, the political issues which divided the country's statesmen and almost tore the land itself asunder.

The news of the *Chesapeake* affair, narrated in the previous chapter, aroused the greatest excitement in the city.

The merchants called a general meeting and passed resolutions telling the President—still Mr. Jefferson—that they would uphold his hand in any step he chose to take.

Their assumption that he would go to war against Great Britain was a little shaken a month or two later when news leaked out of a somewhat unpleasant incident in the bay. A group of French sailors, on the beach in Baltimore, had somehow managed to fit out and arm a small schooner for commerce raiding. On their way down the bay they came upon the British ship *Othello*, Captain Glover, inward bound from London. The Frenchmen were more valiant than wise. They assumed that if the United States wasn't already at war with England it soon would be, so they fired on the *Othello* and took her. But there were not enough of them to man her, and so when a storm came up they abandoned her to her own captain and crew.

This was too much like piracy even for Baltimore opinion. An expedition was sent after the Frenchmen, and they were captured and brought back. Nobody was quite sure which law they had broken, if any, and they were discharged. But in the next resolution passed by the townspeople it was carefully stated that if the President wanted to make war against the French as well as the British, or with either of these nations separately, it was all right with Baltimore.

Through the embargo Baltimore carried on. It is likely that her merchants evaded the law to some extent, but it is not likely, considering the general feeling in their class, that they went as far as did the New Englanders and deliberately supplied the British at great profit to themselves. Indeed, the embargo laid a heavy hand upon the trade of the port, and its abandonment was received with joy.

Baltimore on the Chesapeake

The non-intercourse decree of November 2, 1810, was more to Baltimore's taste, for trade with Great Britain, though important, was not her mainstay, and dogging frigates was a risk her merchants and skippers were prepared to assume. Still, when they got wind in advance of the impending decree they loaded their ships with goods for Britain and sent them forth in great numbers, thereby turning a pretty profit. The clippers were safely home and back on their accustomed routes long before war was declared. It was the bigger, slower ships of the Northern ports which suffered most from non-intercourse.

Baltimore heard with enthusiasm of the fight between the *President* and the *Little Belt*, a swift sloop-of-war which many of them had found it difficult to escape. Moreover, Rogers, commander of the *President*, was a Marylander, rapidly rising in the public estimation as a worthy successor to Barney. This encounter made it even more likely that war was close at hand, and the merchants, knowing what it meant to them, began to fit out ships in preparation for the expected issuance of letters of marque. The shipyards rattled with activity. Sailors thronged about the shipping offices. From the rivers down the bay the local shipbuilders and designers sent up newly finished craft and offered them for sale, getting high prices without difficulty. The town, in fact, was in the throes of another speculative fever. It could hardly restrain its impatience at the slow functioning of the Congress and on May 21, 1812, it held another meeting and passed another resolution, the purport of which, if not the precise wording, was an appeal to Washington to declare war immediately and never mind the detail of choosing between England and France as the enemy.

Baltimore's Own War

Madison signed the war act on June 8. On June 18 war was formally declared. Three days later George Stiles, a merchant of Baltimore, owner of the fast clipper schooner *Nonesuch*, sent his son to Washington to see the Secretary of State, Mr. Monroe. Monroe was out of town, but Congressman Alexander McKim, a Baltimorean, took the young man to call on President Madison. What Stiles wanted was the honor of holding privateering commission no. 1. He learned from this highest source that letters of marque when and if issued would be handled at the local customhouse. It wasn't until Friday, June 26, that Congress got around to authorizing privateering. The blanks arrived in Baltimore the next day but after the customhouse was closed. Early Monday morning Captain Stiles appeared at the customhouse and got from James McCulloch, collector of customs, the bit of paper he had so persistently sought.

Later it transpired that he had been given something of a run-around. Joshua Barney, who had been vegetating impatiently on a farm owned by his wife in Anne Arundel County, had been promised commission no. 1 by the President. He was to have the schooner *Rossie*, whose chief owner was Isaac McKim, later to build the most beautiful if not the most successful of all Baltimore clippers. There was a considerable excitement when the mix-up was discovered. But the net result was the issuance of two commissions, both with the coveted number.

This might have led to complications had the British discovered the duplication. But they didn't, and both Barney in the *Rossie* and Henry Levely, who had been given command of Mr. Stiles's *Nonesuch*, put to sea. Levely picked up a British vessel, masquerading under Swedish colors, at the very entrance to the harbor. That was the first capture. But Barney, in the *Rossie*, was the first to clear the capes and operate in the open sea. The *Highflyer* was right behind him.

While this excitement was going on on the water front the town was going through one of the most painful (and perhaps the most disgraceful) episodes in its history.

The Federalists in Baltimore had a newspaper called the *Federal Republican*. Its chief owner was a young man named Alexander C. Hanson. He was the grandson of John Hanson, a signer of the Declaration of Independence and, as presiding officer of the Congress under the Articles of Confederation, in one sense the first President of the United States.

On June 20, two days after the formal declaration of war against England, the *Federal Republican* printed a highly provocative editorial. In New England that editorial would have expressed perhaps the opinion of most of the people. It denounced the war, the motives which had inspired the declaration, declared its undying hostility to Madison, and hinted that he was playing the game of Napoleon. It ended with an ardent insistence that it would cling to this position, come what might.

The paper was issued on Saturday. On Monday evening a mob assembled before the wooden house in Gay Street which housed the presses and other machinery of the paper and proceeded to tear the building to pieces, bit by bit. The type was scattered, the presses smashed, the paper tossed about. One man, engaged in pulling out the window frame on the second floor, lost his balance and fell to the street and broke his neck. Apparently the mayor, Mr. Edward Johnson, a judge or two, and several magistrates were present during the whole of the excitement. Some accounts say they tried to dissuade the mob but that their efforts were unavailing. Others say that the notables encouraged the work of destruction. There were no arrests.

The town was quite willing, perhaps anxious, to forget the whole affair, but Mr. Hanson was a headstrong and passionate young man who knew his rights and was willing to risk destruction to gain them. He repaired to Georgetown, a community much frequented by Federalists and others who had no love for Baltimore, and there concocted his plans. On a press in that community he set up a new edition of his paper and printed it. His partner in Baltimore, a man named Wagner, had a house on Charles Street. When all was in readiness Hanson, accompanied by a group of about twenty-five friends, took his supply of copies of the *Federal Republican* over to Baltimore and moved into the Wagner house. In the group were representatives of some of the proudest of Maryland's families and at least two outstanding Revolutionary heroes, Generals Henry (Light-Horse Harry) Lee and James M. Lingan. General Lee was the father of Robert E. Lee. There were, in addition, representatives of such leading families as the Gwinns, Gaithers, Warfields, Winchesters, Murrays, and Pringles. All were well armed. The Wagner house was sturdily built of brick and well able to withstand a siege.

On July 27 the *Federal Republican, redivivus,* came forth. Its chief feature was an editorial castigating the town, the police thereof, and the mayor especially. It argued, moreover, that the destruction of its property had been plotted long in advance and that the stimulus for the plot came from Washington. It concluded its denunciations with a special blast at the governor of the state for his failure to take steps to bring to justice the members of the mob and those who incited them.

By nightfall a new mob had gathered in front of Mr. Wagner's house, now become a fortress. A few calmer persons suggested its dispersion, but that meant only that more men joined the boys who up to now had been in the majority. A little later a carriage drove up. Several persons got out and went into the house, carrying arms with them. Someone in the mob threw a stone. Shots rang from the house. More stones were thrown. A gang detached itself and rushed the door, seeking entry. A volley from within, and one man fell dead and several wounded. There was a call for the militia and more rushing and shooting until it arrived. Another man urging on the mob in the street, a Dr. Gale, was shot dead.

Whereupon a cheering crowd appeared, dragging a field piece after them. They were preparing to fire it, but a troop of cavalry rode up under Major John Barney (not Joshua, who was already at sea in the *Rossie*), and the mob rushed away. But Barney was politically on the best of terms with the crowd in the street, and they soon gathered about again, though Barney stood in front of the field piece and told them that if it were fired they would have to kill him.

This sort of thing went on all night. At six in the morning Mayor Johnson showed up, accompanied by General Stricker, commander of all the town militia. A parley ensued between him and the occupants of the house. Hanson was against any kind of surrender, but the night-long assault had worn down the spirits of all of them, and there had been several outright defections. His friends, one of whom had already been wounded, prevailed upon him to accept for them all the safe-conduct to the jail which the mayor and the general offered. Between eight and nine o'clock the whole party, now about twenty in number, was escorted to the jail "for safekeeping" by a party of horse-and-foot militia.

But the worst was yet to come. After the political prisoners were safely in the jail the mayor allowed the militia to keep out of sight. He said he thought the danger was over. The mob reformed several times but was persuaded to disperse. The more sober citizens had got themselves into some sort of organization by this time, but even they were brought to believe, by General Stricker's reassurances, that there was no possibility of more disorder.

Sometime in the night, by obvious prearrangement, the mob formed again. It stormed the front door of the jail and was finally mysteriously admitted. The prisoners, all in one large cell, defended themselves as best they could in the darkness and excitement. But those who managed to get as far as the door without being recognized found the way barred by a gigantic fellow named Mumma, a butcher. Mumma knew every one of the prisoners by sight. He signaled the arrival at the door of each of them by delivering a mighty blow with his fist. Whereupon the crowd rushed upon the unfortunate if he stood after the blow or rolled him violently down the jail steps if it felled him. Once at the bottom, he was set upon, beaten, kicked, and generally maltreated until no sign of life was apparent.

One by one the victims were thrown upon a growing pile. If an arm twitched or a leg moved it was the signal for another attack. Knives were freely used in this little scene in the drama, and many of the bodies were pretty well hacked about before the blood lust was satiated.

Baltimore on the Chesapeake

Normally enough, the mob got tired of the sport before many hours had passed. Whatever spirit gave unity to the monster was dissipated. Bit by bit it fell apart, the shamefaced individuals who had composed it slinking off to their homes. Two or three even found some room in their hearts for mercy and helped several of the wounded to escape. Bit by bit decent people recovered their courage, approached the scene, and began some sort of humane ministrations.

It is a commentary on the toughness of the human frame that of all those attacked only one died immediately as a result. This was the aged General Lingan. Light-Horse Harry Lee never fully recovered, although he survived until 1818. The younger men, including Mr. Hanson, managed to feign death so realistically that their drunken assailants did not realize that they were being deceived.

Members of both sides were indicted and brought to trial, the Federalists in Annapolis and the mobsters in Baltimore. There were no convictions.

No incident in the early history of Baltimore throws into higher relief the special nature of the conflicts which came to a head at that time in this not overly distinguished city. But in order to understand the incident it is necessary to examine the interests in conflict. Baltimore, though as mercantile in its outlook as New England, was, nevertheless, not Federalist in politics but Republican, i.e., Democratic. The landowners of the surrounding country, those whose political fanaticism had precipitated the riot, were not Republican in politics, like their agricultural brethren in the South, but Federalist, like mercantile New England. It is probable that fear of commercial Baltimore was responsible for their political allegiance.

The party labels are thus confusing, and so, too, are the economic motives of the contending forces. The New England Federalists up to this time had stood for a strong national government. It was the prospect of a war for which they thought the country unprepared and almost certain to be a loser which made them, for the time being, willing to wreck the central authority, by secession if need be.

The Republicans of the South, of course, had stood stanchly for States' rights, for in times of peace they were fearful of the wealth and power of industrial and commercial New England and did not want it to dominate a government which in turn might dominate them. But they favored this particular war because they had found in their hinterland on the other side of the mountains new and vigorous allies who, for their own purposes, found the idea of war against England politically agreeable.

Baltimore, fighting an uphill battle for a position in the commerce of the country, found its way made difficult by the commercial competition offered by the older and richer cities to the north and also by the condescension and outright opposition offered by the agricultural interests in Maryland itself. That vote in the General Assembly flatly refusing the city the additional representation to which it was so clearly entitled had rankled. Thus a purely intrastate town-versus-country conflict had scrambled the national issues and left things in a mess for the historian.

Moreover, it should not be forgotten that some of the solider and less venturesome of Baltimore's merchants looked on the war in much the same light as did the New Englanders in the same line of business. In 1800 Baltimore attracted a rather unusual figure in the person of Alexander Brown. Like so many others of the merchants of the town, he was an Irishman. His choice of Baltimore as his place of future enterprise went back in all probability to the influence of old Dr. John Stevenson, whose venture in flour had attracted the attention and perhaps aroused the cupidity of a good many sons of Erin. By 1812 Mr. Brown had become a substantial figure, adding banking to his numerous commercial interests. His sons were beginning their dispersal to other cities and towns, setting up those houses in Philadelphia, New York, Boston, and London which were destined to make the name of Brown a synonym of banking prudence and integrity for more than a hundred years.

On April 7, 1812, Alexander, the founder, wrote his son George, then in London, a letter of advice in which he said:

I still think it impossible that our Executive can have any serious intention of going to war with England, in the unprepared state of this country, and particularly so, as we are equally as ill treated by France as respects capturing and burning American ships. . . .

But Mr. Brown was a special sort of merchant. It probably would have suited him just as well to have carried on his business from New York or Philadelphia or Boston. He hadn't been in town long enough to get into the emotional state which many of the merchants had reached over the condescensions of New England on the one hand and of the tobacco planters on the other. Anyway, his business was almost entirely with England and Ireland. The special problems and opportunities of the West Indian and Mediterranean trade concerned him but little.

There was another factor, probably as important as any. Because his trade was legitimate in every sense, because he was running no blockades, violating no orders in council or Berlin decrees he trusted his goods both ways to simple, straightforward, high-sided, workaday ships capable of carrying huge cargoes but making no pretensions to speed or class. He had little need for and hence no particular pride in the Baltimore clipper. He had never felt the thrill of owning a vessel capable of outpointing a frigate or running a blockade. He had not yet come to believe, as so many Baltimore merchants had, that trading on the seas was a gamble and that the bigger the risk the greater the gain. So, after all, he wasn't a typical Baltimorean—not at that time, anyway—and could take a view with which a New Englander could sympathize. But many of the other merchants *had* been engaged in trade that was dangerous and at times somewhat illegitimate. Some of them recalled the great days of privateering in the Revolution. Like golfers who remember their good shots but conveniently forget those which are dubbed, such Baltimoreans remembered the successful cruises of their sightly schooners and forgot their losses.

They believed that in the clipper they had an instrument which, properly used, could be turned to great advantage in time of war, for it could give them something close to a monopoly in a dangerous trade. They longed for a chance to show the uppity Yankee sailors and their own haughty planters what they could do.

Such sentiments, however lacking in ethical value, have a special persuasiveness when mulled over in simple minds. They would be especially warming to sailors cast on the beach by the embargo, to workmen dependent on the shipbuilding industry, to longshoremen, and to the habitués of grog shops and public houses. Moreover, there is nothing like the shedding of a little blood to give moral sanction to a doubtful enterprise. However unconvinced before the attack on the jail, Baltimore had few doubts after that affair.

CHAPTER XVI

"Nest of Pirates"

FOLLOWING HIS ORDERS, Barney, in the *Rossie*, sailed north to the Grand Banks. It was an error in judgment on the part of his owners to send him there, for the rich prizes were all to the southward. His first prize was the *Nymph* brig of Newburyport. She was violating the non-intercourse act by trading with the English, and he sent her in, probably with a sense of satisfaction, for he harbored a grudge against the English and had an especial dislike for traitors.

Soon after, he was off the banks, playing havoc with the fishing schooners. As prizes they were not worth a thing, but Barney followed orders and sank or burned them in succession, sparing an occasional one to carry ashore his numerous prisoners.

A month of this, and he considered his obligations to his owners filled and turned south, stopping for supplies in anti-war Newport, where he got anything but a cordial welcome. A day or two later he was chased by three men of war, escaped them with ease, and then found himself in sight of a trim brig which instead of heeding his warning

[171]

gun fired in return. It was a warm contest in which Barney
lost his first lieutenant, Sylvanus Long, but killed the captain and sailing master of the brig and wounded several
sailors. The courageous fight put up by the English vessel
was explained by the fact that she was a post-office packet,
the *Princess Amelia*, under order to fight to a finish. There
were some female passengers aboard, and, out of consideration for these and for the wounded, he sent her in rather
than burn her.

Off St. Thomas he hung for four days around the edges
of a convoy guarded by a schooner-of-war, seeking to cut
out at least one of the ships. The schooner gave battle finally and sent aboard an eighteen-pound shot which dis-
abled the *Rossie's* pump. He was forced to withdraw.

After this he took one schooner, the *Jubilee*, in Mona
Passage between Haiti and Puerto Rico before setting out
for home. On the way thither he picked up the *Merrimac*
brig, another American lawbreaker, and sent her in.

That was enough privateering for an ex-naval hero. He
had taken twenty vessels, most of which were worthless.
He had learned that a privateer captain gets little credit for
patriotic endeavor outside his home port and that most of
his captures are defenseless merchantmen or fishermen. So
Barney called it a day and wrote to Washington asking for
a commission in the regular navy. The *Rossie*, under Barney, is frequently hailed as the storybook privateer. But
she made little or nothing for her owners, and even Barney
couldn't live on gallantry.

Baltimore's most noteworthy privateer captain was not
Baltimore-born. He was, instead, a Marblehead Yankee, of
Irish origin, attracted to the city in 1794 by tales of the
boom. He had commanded a ship at sixteen and with that

reputation behind him had little difficulty finding a place for himself in his new home. He found a wife, too, and got a special liking for and skill in handling the Chesapeake schooners. His name was Thomas Boyle.

From the very beginning of his long career out of Baltimore Boyle had qualities which set him apart from the ordinary run of sea captains. They all had courage. But Boyle had courage plus discretion. All of them were good seamen, but Boyle had forethought as well as skill, as we shall see. Many of them were illiterate or nearly so. But Boyle was almost a learned man and had resources in the way of self-expression, both by word of mouth and with the pen. They all drove their crews, but Boyle had the art of imposing discipline and inspiring affection at the same time.

His first command, in the War of 1812, was the privateer schooner *Comet*. She was a tiny vessel, just over ninety feet in length, with a tonnage of only 187. We have no account of the quality of his crew, but it was probably much like that of another vessel, the *George Washington*, which went out just behind the *Comet*. Of the *George Washington's* crew, her lieutenant, George Little, another New Englander, wrote that they "were a motley set, indeed, composed of all nations; they appeared to have been scraped together from the lowest dens of wretchedness and vice and only wanted a leader to induce them to any acts of daring and desperation."

Boyle was a leader and he showed it by putting his men to hard drill as soon as he was outside the capes. They were in fine fettle by July 25 and so smart in the handling of sails and guns that they took their first prize, the ship *Henry*, four hundred tons, before she had a chance to unlimber and fire a shot.

Three weeks later he ran down on the ship *Hopewell*, fourteen guns, laden with a rich cargo of sugar, molasses, cotton, coffee, and cocoa. Anderson, her skipper, had no desire to surrender to a vessel so much smaller than his own and with an armament no heavier. But Boyle's maneuvers gave him little opportunity to use his weight of metal, and he had no effective answer to the rain of musket fire from the landsmen on the deck of the *Comet*. After an hour, with one man killed and six wounded and most of his guns out of commission, he hauled down his flag.

Two weeks later Boyle outsailed and took the *Industry* brig off Bermuda and two weeks after that the ship *John*, 372 tons, Demerara for London. With a crew depleted by the necessity of manning prizes and supplies running low, he turned back to Baltimore. Every vessel he had captured came in safely; the total value of his prizes was over $400,000. Though about half this went to the government, his own share was enough to enable him to buy an interest in the little schooner which had served him and his owners so well.

The second cruise of the *Comet*, with her captain now enjoying the feeling of being part owner, began in November of 1812. It was full of excitement and glory. Off Pernambuco Boyle heard of a convoy about to go out. He lay in wait and saw four vessels come out of the harbor. Giving them time to get well to sea, he bore down to discover that one of them was the Portuguese man-of-war brig, *Libra*, obviously acting illegally as protector. He nevertheless came up with the fleet, only to be challenged by the Portuguese. The two masters held a spirited colloquy, but Boyle was not intimidated. He knew his rights as bearer of a privateering license. In the falling darkness he attacked the three merchant vessels, a large ship, and two brigs, and captured all of them, despite the constant interference of heavy broadsides from the man-of-war. Unfortunately for him, the action was so severe, and the merchantmen, their courage raised by the presence of professional help, fought so hard, he all but sank two of them before they surrendered. The Portuguese captain got into trouble later over this affair, but his presence and his activity did prevent Boyle from enjoying the full fruits of his bravery. Still, he got away with one of his prizes.

For a few days he dodged warships and then early on the morning of January 29 came up with a large ship. A sharp battle ensued, and Boyle himself was slightly wounded, but the ship *Adelphi*, 361 tons, Liverpool to Bahia, struck her colors just before she was boarded.

After shipping into St. Barts for water Boyle ran into a series of difficulties and had the mortification of seeing a Baltimore schooner, the *Newton*, which he had agreed to protect, taken by a large brig-of-war, apparently H.M.S. *Swaggerer*. A day later he sighted two sails. The first was the brig *Alexis* from Demerara with a rich cargo. She was taken with no difficulty. The second turned out to be the brig *Dominica Packet*, of Liverpool.

While she was being chased another sail came up. It turned out to be the *Swaggerer*. Boyle had to rush the capture of his quarry, man it, and send it off quickly, in order to turn and face the *Swaggerer*. Of course he had no idea of giving battle but he was bound to try to save his prize. For hours he made the man-of-war look ridiculous while he darted about, firing an occasional shot and pretending to prepare for battle. The prize crew was making off with the *Dominica Packet* all the while. When he regarded her distance as sufficient Boyle stopped his maneuvers and drew away, taking another small schooner while his lumbering pursuer was still in sight.

On March 17 Boyle sailed into the capes again on a foggy day, completely in ignorance of the fact that a blockade had been established during his absence. This voyage was a complete failure as far as profit went, for not a single one of the vessels he captured ever made an American port. All were retaken by the British cruisers which were patrolling American waters in ever-increasing numbers.

For the next six months or thereabouts Boyle held a naval commission. His *Comet,* along with three other privateering schooners, was leased by the government for patrol duty in the bay. On October 29, provided with new letters of marque, she was off again on another cruise.

By this time the Spanish Main was swarming with British men-of-war on the lookout for the *Comet* in particular. It was a spectacular five months for Boyle. He reported after his arrival in Beaufort, N.C., in March 1814 that he had been chased by no fewer than thirty-four frigates and brigs-of-war and had in each instance outsailed them with ease. His biggest failure was to take the large ship *Hibernia.* The captain and crew of this vessel were doughty fellows and they took advantage of their size by refusing to surrender and by fighting off, from the great height of their deck, every effort at boarding made by Boyle and his men. Both vessels were badly mauled, but the *Comet* had so much damage to spars and rigging that she had to retire to San Juan to refit.

During this cruise Boyle made twenty captures, of which four were ransomed and nine destroyed. Only four actually made American ports. But Boyle's reputation was so enhanced by the havoc he had wrought and by the obvious terror which his name aroused in British shipping and naval circles that the owners offered him the *Chasseur*, a much larger and more formidable vessel.

The *Chasseur* was built in the shipyard of Thomas Kemp, on the Point. Her burden was 356 tons, and she was just under 116 feet long. She was thus the largest Baltimore clipper built up to that time. She was also one of the fastest sailing vessels of all time, as she later proved when engaged in the China trade. She was put overboard on December 12, 1813, which is pretty good evidence that she was built primarily with privateering in mind.

Her first effort, however, was to sail as a letter of marque to Bordeaux. Unfortunately her commander, Pearl Durkee, was unable to run the blockade at the capes. Her luck was so bad that her first owners, Hollins and McBlair, lost heart and sold her to a new syndicate which refitted her, strengthened her armament, and got her a new captain, William Wade, who had been Boyle's second officer in the first cruise of the *Comet*.

Wade shipped a crew of 148—if the crew had been 150 the bond would have been doubled—and slipped down the bay and through the reinforced blockading fleet in a snowstorm. On this voyage Wade took eleven prizes—of which few got safely in—but he did prove the sailing qualities of his vessel. In June 1814 he brought her into New York, the blockade of the Chesapeake being complete at that time. Her owners had in the meantime sold her at auction, deliverable at New York. Boyle had bought a share in her, and it was natural that the command should be turned over to him.

Baltimore on the Chesapeake

He had grand ideas for this cruise. Taking advantage of the summer weather, he planned to go, not to the Spanish Main, where the British patrol was thick, but to the British Isles themselves. It is also likely that he was cherishing at that time the notion which he later carried out with great éclat.

But the Northern waters, even in summer, are not those in which the Baltimore clipper is at her best. She is wet in a sea, and, especially, her light spars, with their weight of canvas, are subject to strain in heavy weather. So Boyle provided himself with a whole supply of extra spars and sails so that he could, on occasion, turn his schooner into a brig, a brigantine, or a hermaphrodite. Cranwell and Crane, from whose *Men of Marque* most of this material about Baltimore privateers in the War of 1812 has been drawn, think that Boyle had in mind also the possibility of disguise in thus providing the means to change his appearance. For armament he had sixteen long twelves which gave him hitting power at a distance much greater than that of any other privateer of the time.

He weighed anchor first on July 24 but immediately outside Sandy Hook found himself confronting a ship of the line and three frigates. It would have been foolish to attempt to outmaneuver them, so he put back. It was not until the twenty-eighth, when the weather thickened, that he managed to elude their vigilance.

His men were immediately put into hard training. No naval commander exacted a stricter discipline than this privateersman. Off the banks he picked up the brig *Eclipse*, trying out his long twelves in the process. She wasn't worth so much, but he sent her in. His next capture was the *Commerce*, a new vessel, her hold loaded with codfish.

That wasn't of much value, either, but because the craft was new he sent her in instead of destroying her.

On August 21 he ran down on the *Antelope* brig and took her without a shot. On board he found not only eight eighteen-pounders and a long gun but also a letter of marque. So disgusted was he with her failure to put up a fight that he wrote a letter of protest to the British Admiralty. Next day he picked up another fisherman. On August 24 he overhauled a Scotch sloop, the *Canary*, unloaded all his prisoners, and sent her to England as a cartel.

By now he was off the Scilly Isles, his real hunting grounds. There were merchant ships aplenty, but the British navy was active too. He had to make captures, elude capture himself, and, if possible, see that his prizes were not retaken. He was thus a very busy man.

He sighted a large convoy on August 25 but as he approached it from the windward he discovered that two of the fleet were warships. He hauled in his sheets and sailed up the wind, giving them the slip. The following day he took and burned two small vessels unworthy the risk of manning and sending in. His next capture was the *Marquis of Cornwallis* brig, equally valueless. He utilized her, however, to put in effect the plan he had concocted while still ashore.

Putting all his prisoners on the *Marquis of Cornwallis*, he sent her in as a cartel, commissioning her captain to post at Lloyd's the following proclamation:

Whereas, it has been customary with the admirals of Great Britain commanding small forces on the coast of the United States, particularly with Sir John Borlaise Warren and Sir Alexander Cochrane, to declare the coast of the said United

States in a state of strict and rigorous blockade, without possessing the power to justify such a declaration, or stationing an adequate force to command such a blockade.

I do, therefore, by virtue of the power and authority in me vested (possessing sufficient force) declare all the ports, harbors, bays, creeks, rivers, inlcts, outlets, islands, and seacoasts of the United Kingdom of Great Britain and Ireland in a state of strict and rigorous blockade, and I do further declare that I consider the forces under my command adequate to maintain strictly, rigorously and effectually, the said blockade.

And, I do hereby require the respective officers, whether captains, or commanding officers, under my command, employed or to be employed on the coast of England, Ireland and Scotland, to pay strict attention to this my proclamation.

And, I hereby caution and forbid the ships and vessels of all and every nation, in amity and peace with the United States, from entering or attempting to enter or from coming or attempting to come out of any of the said ports, harbors, bays, creeks, rivers, inlets, outlets, islands, or seacoasts, on or under any pretence whatever; and that no person may plead ignorance of this my proclamation, I have ordered the same to be made public in England.

Given under my hand on board the *Chasseur*,

THOMAS BOYLE

By Command of the Commanding Officer,

J. B. STANSBURY, *Secretary*

The captain of the *Cornwallis* carried out his mission, and the proclamation was duly posted at Lloyd's. The story says that insurance rates were immediately raised to an unprecedented height and that the cost of carrying linen from Belfast to Liverpool went up to thirteen guineas the hundred. But Britain was still mistress of the seas, and Boyle's bravado made his task even more difficult than it had been before. The seas in which he was operating soon became alive with vessels of war.

He had dispatched his proclamation on August 27. On the twenty-eighth he took two valuable prizes, the ship *Atlantic* and the *James* brig. Two days later he picked up the sloop *Christiana*, which he had sent in earlier as a cartel. By her he sent in a repetition of his proclamation. But that very afternoon, trying to protect his prizes, the *Atlantic* and the *James*, he had to take on, for a brush at least, a second-class frigate with sharpshooting crew.

Next morning at dawn, in full sight of a tempting convoy, he found himself being chased by no less than four of His Majesty's ships, two frigates and two brigs. He had to run for it, losing his *Atlantic* in the midst of the race. Two days later he found the sharpshooting frigate convoying the retaken *Atlantic*. He tried to lure the frigate away, but she wasn't playing that game.

Next day, just for the fun of it, he pretended to be deceived by two brigs-of-war masquerading as merchantmen. They thought they had him, but he was sure of his sailing qualities and gave them a lot of trouble for nothing. On September 6, in the midst of almost a dead calm, he rose at dawn to find himself in the middle of a triangle composed of two brigs-of-war and a frigate. His fear was that they would send their boats to take him, but his lofty sails, with their ability to catch and utilize to the full every breath of wind, finally enabled him to work to windward of his enemies. The next day—he was now just to the west of the Scilly Isles—he was chased by four men-of-war but on this occasion he had a sailing breeze and hence had no difficulty. The next day the same story was re-enacted with the brig *Fly*, one of five sent out by the Admiralty to take him after the posting of that impudent proclamation.

A man less convinced of his own good fortune might have quit at this point, but Boyle kept on, alternately chasing and being chased, taking prizes and losing them, filling his own cargo space with the most valuable goods, until almost the end of September. Heading west, he reached New York late in October, turned his cargo over to the Federal authorities, and went to Baltimore to report.

On Christmas Eve—peace had been made at Ghent the same day, but he didn't know it—he went out again, this time to the West Indies, for the Northern waters would have been too much for him at this time of year. This cruise was a short one but it was filled with incident. Damaging gales accompanied him all the way to Barbados. Outside the harbor of Bridgetown he deliberately gave battle, of a sort, to a ship-of-war, with two other war vessels in sight, and in the very midst of the engagement took and searched the *Elizabeth* schooner, afterwards setting her afire. The admiral of the fleet, on board his flagship in the harbor of Bridgetown, must have observed the whole incident. The old game of hare and hounds began again, with the hare, because of her unrivaled sailing ability and the courage and resourcefulness of her captain, invariably getting the better of it.

On February 26, running along the north shore of Cuba, Boyle sighted a sleek topsail schooner making good time before the wind. The *Chasseur* was rigged as a brigantine at the time, and Boyle knew therefore that he would have to watch his quarry carefully lest she get to windward of him and so escape. Eying her through his glass, he saw that in her endeavor to get the windward berth she had overstrained her light spars and that her fore-topmast had actu-

CAPTAIN THOMAS BOYLE'S *CHASSEUR*

A contemporary model of the Baltimore clipper with which Boyle "blockaded" the British Isles during the War of 1812. She is here rigged as a brig. but Boyle carried extra sails and spars which enabled him to convert her into the characteristic topsail schooner if prudence demanded. The model is the property of the city of Baltimore and is displayed in the Municipal (Peale's) Museum.

ally carried away. Though her crew made quick work of cleaning up the wreckage, his suspicions were not aroused. This accident meant that he drew up more quickly on his quarry.

At close view she turned out to be a typical Chesapeake-built schooner, with but a few men on her deck. He drew up alongside, estimating her possible armament as he did so. Just when he was ready to order his boarders to go into action—when, in fact, only about fifteen yards separated the two vessels—the deck of the schooner suddenly swarmed with men. Ten gun ports, rather than the three he had counted, were suddenly triced up, and the *Chasseur* reeled with the impact of a full broadside. The biter was bitten. Boyle had been deceived by a man-of-war masquerading as a merchantman. He was in a real naval battle.

Now, in the emergency, the arduous training and strict discipline which prevailed on every ship which Boyle commanded, and especially on the *Chasseur*, proved its value. His men did not lose their heads any more than he lost his. The thunder of the carronades, the rattle of the musketry from the marines who swarmed on the deck of the war vessel were answered with a steely precision from the privateer. The schooner luffed, and Boyle countered with a jibe—a maneuver often practised by his men—keeping the weather berth. Running up on his opponent—he still had the advantage of speed—and ignoring both her guns and her muskets, he ordered his boarders into action. As the first of them reached the schooner's deck her colors came down.

He had captured H.M.S. schooner *St. Lawrence*, formerly the privateer *Atlas*. She mounted fifteen guns and carried a crew of seventy-five. Her total complement, including several naval officers bound for the squadron off New Orleans, amounted to eighty-nine men and several boys. She reported six killed and seventeen wounded, several of them mortally. Boyle was inclined to think that her losses—and consequently the size of her crew—were greater than the commander, Lieutenant J. C. Gordon, admitted.

He was very apologetic in his letter to his owners recounting this affair, for a privateer whose motive is profit is going beyond his province when he deliberately engages in a battle to the death with a war vessel. Moreover, he lost five men killed and eight wounded on his own ship, which was something that took explaining.

With a prize master on board, the *St. Lawrence* was sent on to Havana in the hope that her wounded could receive attention. On the way she was stopped by an English privateer. A British warship in the harbor, hearing Lieutenant Gordon's account of the battle, compelled the privateer to release her, and her case was adjudged by an admiralty court in Bermuda. The court decided that she was a legitimate prize to Boyle.

Meanwhile her captor, working north, learned from an American vessel that the war was over. On St. Patrick's Day, 1815, he came in the capes and the next day was the hero of a triumphal reception at Fells Point.

Boyle in the *Comet* and the *Chasseur* was by far the most picturesque, as well as the most articulate, of all the privateer commanders out of Baltimore during this war. But the Baltimore clipper was the favorite of all privateering syndicates, for the bay shipbuilders turned out their craft on almost a mass-production basis, selling them to adventurers all along the coast. The *Atlas*, which became the *St. Lawrence*, is a case in point.

During the thirty months of the war Federal licenses were granted to 250 private-owned vessels, of which Baltimore owners accounted for 126. Of this number seventy-eight were letters of marque, which means that they captured but few prizes. Twenty-seven were privateers, pure and simple. Twenty-one, including the *Chasseur*, pursued both callings. Of the total, fifty-four were either captured or lost. But, altogether, the 126 accounted for 556 of the enemy's vessels. Their activities helped supply the country's needs for imported goods during the war and made it possible for the American representatives to negotiate a more honorable peace.

But it is also true that their successes aroused in England a special hatred of the Chesapeake Bay and of Baltimore in particular. The communities on the bay paid in full for the escapades of their ships at sea. Of all of them, including Washington itself, only Baltimore had the satisfaction of turning back the invader.

CHAPTER XVII

"Oh, Say Can You See?"

THE ATTACK on the jail and the bestiality of the scenes which followed had one interesting result in Maryland. At the next election it elected a Federalist governor. The breach between town and country naturally was not healed by this change in sentiment. But the sufferings of the war were soon to become acute, and they had to be borne not only by Baltimore City but by every community and almost every plantation along the shores of the bay and its rivers. Misery, rather than politics, was the cementer of friendship during the next three years.

Which was just as well. For in the country as a whole the war did not become more popular as it progressed. New England was never won over, and the almost complete failure of the several expeditions into Canada had unpleasant repercussions. More and more Baltimore felt alone and friendless. If the state as well as the country had joined in the general execration which was being showered on the city it could hardly have survived. As it was, it just gritted its teeth and hung on, cheering wildly at every report of a capture by one of its privateers and, in calmer and soberer moments, trying to adjust itself to the almost complete stifling of its more peaceful trade.

British enmity toward Baltimore was specific. One speaker in the House of Commons solemnly pronounced it "the great depository of the hostile spirit of the United States against England." Boyle's escapades in the Channel brought a London newspaper to declare that "the American navy must be annihilated; their arsenals and shipyards must be consumed, and the truculent inhabitants of Baltimore must be tamed with the weapons which shook the turrets of Copenhagen."

The Northern cities were hardly more friendly. They reported the captures, real or imaginary, of Baltimore privateers with only slightly less glee than the English newspapers. Once when a New York paper carried a story about the taking of Boyle's *Comet* a Baltimore contemporary remarked, bitingly, that it was the third time the New York printers had sunk that busy raider.

In any event, the first blockade was proclaimed early in 1813. Ten vessels, under Admiral Cockburn, pretended to be able to cut off the whole coast south of Rhode Island. As a matter of fact, most of these vessels were not far from the mouth of the Chesapeake during that year. Privateers were willing to take the chance of getting in and out, but few peaceful merchantmen dared try it.

One result of this stifling of foreign trade was a new development of local industry. One finds all sorts of indications in the record of the spirit of enterprise turned inward. For instance, Mr. Charles Gwinn, a leading exporter of flour, built a mill in his warehouse on the end of Commerce Street wharf, the power to be supplied by steam. Mr. Job

Smith, who had a sawmill on Chase's wharf, abandoned horse power for the new steam engine. And William McDonald & Co. commissioned Mr. Flanigan, at the end of McElderry's wharf, to construct for them the first steamboat ever to operate out of Baltimore. This vessel, called the *Chesapeake*, was put on the line from Baltimore to Philadelphia. It carried passengers and freight as far as Frenchtown, at the head of the bay. There the passengers took a stage to Newcastle, on the Delaware, whence they took another steamer to Philadelphia. The most elaborate undertaking of the period was the erection of a new group of mills on Gwynns Falls, in a village called Calverton, just to the west of the city, but the most significant was the erection of three cotton mills, the Union, Powatan, and Washington, all of which derived their power from the streams in the neighborhood.

Most of these enterprises had to be carried out with one hand, so to speak. Cockburn's fleet was the main concern of the people. They knew they would be attacked sooner or later and they tried to put themselves in a proper state of defense. The first move was to find money. The mayor and city council appropriated $20,000, as a sort of start, and followed this by borrowing from the citizens and the banks an additional sum of $500,000. They thought they could get this back from the legislature, due to meet in May, but that body, though wordily sympathetic, could find no legal warrant for dipping into its own treasury for such a purpose. Thus Baltimore acquired its first debt.

The Federal government also found that sympathy was the only commodity which it could deal out freely. Its greatest contribution was to commission Joshua Barney to refit the old flotilla of gunboats and take command of them. That aging worthy, energetic as always, did his job well. The flotilla wasn't much but it was able to defend some of the waterways against forays by boats from the British fleet. In the course of time Barney managed to instill a sense of discipline and loyalty into several hundred men and created thereby a body of fighters who were later to stand the community in good stead.

Washington also sent over several officers out of the regular army, such as it was, to advise and help the city in the preparation of its defenses. Governor Winder named General Sam Smith, of Revolutionary fame, to be commander of the city's militia.

Acting under the advice of the Federal officer, General Smith first set about renovating Fort McHenry, on Whetstone Point, at the entrance to the harbor. He found it fallen to a low estate. Fortunately a French frigate, *L'Eole*, which had been abandoned in Baltimore after a punishing storm off the capes, had on board twelve forty-two-pounders. These were purchased and mounted. Two supporting batteries, called Forts Covington and Babcock, were set up a little farther up the Middle Branch, in the event the enemy should try to slip past Fort McHenry's guns and land a party to attack it in the rear.

On the other side of the harbor, where it is narrowest, a battery was erected alongside the quarantine station, called the Lazaretto. Further to protect the entrance, several supposedly worthless hulks were filled with stones and sand so that they could be sunk if necessary and effectually bar the not-too-deep channel. It transpired later that these hulks took on added value after they were so used and that their owners made exorbitant claims for them. There were preparations for furnaces for heating shot, for movable batteries on pinnaces which could be towed to the point needed, and so on.

As to the protection of the city against a land attack, the assumption was that the enemy would debark on the north side of the Patapsco somewhere near its mouth and so approach the city from the east. For defense against this contingency a height called Hampstead Hill (now Patterson Park) was fortified with a series of embankments, with occasional redoubts or bastions. This, it transpired, was the most effective of all the defense undertakings.

Manning all these positions was a considerable problem. General Smith could command only the services of the city militia, who were quite numerous. The help he could expect from the rest of the state, from neighboring states, and from the national capital was uncertain in both numbers and quality. But he was politician as well as soldier and he maneuvered and begged until he actually had several thousand men who one way or another were in training.

There was no real threat until April 16, 1813. Cockburn, only slightly hampered by Barney's flotilla, had moved leisurely up the bay. By night smaller vessels of shoal draft had not hesitated to slip by him. But now he anchored at the very mouth of the Patapsco. Thus all the bay trade with Baltimore was wholly cut off. Moreover, panic spread through the back country, and the farmers, accustomed to bringing their supplies in for sale in the three markets recently erected, feared to find themselves running into a real battle and stayed away. Mr. Hezekiah Niles, editor of the famous *Niles Register*, decided it was not only natural panic which kept the farmers. He guessed, rather, that it was "internal foes of the city cooperating with the enemy" who were fomenting these fears.

This may have been true. Not all the passions aroused by the mob had been allayed. Moreover, there were those in Philadelphia and in New York who could look with equanimity on the destruction of Baltimore and perhaps might not be averse to doing what they could, in the safest possible way, to spread the notion that Baltimore was doomed. In any event, there wasn't enough food to go round, and a good many of the well-to-do, especially, moved into the country or sent their families out to stay with friends.

This first threat, it transpired, was a false one. Cockburn had little or no knowledge of the state of the city's defenses. He sent a flag up the river, pretending he had a letter for the Secretary of War. But General Smith, suspecting that he was sounding the channel and perhaps seeking other information equally valuable, sent an aide to stop the British messenger four miles below the fort. The aide was Captain Chaytor, in command of one of Barney's gunboats. While he and the messenger awaited a reply to the letter, which was sent up in another vessel, the Englishman asked many questions. He particularly wanted to know if the guns of the French frigate *L'Eole* had been mounted. Chaytor assured him that they had been well mounted and that a furnace was ready to serve them up red hot.

This news was carried back to Cockburn. He thought better of attacking the city and spent his energies for the next few weeks raiding the islands, plantations, and settlements in the upper bay. It was a real reign of terror for the people affected, and it is not surprising that on one occasion word came to Baltimore that a land attack was impending.

This was only another rumor, but no one knew that at the time. The alarum guns were fired. Bakers left their ovens; carpenters dropped their hammers; lawyers slammed their dusty tomes, and in less than an hour something like five thousand men were not only under arms but at their appointed stations. There have been many sarcastic flings at the capabilities of General Sam Smith. But this little try-out of his mobilization plans indicates that he had done a good job so far. His real test was yet to come.

In June Cockburn was reinforced with more vessels and a considerable number of troops. The British fleet in the bay now consisted of eight ships of the line plus twelve frigates and a large number of smaller vessels, many of them captured from the Americans. Such a piling up of forces could only mean that a major attack was impending, and the general impression was that Baltimore was the goal. This view was sufficiently widely held to impress the authorities at Annapolis. Several companies of county militia were sent in, thus relieving some of the citizens for a while at least of the double duty of serving as soldiers and carrying on their daily tasks.

In August a large part of the augmented British fleet appeared again off the mouth of the Patapsco. Once more the general mobilization was ordered. This time the troops not only manned the forts but actually sent out a skirmishing force to delay the British if they should land at North Point and march on the city. Behind this force the others took their positions in the earthen fortifications on Hampstead Hill and manned the forty-eight pieces of artillery which had by now been gathered together. Once more the British, still remembering those forty-two-pounders, thought better of it, but by now the Baltimore force had learned something.

The real attack upon the city did not come until the

following year. It had to await the fall of Napoleon and the release of the ships and men which had brought about that fall. When Britain found her hands freed she set herself immediately to the task of bringing the United States and especially Baltimore into a proper frame of mind. The troops were placed under the command of General Robert Ross, who announced that he would spend the winter in Baltimore though the heavens "rained militia." "Baltimore," proclaimed Admiral Warren, "is a doomed town."

As fast as ships and men could be gathered they were dispatched to the Chesapeake. By the middle of August the lower bay was crowded with ships of the line, frigates, smaller boats of all descriptions, and three transports with regulars to the number of at least three thousand, all hardened by the peninsular campaign. Cockburn had already established a base at the mouth of the Potomac, and it was there, after consultation with the man who had already laid much of the bay country waste, that it was decided first to attack Washington.

That affair is not part of our story. But it is worthy of a note that Barney, with his flotilla, made a gallant effort to stop the force coming up the Patuxent for the attack on the capital and that after he had been forced to scuttle his little fleet he took his men ashore and made the one really creditable stand at the Battle of Bladensburg, being himself wounded and captured in the melee.

Having shown up the Americans, as they thought, the British took counsel once more. If they had decided to march overland to Baltimore, a distance of some forty miles, they might have taken that perturbed city. But they chose, instead, to go back to their boats and make the Baltimore campaign a joint action from the water side. To deceive the city as far as possible they sailed first down the bay and anchored in the Potomac while the soldiers rested. It wasn't until the night of September 10, nearly three weeks after Bladensburg, that they weighed anchor and stood up the bay.

Baltimore profited by the delay. The soldiers who had escaped from Bladensburg were re-formed and marched to the city. Special pleas were sent to the farmers round about to bring in food for the expected siege. Assurances were given that no man who came in on such an errand need fear impressment, either for himself or his horses and wagons. General Smith disposed both his officers and his men so as to secure the best results. The hulks were sunk across the channel. The furnaces for heating the shot were lit in Fort McHenry, in Forts Covington and Babcock, and in the little four-gun battery by the Lazaretto.

The British fleet arrived off the mouth of the river on Sunday afternoon, September 11, while a good many of the townspeople were in church. When watchers on the river shores gave the alarm it was flashed by prearranged signals to the city, where General Smith gave orders for firing the signal guns prepared for the purpose on the courthouse plaza.

The three detonations meant only one thing. The congregations were dismissed before the parsons had reached their fourthlies and lastlies; the drums began to roll; the militiamen donned their uniforms and rushed to their appointed rendezvous. By three o'clock the first proud contingent was marching out of Baltimore Street, under command of the same General Stricker who had failed at the time of the mob, with instructions to "feel out" the enemy if, as expected, he came in on the North Point road, then known as Long Log Lane. This contingent consisted of 3185 citizens of Baltimore plus a few of the ever-helpful militiamen from York and Hanover. They bivouacked for the night at the junction of the North Point road and the Philadelphia road, sending a few riflemen still further forward to watch for movement by the enemy.

It was not until daylight that the watchers reported that he was methodically disembarking his men under cover of gunboats precisely at the point which General Smith had hoped for and planned for—"a remarkable example of accommodating generalship," as someone has remarked.

Save for some details, the ensuing battle was likewise according to plan. As soon as the news of the enemy's approach reached Stricker's skirmishers he moved forward, his advance screened by riflemen. The British regulars, on the other hand, marched stolidly up the road. Finding themselves confronting sporadic rifle fire of unusual accuracy—Baltimoreans of those days were close enough to frontier times to know how to shoot—they sent forward scouts who reported back that the militia was firing from behind incompleted breastworks and other cover.

The delay being reported to General Ross, in command of the land forces, he rode forward to investigate for himself. Herein he made his great mistake, for two members of the advance guard of riflemen were very good marksmen indeed. These two young fellows, Daniel Wells and Henry G. McComas, hidden behind trees, suddenly found the general himself riding full into view. Simultaneously they aimed and fired. The general reeled in his saddle and, had he not been caught by his aide, would have fallen from his horse. He was lifted down as tenderly as possible but died in a few minutes on the roadside. Both Wells and

McComas had fired their last shot, however. The British picked off both of them.

Command of the invading force now devolved on Colonel Arthur Brooke, a more cautious man than his late commander. Adopting classical battle tactics, he sent out a force to flank the American advance guard and drive them from their thinly held position. Stricker saw the maneuver and tried to rearrange his front to meet it. But this meant some rather complicated orders and still more complicated maneuvers. Before the Americans could be entirely reformed the British were charging them, seeking to come to close quarters where they could use the bayonet. This was too much for the raw militiamen. A few of them fired in a desultory fashion at the oncoming redcoats. The rest simply turned tail and fled.

But both Smith and Stricker had foreseen such a contingency. They did not expect this small body to turn back the British army. All they had hoped for was a delaying action. Back of Stricker's men was a battery of small guns, loaded with "grape and canister, shot, old locks, pieces of broken muskets, and anything they could get into their guns." Tremendously anxious to retrieve the honor of the city, the gunners stood firm and fired as often and as accurately as they could at the advancing force. This shook the British almost as effectively as the fear of the bayonet had shaken the Americans. They stopped their advance, and meantime Stricker was able to withdraw his exposed units.

Thereafter the retreat was regular and strictly according to plan. As the Baltimoreans drew back they felled trees across the road. Brooke had to send pioneers forward to open the way, and as they sawed and chopped and pulled they were subjected to deadly fire from the riflemen of the rear guard. It was a hot and sultry day, of a sort that always gets Englishmen down and dulls their interest in life. So Stricker and his men were able to reach the junction of the North Point road and the Philadelphia road and then move in toward Hampstead Hill, where the real defense was to be made. The British toiled painfully after them.

Ross and his staff had known of the fortifications on Hampstead Hill. It was not their plan to attack the works directly, for they knew that raw troops, when protected by breastworks, have a valor equal to that of seasoned regulars. They proposed instead that the fleet should move up the river, silence Fort McHenry or ignore it, and pour its main fire into the little battery on Lazaretto Point. If that were reduced the land forces could take it and thus attack the hill on the flank.

Therefore, having reached the foot of the ascent and seen how closely it was held and how carefully the bastions and *flèches* had been prepared so as to pour a cross fire on troops attempting to storm the position, Colonel Brooke ordered a halt until he could be certain that the fleet had done its part. That halt proved his undoing, for the muggy day was followed by an even worse night. It rained unceasingly. There was no shelter; the men were not provided even with blankets for gypsy tents. They just had to take it.

Brooke waited for the sound of the cannonading which would mean that the fleet had come up to do its work. It wasn't until nearly midnight that he heard any firing at all, and that was at such a distance that he knew it could not be what he was hoping for. As he waited his spirits fell. After an hour or two he sent messengers to see if they could find out what was wrong. Down near the riverside they met a group from the fleet on a similar errand. The message from Admiral Cockburn was that "no effectual support could be given to the land force, for such was the shallowness of the river that none except the very lightest craft could make their way within six miles of the town, and even these were stopped by vessels sunk in the channel and other artificial bars, barely within a shell's longest range of the fort." The ordnance officer from Washington and General Smith had made their preparations well.

Poor Brooke held a council of war in the early-morning darkness. He looked over his drenched and dispirited forces; he glanced once more at the fortified heights they would have to storm. Then, with a heavy heart, he gave the retreat, consoling himself with the thought that, since there were no ships to carry away the booty that might result from the taking of the town, the whole adventure probably was not worth the trouble it had caused. The defenders didn't know he had gone until he was miles down the road.

This was the end of the land campaign. What had meantime been going on in the river? Admiral Cockburn had told the exact truth when he said the water was shallow. There was a deep natural channel, but it was difficult even for those who knew it well and almost impossible for the heavy, deep-draught vessels which composed the strength of his fleet. The best he could do, therefore, was to take some of the smaller local vessels which he had captured— he chose sloops, for the most part, because their draught was less—mount mortars on them, and send them up as close as he dared.

This meant that they anchored about two miles below

"THE BOMBS BURSTING IN AIR"

From a contemporary, or almost contemporary, conception of the British attack on Fort McHenry on September 13 and 14, 1814. The view is apparently from Federal Hill, looking down toward Whetstone Point, on which the fort was built. The scale is very bad, but the little encampment to the far right is supposed to represent Fort Covington and the wrecks between that and the point the remains of the landing force which was driven off. The point on the far right is apparently the Lazaretto, and the vessels between that and Fort McHenry the hulks which were sunk to block the way into the harbor.

Fort McHenry, out of range of the forty-two-pounders from *L'Eole*. From this safe position they began, about two o'clock Tuesday morning, the bombardment which Colonel Brooke heard. All night long they fired high into the air, their shrieking shells falling into the silent fort, entirely harmlessly, for the most part. Some of these shells weighed as much as two hundred and twenty pounds, and the noise of the guns and of the explosions of the falling missiles kept the town in an uproar. It is said that something over eighteen hundred shells, plus a multitude of round shot and rockets, were thrown. The bombardment kept up all day Tuesday and most of that night.

About midnight Tuesday, while the din was at its height, a few vessels detached themselves from the fleet and, accompanied by a large number of barges carrying some twelve hundred men, slipped up Middle Branch and tried to make a landing in the cove behind the fort. But they had forgotten or else were ignorant of Fort Covington and the supporting batteries. A rocket disclosed what was going on, and for once the men manning the guns on shore —Barney's flotilla men were among them—had some action. They fired into the advancing boats and wrought such havoc that the whole effort was abandoned by the British. During this brush, which didn't last long, the people of Baltimore heard a barrage which must have rivaled that which the people of London endure while their anti-aircraft batteries are working.

At six in the morning, having utterly failed either to reduce the fort or to make a landing, the whole British force withdrew to the mouth of the river where Cockburn was taking on board the dispirited men who had tried the land attack.

Baltimore on the Chesapeake

During their various forays on the shores of the bay the British had captured and detained a number of well-known Marylanders, including a Dr. Beanes, of Upper Marlborough, in Prince Georges County. Beanes was an outstanding practitioner with many friends. One of them, a reputable lawyer of Frederick, named Francis Scott Key, heard of his plight and sought to effect his release. Mr. Key, accompanied by Colonel John S. Skinner, boarded a small vessel, ran up a flag of truce, and approached the British anchored in the Patapsco. They were well received and taken aboard H.M.S. *Surprise*. But the attack on Fort McHenry was in preparation, and the British were fearful of letting Key and his friend go ashore before it was concluded. Accordingly, they were carried up the river and after the attacking vessels had taken their positions were put aboard their own little cartel and bidden to stay there until the fight was over.

Neither Key nor Colonel Skinner slept that night. The confident British had led them to believe that the city would surely fall, and they could hear little evidence that it was making any real resistance. During the night an occasional rocket showed them that the flag was still flying, but when dawn came they were able to see, through the smoke, that McHenry was practically unharmed. Key was a highly strung man, capable of great emotional heights, and when finally the British gave up the effort and dropped down the river, he was in a state of poetic exaltation. On his way back to the city in his cartel he began the composition of some verses to express his feelings. He made his notes on the back of a letter he had in his pocket. By the time he had stepped ashore in the jubilant town the form was pretty well blocked out.

That night, working from his notes, he finished the effort and gave it its title, "The Star-Spangled Banner." Next morning he showed it to his uncle, Judge Joseph H. Nicholson, who had spent the night in the fort. The judge was so delighted that he rushed around to the printing house of Captain Benjamin Edes, on North Street, to get it printed. But Captain Edes hadn't yet been mustered out of the regiment in which he served, and his pressroom was closed. The judge, breathless by this time, took it to the office of the *Baltimore American* (successor to Mr. Goddard's *Commercial Advertiser*) and had it struck off in the form of handbills. It was Judge Nicholson also who made the happy discovery that Key's verses could be sung to the tune of "Anacreon in Heaven," a highfalutin drinking song recently brought over from London and much in vogue among the gay fellows of the town.

The story says the new song was first sung publicly at a celebration in a restaurant next the Holliday Street Theater, the soloist being Charles Durang. The next night it was tried out in the theater itself and after that was rapidly taken up by the whole town. In short order both the army and navy adopted it as their national anthem, but it wasn't until March 4, 1931, that Congress formally pronounced it *the* national anthem.

CHAPTER XVIII

Perversion of Talents

ALTHOUGH not quite certain that the British might not come back and try again, Baltimore celebrated the immediate relief from attack with justifiable self-congratulation. For the most part, it had done the job without Federal help. It was Baltimore troops, aided, as always, by friendly Pennsylvanians from York, Hanover, and the southern Pennsylvania counties, who had fought through the day along the North Point and Philadelphia roads. It was Baltimore volunteers, under Colonel Armistead, who had withstood the twenty-four-hour bombardment in the fort. It was Barney's flotilla men who had provided most of the little garrisons of Forts Covington and Babcock which had foiled the British effort to force a landing on the flank of Fort McHenry. The rest of the country might regard the three-day affair as a mere skirmish, but Baltimore had shed her blood. Her losses were not heavy—perhaps twenty killed, ninety wounded, and forty or fifty prisoners—but she had inflicted losses on the enemy many times her own, perhaps to the number of five hundred in all, including the general in command. She had reason for pride.

The setback which the British received had its effect at the conference table in Ghent, where the commissioners to negotiate the peace were already assembled. Up to the news of the Battle of Baltimore the British representatives had been almost contemptuous in their treatment of the Americans. But when that news arrived, almost at the same time as that of the battle at Plattsburg, the British attitude changed. Matthew Page Andrews, a conscientious historian, believes that the terms finally agreed upon would have been much less advantageous to the United States without these victories. This, however, the Baltimoreans did not know. All they knew was that they had turned back a formidable British army, composed of hardened regular troops and supported by a strong fleet.

They had less reason for being cocky about their future. Several things had happened elsewhere which, had they appreciated their significance, would have thrown a chill over the exuberance with which they went about trying to re-establish their former trade connections.

The first of these was the invention of the steamboat. When the purchase of Louisiana opened up the Mississippi produce could be floated down the river and there loaded on ocean-going vessels, but floating back the manufactured articles was a different story. It was customary for a Western merchant or planter to take his crop to New Orleans to sell and then go by ship around Florida to Baltimore to purchase his supplies. Thence, by Conestoga wagon over the national pike or one of the other roads, he could get back to his home in much less time than if he had tried the difficult passage up the river. But when steamboats capable of fighting the current were built on the Ohio the story was altered. Baltimore didn't appreciate this alteration for quite a long time.

The second factor in the situation was this: For nearly fifty years the European world had been almost continuously at war. All the Eastern cities of the United States had profited by the situation. They owed their rapid growth largely to the fact that they had all but monopolized the carrying trade of the world. In this trade Baltimore was especially favored, not only by its geographical position but also because it had developed a vessel peculiarly suited for wartime adventuring. It might almost be said that the prosperity of Baltimore was dependent for its increase upon the continuance of war.

Certainly it soon began to look that way. When peace came the privateers and letters of marque, so long forced by the blockade to make their runs from Northern or Southern cities, began to come back to their home port. One by one they discharged their crews. Each discharge augmented the number of idle men hanging about the taverns along the water front.

The tobacco trade also was in the doldrums. The blockade had effectually prevented the shipping of this bulky cargo on any real scale, and the discouraged planters had begun to abandon its cultivation. A large part of Europe had apparently forgotten its taste for the weed. It was years before the ancient craving reasserted itself, and in the meantime the planters, and the tobacco merchants, too, grew poorer and poorer.

Finally the new factories, especially the new cotton mills, soon found that the return of peace meant increased competition from the English. The ventures which had begun so bravely and carried on for two or three years so successfully were slowed down and in some cases even stopped. The flour trade, the backbone of the port's commerce, began to suffer. It wasn't that the flour wasn't still needed in the West Indies. It was rather that the British made laws under which their ships which brought in cotton goods and cheap metal wares took over the transport of the staple to the islands.

Counsels in Baltimore were sharply divided as to the proper course. It was natural, however, that some of the owners of these vessels which had distinguished themselves so brilliantly during the war tried to believe that they still had a future on the sea. It was natural also that with little legitimate cargo to handle they began to think in terms of the more reckless kind of commerce.

It so happened that the revolutionary spirit which manifested itself in North America in the 1770s and reached its height in France in the 1790s finally rebounded and found a lodging in certain Latin American hearts. Along the shores of the Spanish Main, so well known to Baltimore skippers, the revolt was in full swing. It had leapt over Brazil, for reasons which will concern us a little later, but throve in Buenos Aires and the country thereabouts. It was alive also in Chile, on the west coast. Peru was still loyal to the regime in Spain but was being pressed from the north and the south. From Buenos Aires, in particular, the battle against the Spaniard was being carried on on sea as well as on land.

But the people of Buenos Aires were not themselves seafarers nor sea-fighters. They had to have mercenaries with ships to do their fighting for them. Accordingly—and here we draw on the careful researches of Charles C. Griffin of

Vassar College—early in 1816, less than a year after the peace, a certain Thomas Taylor, formerly of Wilmington, Del., but now of Buenos Aires, began to be seen in the taverns and coffeehouses of Baltimore. The despondent shipowners and merchants heard him talking about the easy money to be made privateering under the flag of the United Provinces of Rio de la Plata. He orated also about the glory of fighting in the cause of American—South American—liberty. But the chances are that it was the easy-money talk that captured the ears of most of his hearers. Then after he had made a few intimate friends and could afford to be confidential he let them in on a secret. He had six privateering licenses signed in blank, to be given to those ships whose owners knew a good thing when they saw it. There were more where these came from.

It is hard to know precisely what Baltimore ships, how many of them, and what capitalists participated in these dubious undertakings. The very minimum, according to Dr. Griffin, was twenty-one, for that many were involved in legal proceedings of one kind or another in the Federal courts at New York, Philadelphia, and Baltimore. They changed their names frequently. The *Orb*, a small schooner of about 175 tons, which had been a letter of marque during the war, was one of the first equipped for this new duty. She was known also as the *Congreso, Tyger*, and *Pueyrredón* and appears in the records under all these aliases. Her first commander was Joseph Almeda, alias Don José Almeida, next to Boyle perhaps the most colorful of privateer captains during the war just ended. The *Romp*, also the bearer of one of the first licenses peddled by Taylor, got into trouble as the *Santafecino*, the *Atrevida*, and the *Altavela*.

It is hard to find out also who was responsible for and who profited by these ventures. Merchants and politicians seem to have agreed that all possible anonymity was desirable. There was something called the American Concern, a sort of holding company, involved. But it changed its stockholders and its ship holdings with considerable ease and frequency. Sometimes it was the Old Concern and sometimes it was the New Concern. John S. Skinner, the gentleman who held Francis Scott Key's hand while he composed the "Star-Spangled Banner," had by now become postmaster. He had a share in several of these undertakings. So, too, had Mr. James McCulloch, the collector of the port. Some have suspected the sitting judge of the Federal court, the Hon. Theodoric Bland, of having more at stake in some of the legal proceedings than a mere desire to do exact justice, but President J. Q. Adams later accepted Judge Bland's denial, and perhaps we should too. But it is worthy of note that the privateer captains preferred Judge Bland to hear their cases rather than his Philadelphia colleague, Judge Peters. There was never any lack of able counsel for the adventurers. Lawyers, like shipowners, were feeling the pinch of the times.

All of this legal to-do grew out of the handicaps under which the privateers worked. Except in the very early days, their difficulties began with the shipping of their crews. Men had to be decoyed aboard. The boardinghouse keepers, often stuck with idle sailors who had run up big arrears in their room rent, were helpful in this respect. So were the saloonkeepers and crimps. Baltimore began to get a bad reputation among sailormen at about this time. Even an honest and sober seaman, shipping decorously on what he thought was a reputable merchantman, was likely to discover, once the vessel was beyond the capes, that she was a privateer in disguise and that he was expected to fight and even to run the risk of arrest for piracy—all this in return for a minute share in some rather illusory booty.

The booty was illusory, not because the ships didn't make captures, for they made many of them. The problem was that of disposing of the goods taken, of reintroducing them into the channels of legitimate trade. The prize courts of the several South American countries under whose flags the clippers operated were very sketchy affairs. Some of them seemed to have no clear national authority behind them. The sales of cargo were thus not necessarily acceptable in the courts of the older and better-established nations. The captain of an honest merchantman might pick up, in all innocence, a cargo of sugar in Haiti and bring it to the United States, only to discover on his arrival that what he had bought was in reality the property of another.

The Spanish consuls were very much on the lookout for this sort of thing. Hence the cluttering up of the courts with all sorts of libel suits. Hence also the uncertainty of the profit to the privateersman. Hence the frequent desertions and hence, finally, the growing use of shanghaiing. Baltimore developed this practice to such a point that in later years it was a common method of shipping crews even for oyster boats.

The difficulties of this kind of privateering were great and the returns so uncertain that only a few prospered at it. Moreover, the wars which gave it even its small semblance of legality came to an end. It became necessary for the ships to take increasing risks, to venture further and further to the wrong side of the vague line which separates privateering from piracy and slave trading. None of the

Baltimore skippers went in for outright piracy, so far as we know, but there is some evidence that a few of them found themselves involved almost against their wills in the slave trade and that, once in it, they found it easier to continue than to quit.

In the early days, before the slave trade was proceeded against in England and while it was still accepted as legitimate business in the United States, any vessel capable of crossing the ocean and carrying cargo was good enough to bring its human freight to these shores. At this period Baltimore probably did its share of slave carrying and no more. The agitation that began in the late eighteenth century and continued on in the nineteenth found expression in the general agreement reached by the Congress of Vienna in 1816. The United States went through the form, at least, of outlawing the trade and contributing to its suppression. The British got at the business more seriously and maintained a squadron of fast ships in service off the African coast.

The trade thus became a highly speculative business. Those venturing their capital in it ran the risk of losing it all through one piece of ill luck. To escape the British fleet they needed vessels able to show their heels to the smart sloops-of-war which the British assigned to the patrol. To the slaver the Baltimore clipper seemed the divine answer to his prayer. Both British and American forces captured many ships that were known to be Baltimore-built though perhaps owned in New York or New England. Occasionally in the record one finds the name of a Baltimore firm, a sufficient indication that the merchants of the city were not immune to the temptation to which their colleagues in other cities yielded.

Capable as was the Baltimore clipper in the eyes of her

owners, she must have been a hell afloat to the black wretches who were taken aboard her on the Gold Coast for shipment to the West Indies or to the Southern states. As we have seen, her hold was relatively shallow. Most of what space there was had to be used for the stores, including the trading stock necessary for the long voyage across the Atlantic and back. While the deal was being made on the coast with some Negro chieftain for captives brought from the interior the crew prepared the accommodations for the live cargo. A sort of scaffolding was erected below decks and planks laid across its topmost members. This made a temporary deck usually three feet or three feet, six inches below the main deck. On the platform thus improvised the captives were stowed away.

Ordinarily they were chained in pairs, the gyves on both ankles and wrists. As they came aboard, already chained, they were forced down the hatch and made to take their positions lying flat on the temporary deck. Usually they were so closely packed that it was necessary for them to lie "spoon fashion." They lay in this enforced position during the whole voyage, often rough and stormy, to the American coast or the Caribbean.

Now and then, of course, one of them would die. There are accounts which say that when this occurred the live companion of the dead Negro would be forced to carry him to the deck. The dead man would be laid on the rail, and the mate or perhaps a member of the crew would chop loose the arms and legs so as to save the trouble of removing the rivets in the irons. The survivor would then go below again and take up his accustomed place.

Strangely enough, this method of transportation did not result in a mortality rate sufficiently costly to force the management to revise it. It is said, however, that a ship passing to windward of a loaded slaver could detect the character of the ship, even at nighttime, at a distance of several miles.

The demand for slaves was enormous and grew constantly from the time Eli Whitney invented the cotton gin up to the outbreak of the Civil War. It continued even after that melancholy year. The *Storm King*, of Baltimore, landed 650 slaves in Cuba in 1861. The *Ocilla*, of Mystic, Conn., landed a cargo there in 1862, and the *Huntress*, of New York, landed one in the same place as late as 1864.

The trade could not be put down completely, because it was supported by a strong public opinion. The market for cotton grew by leaps and bounds. Labor to work the fields was essential. Breeding slaves, in Maryland as in Virginia, was a business of considerable size, but the process was slow, and, moreover, the planters soon discovered, or thought they did, that it was cheaper to buy full-grown men or women, fresh from Africa, and work them violently for a few years until they died than to nurture them to adulthood, treat them kindly, and then be under the necessity of supporting them during a long and relatively unproductive old age. A high initial price was endurable when the purchase was first class.

However, not all the merchants of the city were willing to take this completely businesslike view of the situation. One of them in particular, a Quaker of German descent, Elisha Tyson by name, came into Maryland and set up in Harford County some time before the Revolution. The lure of the city called him, and he was soon established in a business way in Baltimore. From the very beginning the idea of slavery revolted him, and he began a lifelong campaign to build up public opinion against it. He endeavored, though with scanty success, to organize societies of men of like mind and seems to have been at the head of several vest-pocket pressure groups working on both the Legislature and Congress.

He was adroit in the utilization of such sketchy and halfhearted laws as were enacted and was particularly successful in challenging the title to various individual Negroes claimed as slaves by some of his fellow townsmen.

Tyson was a man of great personal courage. On one occasion he heard that a Negro who was probably a freedman was being detained on board a ship lying in the harbor. Getting a pair of bailiffs, he had himself rowed out to the vessel and demanded of the captain that the Negro be put ashore. The owner stepped up and, drawing a knife, challenged him to set foot on the vessel.

"The first man who dares come aboard," he shouted, "will be a dead man."

"Then I'll be that man," said the aging Tyson, and clambered upon the deck.

The trader was so surprised at this bravado that he retreated, whereupon Tyson ordered his bailiffs to take the Negro and put him in the boat, meanwhile telling the alleged owner that he could come along also if he wanted to press his claim. That worthy thought it wise not to get too intimate with the law, and so it was possible for Tyson to have the Negro provided with papers establishing his freedom.

The slavers used various devices to bring their captives into the harbor of Baltimore and dispose of them there. A ship, outfitted in Baltimore and provided with a Baltimore crew, might sail for some South American port and there be the object of a wash sale. Then, provided with a Venezuelan or Colombian flag, she would acquire a cargo of slaves—sometimes by purchase or more often perhaps by capture—and bring them to Baltimore, under the pretense that they were members of her crew. This was a recognized subterfuge and one with which the authorities made little effort to cope.

One such ship, well known in Baltimore and licensed as a privateer, had transferred to the Colombian flag. Her master had even taken the precaution to become a Colombian citizen. Thus provided, he fell in with a Spanish slaver just coming into Havana from Africa, with forty-two slaves aboard, captured her in a running fight, and brought her cargo directly to Baltimore. The procedure was so common that no one, save Tyson, paid much attention to it. He, however, was determined to break up the practice if he could and made this a test case.

His legal maneuverings were difficult and devious, not only on account of the weakness of the law but also because none of the Negroes could speak or understand English. Importation was forbidden, of course, and if the Negroes could be persuaded that they were not legally bound to stay on board he might, he thought, procure their freedom. Writs, counterwrits, petitions to Washington, and counterpetitions flew back and forth. The Negroes were finally lodged in the local jail. But the United States marshal, being certain of his powers and perhaps regarding Tyson as an interfering busybody, turned them loose in the presence of an agent of Tyson and the captain of the ship. One pleaded with them; the other threatened. The Negroes, fear in their hearts, vacillated. Finally eleven of them decided that, on the whole, they would risk the threats of the captain and so followed Tyson's representative. This group, incidentally, was finally sent back to Africa by the African Colonization Society and, apparently, restored to relatives there.

Anti-slavery sentiment undoubtedly increased in Baltimore as a result of Tyson's endeavors. Thanks to him, a town meeting was convoked at the time of the fight in Congress over the admission of Missouri, and, though the vote was close, a memorial was adopted *against* the admission of another slave state. When he died, in 1824, three thousand Baltimore Negroes—one enthusiast counted ten thousand—attended his funeral and listened to the reading of a somewhat lengthy message to them which he had written only a few days before his death.

CHAPTER XIX

Divine Schizophrenia

SUCH ACTIVITIES as privateering under dubious flags and trading in slaves are interesting psychologically because they show that it is difficult for men habituated to certain crafts to abandon those crafts, even when the ends which justified them have ceased to exist. The decline of the Baltimore clipper and her gradual perversion to unworthy ends perhaps is the most melancholy chapter in all the history of Baltimore. The merchants were coming to realize that she was no longer, as the mellifluous Brantz Mayer says, the "Aladdin of their countinghouses." What was to take her place?

No one quite knew. The spirit of enterprise was there, and the money, or some of it, was there. When, after the close of the war, it was decided to build a monument to honor the memory of the fallen heroes of the Battle of North Point the subscriptions came out by the thousands. When the new Bank of the United States was chartered in 1816, with a capital of $28,000,000, Baltimoreans bought stock to a total face value of $4,010,000. In person or by proxy, 15,160 persons subscribed. Someone got the notion that there was coal under the city itself, and money was put up to dig a deep hole at the corner of Saratoga and North streets, almost in the bed of the old bend of the falls. The coal wasn't found, and the money was lost, of course. But the subscribers proved they were willing to take a chance.

In the early days of the century Rembrandt Peale, Charles Wilson Peale's son, showed up in Baltimore with one of the skeletons of the two mastodons his father had excavated in New York State and was so pleased with the reception he got that he came back in 1813 with a general collection of curios he had somehow acquired and began the erection of a Museum and Gallery of the Fine Arts in which to house them. The building, still standing in Holliday Street in what used to be Steiger's Meadow, is a charming one and is now the home of the Municipal Museum of the City of Baltimore. Peale used the largest chamber in it as a studio and painted there some of his most pretentious canvases. He was an enterprising fellow, and Baltimore appreciated him.

One of his memorable undertakings was to set up a small gas plant sufficient to illuminate his gallery with a brilliance such as no one had ever dreamed of before. In 1816, with this success as his chief selling point, he organized a company for selling the gas to those who wanted it. The necessary money was subscribed, and by 1820 a considerable plant was in operation near the site of the ill-fated coal mine, and three subscribers were having the "fluid" piped to their dwellings or places of business. This is usually regarded as the first commercial use of gas in the United States. A little later it was being used to light the streets.

Divine Schizophrenia

In 1816, also by legislative fiat, the town was greatly enlarged, to the complete disgust of the countrymen who were thus turned urbanite. But the legislature which set the new bounds was careful not to give the city any increase in its voting power. In the same year a medical school was set up, and the physicians banded themselves together into a medical society.

The flour trade got a fillip in 1817 because of the failure of the European crop. Prices skyrocketed, and the growers, millers, and merchants, all had a brief splurge of prosperity. Those among them who were of Irish extraction banded together into a society, called the Hibernian Society, whose chief object was to look after the welfare of the constantly increasing flood of Irish immigrants.

There was a sort of rage for corporate organization at the time. The well-meaning who opposed the institution of slavery and still hoped it might be possible to eliminate it by rational means organized the African Colonization Society to ship those Negroes who cared to go back to the Africa of their ancestors. Francis Scott Key and Elisha Tyson were prime backers of this movement. The society actually sent out many Negroes. One of the counties of Liberia is called Maryland to this day.

Another example of the growth of the rational spirit in emotional Baltimore was the formation of a society of Unitarians, the southernmost expression of this typically New England religious impulse. The church which the group built according to the design of Maximilian Godefroy remains a noble edifice today. Its first regular preacher was Jared Sparks, later to become famous as the biographer of Washington.

There were other developments akin to these. The

wealthy Mr. John McKim died, leaving the sum of six hundred dollars annually to support a free school. His dutiful son, Isaac, erected a proper building to enshrine his father's worthy undertaking. This also survives. It is called an exact, or almost exact, replica in granite of the Temple of Theseus at Athens.

The zeal for improvement affected even the common hangman. Two robbers who had held up a mail wagon were caught and because they had put the driver in jeopardy of his life were duly sentenced to be executed. Up to that time condemned men were suspended in mid-air by driving out from under them the cart on which they had been standing. But on this occasion, for the first time in the city's history, a proper scaffold with a trap door was built for the ceremony. It worked to the satisfaction of everyone, and this method was standard practice thereafter.

There was a rollicking quality in many of the things that happened in Baltimore at this time. Immigrants poured in from Ireland and from Germany, as we have seen, but the city was attracting much in the way of intellect and professional skill from other parts of the country, especially from New England. New theaters created a demand for plays and actors. Newspapers and magazines were issuing from the presses and called for poets and writers to fill their pages. Thus there developed a literary movement, its direction and control mostly in the hands of lawyers and physicians, with a few professional journalists thrown in.

The most characteristic of the several coteries which developed in this postwar period (which resembled in some respects the jazz age of the 1920s and ended in a smash almost as catastrophic) was the Delphian Club. Almost everything is known about the Delphian Club, because its conscientious secretary, Dr. John Didear Readel, kept complete minutes of its meetings for several years. It was a mock-serious organization, lying somewhere between the coffeehouses of the eighteenth century and the Greek-letter fraternities which were soon to sweep the colleges. It had nine members, each of whom regarded himself as the chosen companion of one of the nine muses.

In the first list of members were found, among others, General William H. Winder, commander of the unfortunate Battle of Bladensburg but now become one of the leading lawyers; John Pierpont, then a Baltimore merchant but later to be the grandfather of J. Pierpont Morgan; J. H. B. Latrobe, lawyer, son of the architect of the capital at Washington and soon to be one of the founders of the Baltimore and Ohio Railroad; Dr. Horace H. Hayden, called by some the father of modern dentistry, and John Neal, poet and dramatist. In later years as the fame of the club grew it attracted as active or associate members such figures as John P. Kennedy, author of "Swallow Barn"; Robert Goodloe Harper, Francis Scott Key, Rembrandt Peale, William Wirt (he wrote the accepted version of Patrick Henry's famous "liberty or death" oration); John Howard Payne, a brilliant but eccentric dramatist best known as the author of "Home, Sweet Home," and Samuel Woodworth, author of the "Old Oaken Bucket." It is a strange thing that a single club, and a small club at that, which had an existence of less than a decade should have had among its members the writers of three of the best-known American songs.

The members, naturally enough, regarded themselves

highly. Wit was not only expected of them—it was demanded. They were given to elaborate puns, to impromptu epitaphs on themselves and on their guests, to highfalutin verse, to verbose essays and some others which were quite good, to obscenity (especially if it rhymed) and, above everything else, to eating and drinking.

The president for years was William Gwynn, who lived in a tiny house in Bank Lane, off St. Paul Street. Though small, this house was another copy of a Greek temple. It was designed by Robert Carey Long, one of the architects in the Greek revival. Gwynn called it the Tusculum. He was a hospitable man but not a rich one, and when the club met in his place every member was assessed fifty cents for champagne. The house survived until 1891, and in a way it might be said that the influence of the Delphian Club survived even longer. Several of its members, and especially John P. Kennedy, were friends later on of Edgar Allan Poe. Some of them, notably Jared Sparks, became important figures in the national literary scene. Others were instrumental in influencing the rich merchants of the town, at a much later period, to endow such institutions as the Peabody Institute, the Enoch Pratt Free Library, and the Johns Hopkins University.

No modern student of sociology will have to be told that the incidents and developments here sketched so briefly and inadequately fall into a pattern that could be matched almost in detail in the history of every community in the Western world. Baltimore was being urbanized. It had grown (the census of 1820 showed its population to be 62,738) so that it was no longer possible to describe it as a mere convenience for traders, a geographical area. The merchants were still the most important men in it and, as always, they continued to look longingly toward the lush countryside and to think of themselves as soon-to-be landed proprietors. But the town they had brought into being was no longer wholly their instrument. It was beginning to have a life of its own. It had classes with aspirations other than that of retiring to the country. There was an intellectual seething. The lawyers had come to be a force in the community. So had the physicians. There was a new class of manufacturers, recruited in part from the merchants. Manufacturers and those engaged in foreign trade have disparate interests on occasion. And there was a mob. Fortunately for the merchants, in 1812, the mob had served the merchants' end. They were to discover a little later that mobs can be fickle.

The wheat shortage in Europe which provided the wherewithal for much of the activity of the time continued for two more years. In the meantime the taste for tobacco was re-establishing itself. But now the old business of loading at the planter's wharf was nearly gone. Tobacco had to be inspected and graded. It had to be stored in warehouses where it could be kept under proper conditions until the ships were available for taking it to its European destinations. It had to be "financed." The merchants found themselves lending money on this most precarious of commodities. They built warehouses to supplement the public warehouse which had long existed on O'Donnell's wharf. In 1818 that warehouse burned down, and more private ones were erected, one of them on the made land on Light Street, known as Light Street Wharf. In two or three years there were more than half a dozen of such enterprises, with commission merchants acting between the growers and the foreign purchasers and thereby forming a new tie with the planters, not in Maryland alone but in Virginia and Kentucky as well, and giving Baltimore a bond with the South which was to have its significance later on.

There is nothing simple about this period, stimulating as it must have been to the people who lived through it. The reason, of course, is quite obvious. The country as a whole was going through a transition which first made itself felt in New England. The War of 1812 had turned that important part of the country from an almost purely mercantile civilization into an industrial one. The new class of manufacturers had forced through a tariff of a sort in 1816. It wasn't high enough to give them the protection they wanted, and they were fighting for more. The fight went on, in fact, until 1828, when Daniel Webster, who had represented the old maritime interests in the fight of 1816, shifted his allegiance and became a high-tariff man. Webster, more than any other American, symbolized the change of the character of the civilization of the North.

The South, on the other hand, necessarily remained agricultural. To the farmer engaged in growing a money crop for export a tariff was an abomination in that it meant he must sell cheap and buy dear. The invention of the cotton gin, plus the discovery that in the lowlands of the Mississippi Valley better cotton could be grown than had before been deemed possible, brought new political strength to the cotton country. It also gave a new significance to the institution of slavery hitherto grounded mostly in tobacco culture and made the Southerners, as a whole, feel that the high-tariff movement of the North was aimed at them and their institutions.

Thus the stage was set for a struggle. And, just as Baltimore, on the smaller stage of the little hinterland of Maryland, had found itself between two cultures, so now on the vaster stage of a great and powerful nation it found itself once more between the upper and nether millstones. All the area to the south of it, the region which had provided the form if not the substance of its way of living, was dependent on export. All the area to the north of it and most of that in the West to which it could hope to have access was striving toward autarchy in its organization. The farmers of the growing West sold more and more of their products for consumption inside the country, taking in exchange the manufactured goods from the Eastern towns.

Baltimoreans, like everyone else who has ever lived, wanted the best of two worlds. They wanted to maintain their profitable relation with the tobacco and cotton growers of the South. They wanted to remain in the business of exporting flour on as big a scale as possible. But they also wanted to share in the industrial wealth which New England was creating and of which New York and Philadelphia had learned the secret.

As friends, financiers, and social imitators of the South they were bound to support a low tariff and the institution of slavery. As exporters of flour they were likewise under the necessity of opposing the tariff. But as the city geographically nearest to the Ohio Valley they were wasting their birthright if they didn't use their capital in the exploitation of that market. Thus, in the throes of a sort of divine schizophrenia, they argued among themselves about their future and found release only in intellectual playacting.

CHAPTER XX

Decision

ON MARCH 17, 1819, the Irish were celebrating according to their wont in the saloons and dance halls of the Point. Their spirits were high. They sang as they marched from bar to bar. The noise they made was trying on the nerves of those residents of the neighborhood whose enthusiasm for St. Patrick was under better control. Some boys stuffed old clothes with straw, labeled the effigy "Paddy," and ran it to the top of the mast of one of the idle schooners tied up at the wharf at the foot of Broadway. The figure caught the eye of an Irishman who in patriotic indignation rushed from saloon to saloon summoning his countrymen to the fray. In a few minutes a mob had gathered on the wharf. Because the halyard fouled the figure could not be brought down, whereupon axes were brought, and in a few minutes the mast was hewn through and fell crashing on the deck. The watch arrived a few minutes afterward and chased the frenzied Irishmen from the scene, arresting a few of them before they could escape.

Decision

It was a minor incident and in the trying months to come it was forgotten. But in a way it was significant. In the good days people welcomed the Irish in Baltimore and delighted in their effervescence. In the good days no one, not even the ebullient Irish, ventured to harm a Baltimore schooner, the source of so much of the city's prosperity. Now the Irish, the most submerged group of freemen, were coming to be feared and hated. In revenge they attacked and mutilated the very symbol of the city's pristine prosperity.

Two months later yellow fever broke out on the Point and raged with such virulence that the whole area was soon almost deserted, leaving the section to the very poor and to those too ill to move. While its ravages were at their height the City Bank, a popular institution, was forced to close its doors. The Bank of the United States began having its troubles. The price of flour and of tobacco fell suddenly to ruinous levels. Businesses failed one after the other, and the streets were crowded with men looking for work, any kind of work. There was soon actual starvation. Violent crime became common. The rich took up collections and opened soup kitchens.

Strange fancies filled the minds of otherwise responsible people. Two men, desperate for money, held up the Eastern mail, murdering the driver in the process. The culprits were caught, indicted, and the trial was prepared. The evidence was mostly circumstantial, and the town feared a conviction might not be obtained. Out of the dark recesses of his mind some citizen brought forth a rudimentary recollection of the process known as "trial by ordeal."

The corpse of the murdered mail carrier was put in the center of a room on a table covered with a black cloth, with only a few candles to throw their light on the lifeless face. At midnight one of the prisoners, wholly unwarned, was brought out of his cell and into the presence of the dead man. From behind a screen a voice emerged, sternly bidding him lay his hand upon its breast. The accused man boldly approached the body and laid his hands upon it. Contrary to the hopes of the hidden witnesses, the wounds did not open and begin to bleed. But when the second prisoner was brought in he was so overcome by the sight of the cadaver that he broke down and all but fainted. A few days later this second man—his name was Hutton—confessed that it was he who had shot the carrier, though both, apparently, had been involved in the robbery.

It was difficult for the people of Baltimore to realize the full significance of what was happening to them. They assumed that the good days were certain to return again and they carried on as best they could. In the very midst of the panic a few of them organized the first Academy of Sciences in the town and got themselves a meeting place in the Athenaeum, a fine building which had been put up on the corner of Lexington and St. Paul streets for just such cultural undertakings.

The merchants, also convinced that trade would pick up shortly, finished their great Exchange Building and leased part of it to the Federal government for a custom-house. The task of charting and marking the channel was completed. The monument celebrating the repulse of the British was finally finished, and the statue of civic pride was placed on its summit.

The great cathedral, designed by Latrobe in the Byzantine style, with a broad, shallow dome and two towers with gilded onion minarets, had been begun in 1806 but was held up by the war. It was finally finished and consecrated in 1821.

Out on Howard's Hill, beyond the gully which is now Center Street and in the depths of the primeval woods which covered the summit, the tall Doric column which was the expression of the city's veneration of George Washington finally reached the height planned for it, thanks to a successful lottery. The colossal statue of the father was hauled to its top by an ingenious arrangement of ropes and scaffolds and the dedication ceremony carried out. This is the monument which gave Baltimore its long-time designation of "the monumental city." It is still one of the most beautiful structures in all the world.

A cross-shaped park was laid out around it, and the rich, who had feared it when it was first planned for the downtown location, were proud to build their city houses in its shadow. In a few years Mount Vernon Place became the recognized social center of the community and held that high place until the advent of the automobile.

Mr. William Wirt, then United States Attorney General and so living with his family in Washington, naturally came frequently to the city to visit his constituents and attend his law practice. On November 24, 1822, he wrote a letter to his daughter:

My Dear Catherine:

Yesterday morning I arose before day. Shaved and dressed by candlelight, took my cane and walked to market. There are two market-houses, each of them about three or four times as long as ours in Washington. The first I came to was the meat market; the next, which was nearest the basin, was the fish and vegetable market. O! what a quantity of superb beef, mutton, lamb, veal, and all sorts of fowls—hogsheads full of wild ducks, geese, pheasants, partridges; and then, on one side of the market-house, leaving only a narrow lane between them, a line of wagons and carts, groaning under the loads of country productions; these wagons and carts on one side and the market-houses on the other, forming a line as long as from our house to St. John's church. I must not forget to mention the loads of sweet-cakes of all sorts and fashions that covered the outside tables of the market-houses, and the breakfasts that were cooking everywhere, all around, for the country people who came many miles to market. You may conceive the vast quantity of provisions that must be brought to this market when you are told that sixty thousand people draw their daily supplies from it, which is more than twice as many people as there are in Washington, Georgetown, Alexandria, and Richmond, all put together. Well, and so after I had walked all round and round and through the market-house, I left it and bent my steps toward the country, and walked two miles and a half out to Mr. Thompson's to breakfast. It had been cloudy and rainy for several days, but the night before had been clear, and although the road was still wet, the morning above head was bright and beautiful. After walking about a mile, I came to the summit of a hill that overlooks the city, and there I stopped for a moment to take breath and look back on it. The ground had begun to smoke from the warmth of the rising sun, and the city seemed to spread itself out below me to a vast extent—a huge dusky mass, to which there seemed no limit. But towering from above the fog was the Washington monument (a single beautiful column 160 feet in height, which stands in Howard's Park, and is rendered indescribably striking and interesting from the touching solitude of the scene from which it lifts its head), and several noble steeples of churches interspersed throughout the west of the city, whose gilded summits were now glittering in the sun. Casting the eye over Baltimore, it lights upon the Chesapeake Bay, and after wandering over that flood of waters, it rests upon Fort McHenry and its star-spangled banner. This is the fort where our soldiers gained so much glory in the last war, and the very banner with regard to which Mr. Key's beautiful song of the "Star-Spangled Banner" was written.

After feasting my eyes for some time on the rich, diversified, and boundless landscape that lay before me, meditating on the future grandeur of this city and the rising glories of the nation, I turned around to resume my walk into the country, when all its soft beauties burst, by surprise, upon me. For while I had been looking back on the town, bay, and fort, the sun had risen, and was now so high that its light was pouring full upon hill and valley, field and forest, blazing in bright reflection from all the eastern windows of the hundreds of country-houses that crowned the heights around me, and dancing on all the leaves that waved and wantoned in the morning breeze. No city in the world has a more beautiful country around it than Baltimore in the direction of the west, north, and east. In the direction of Washington it is unimproved, but in the other points all that could have been expected from wealth and fine taste have been accomplished. The grounds, which were originally poor, have been made rich; they lie finely, not flat or tame, nor yet abrupt and rugged, but rising and falling in forms of endless diversity, sometimes soft and gentle, at others bold and commanding. This beautifully undulating surface has been improved with great taste, the fields richly covered with grass, the clumps of trees, groves and forests pruned of all dead limbs and all deformities, and flourishing in strong and healthy luxuriance. The sites for the houses are well selected—always upon some eminence, embosomed amid beautiful trees, from which their white fronts peep out enchantingly, for the houses are all white, which adds much to the cheerfulness and grace of this unrivaled scenery. I hope one of these days to show it to you in person, and then you will be able to imagine what a delightful ramble I had to Mr. Thompson's yesterday morning. I took them quite by surprise, but it was a most agreeable one, and they were rejoiced to see me. Mr. Thompson inquired most kindly after all in Washington, and giving me a good country breakfast (most delightful butter), brought me back to town in his gig, where we arrived by nine o'clock, an hour before court. Was not this an industrious morning?

Your affectionate father,
WM. WIRT.

Mr. Wirt enjoyed writing as much as he enjoyed walking. But his picture, nevertheless, shows that even a city just emerging from its worst money panic and with a very uncertain future still managed somehow to make an impression on an observant man.

CHAPTER XXI

Labors of Hercules

THE POSTWAR DEPRESSION passed because the country had made a decision. It had discovered that its chief job was peopling and developing the interior country. For two hundred years it had been the supplier of foodstuffs and raw materials for Europe and the West Indies. That obligation still lay upon it. But from 1822 up to 1914 the emphasis was to be on the bigger task of turning its own wildernesses into farms, on breeding and importing the human beings to till those farms, and, in the cities, on exchanging the products of those farms for the products of the mills and factories.

New England made the decision first. But New England was geographically remote from the interior, and there was little or no chance that she could be the only supplier of the wants of that vast region. New York was better placed. The Hudson River cut its way through the outposts of the Appalachian ranges, and, from Albany, the way west to the Great Lakes Basin was over a relatively level country.

There had been talk of a canal to the West for many

years. George Washington, as we know, had interested himself in such a scheme before the time had come. But after the close of the second war with England De Witt Clinton saw that the opportunity was ripe. On April 15, 1817, the New York legislature authorized the construction of the Erie Canal, mostly along the course of the Mohawk River, and in 1825, after eight years of digging, the work was completed, and New York City had a waterway from its front door all the way to Lake Superior.

The canal was a success more brilliant than even its promoters had dreamed of. People rushed to fill up the western part of the state. A tremendous volume of traffic moved along it in both directions. Business began to surge upward in New York City, and land values skyrocketed. The two war booms that Baltimore had experienced during its relatively short history were as nothing compared to this. The whole country rejoiced because it understood instantly that a new era was dawning.

The whole country, that is, with the exception of Philadelphia and Baltimore. All they could see as a result of New York's enterprise was decline and perhaps extinction for themselves. Philadelphia answered by starting a system of canals of its own. Baltimore, more than ever of two minds about everything, pondered deeply.

The believers in canals went back to George Washington. In 1824, when it became apparent that the Erie Canal was soon to be a reality, a group of Marylanders and Virginians reorganized the Chesapeake and Ohio Canal Company, got stock subscriptions from the Federal government as well as from Maryland and Virginia, and prepared to make the dirt fly. Since this canal would end at Georgetown, it was not likely to be particularly helpful to Baltimore, and the merchants and manufacturers held a meeting to discuss what they should do about it. One group favored a cross-country branch of the canal to connect it with Baltimore. But those flour-minded folk who still regarded the Susquehanna Valley as Baltimore's primary territory argued so strongly for the old scheme for a canal along the banks of that river that they carried the day. The legislature granted a charter for a ditch from just above Havre de Grace to Mason and Dixon's line and even further if the state of Pennsylvania would give its permission.

There was a group, however, which was not impressed by either of these ventures. The Chesapeake and Ohio Canal seemed to them a visionary undertaking, the Susquehanna Canal one likely to run into all sorts of political difficulties.

One evening in the fall of 1826 Colonel John Eager Howard invited a group of well-to-do Baltimoreans to dine with him at Belvedere, his house on the northern edge of the city. Colonel Howard was one of the biggest landholders in and near Baltimore. He had given the land on which the Lexington Market was built and also that on which the Washington Monument was erected. He grew ever richer out of the sale of land to householders in the expanding city. The colonel was an elderly man in 1826, but his zeal for hospitality was still as unflagging as when in 1791, while he was governor of the state, he had entertained President Washington at a dinner which is still memorable.

On this new occasion the guest of honor was Mr. Evan Thomas, brother of Mr. Philip E. Thomas, president of the Merchants Bank. Mr. Thomas had just returned from England where he had seen the Stockton and Darlington steam railroad in full operation, with clumsy steam engines hauling ore from mines to docks. Colonel Howard thought some of his Baltimore friends might be interested in Mr. Thomas' story.

Evan Thomas wasn't a particularly impressive man, apparently, and his account was listened to with polite interest rather than with enthusiasm. It was his brother, more than the other gentlemen present, who was convinced by the narration that here was the answer to the Erie Canal. It was he probably who had suggested the dinner to Colonel Howard. It was he who kept talking about railroads after the dinner. It was he who finally managed to persuade George Brown, the cautious son of the still more cautious Alexander and the leading financier of the town, to call another and more formal meeting to discuss the city's problem.

No record was kept of this meeting, but only ten days later, on February 12, 1827, also at Mr. Brown's, a third meeting was called to "take under consideration the best means of restoring to the city of Baltimore that portion of the Western trade which has recently been diverted from it by the introduction of steam navigation and by other causes. . . ." William Patterson, father of Betsy, presided at this meeting, thus indicating that those of enterprising spirit as well as the prudent bankers were now becoming interested. The result was the appointment of a committee, headed by Philip E. Thomas, to make a report on the practicability of a railroad from Baltimore to the Ohio River. The other members of the committee were George Brown, Benjamin C. Howard, Talbot Jones, Joseph W. Patterson (William's son), Evan Thomas, and John V. L. McMahon.

Labors of Hercules

In a week this committee had finished its report. It called for a "double railroad" from Baltimore to the Ohio and suggested that a charter be obtained from the legislature at the earliest possible moment so that the work could be begun. No laggards, these committeemen!

They were diplomats also, for their report is careful to give full credit to the wisdom and vision of those citizens who were committed to the Chesapeake and Ohio Canal and to that along the Susquehanna. "But," they continued, "important as this trade is to Baltimore, it is certainly of minor consideration when compared with the immense commerce which lies within our grasp to the West, provided we have the enterprise to profit by the advantages which our local situation gives us in reference to that trade. Baltimore lies two hundred miles nearer to the navigable waters of the West than New York and about one hundred miles nearer to them than Philadelphia, to which may be added the important fact that the easiest and by far the most practicable route through the ridges of mountains that divide the Atlantic from the Western waters is along the depression formed by the Potomac in its passage through them. Taking, then, into the estimate the advantages which these important circumstances afford to Baltimore in regard to this immense trade, we again repeat that nothing is wanted to secure a great portion of it to our city but a faithful application of the means within our own power.

"The only point from which we have anything to apprehend is New Orleans; with that city, it is admitted, we must be content to share this trade, because she will always enjoy a *certain portion* of it in defiance of our efforts, but from a country of such vast extent and whose productions are so various and of such incalculable amount there will be a sufficient trade to sustain both New Orleans and Baltimore, and we may feel fully contented if we can succeed in securing to ourselves that portion of it which will prefer to seek a market east of the mountains."

Then follows a discussion of the relative merits of canals, turnpikes, and railroads, with the conclusion that:

" . . . so decided have been railroads' advantages over turnpike roads, or even over canals, that already two thousand miles of them are actually completed or in a train of rapid progress in Great Britain and that the experiment of their construction has not in one case failed, nor has there been one instance in which they have not fully answered the most sanguine expectations of their projectors. Indeed, so completely has this improvement succeeded in England that it is the opinion of many judicious and practical men there that these roads will, for heavy transportation, supersede canals as effectually as canals have superseded turnpike roads. . . ."

There was much more. Indeed, the further on it got the more the report came to read like a prospectus. The selling talk was so good that the whole group of twenty-five adopted it as it stood and appointed John V. L. McMahon to draw up a charter and itself as a committee to urge a speedy grant from the legislature. On February 28, 1827, the legislature acquiesced and authorized the company to issue stock to the amount of $3,000,000, reserving 10,000 shares for the state if it should decide to participate and 5,000 for the city of Baltimore. The company was to be allowed to charge "tolls" upon both freight and passengers carried over its railroad and to use machines of any sort to convey such persons and freight from place to place. Also—and here is a further echo of the general feeling that this was to be a new sort of turnpike—no person should use the road without the permission of its owners.

On March 20 the subscription books were opened in Frederick and Hagerstown as well as in Baltimore. So well had the promoters done their work that although only 15,000 shares were offered for public subscription individual Baltimoreans immediately offered to buy 36,788. The formal incorporation took place April 24, 1827, with Mr. Philip E. Thomas as president, Mr. George Brown as treasurer, and Charles Carroll of Carrollton (now nearly ninety), George Hoffman, William Patterson, Alexander Brown, Isaac McKim, William Lorman, Thomas Ellicott, John B. Morris, Talbot Jones, and William Steuart associated with them as directors. We already know that most of these men had been merchants and shipowners and that several of them had operated privateers and letters of marque. A significant omen to see them so definitely and firmly turning their eyes and their fortunes inland! Baltimore had been drawn, with the rest of the country, into the enterprise of winning the West.

Nowadays, if, by some remote chance, a group of promoters should decide to build a railroad, raising the money would be the chief problem. Every operation involved in such construction, as in operation, is standardized. But the projectors of the Baltimore and Ohio were working in an absolutely virgin field. They had to decide on routes and grades with no experience to guide them. They didn't know what sort of track to use. They had to decide the question of gauge. There was no rolling stock and no certain idea what that stock should be like. They had heard talk of steam locomotives but they assumed from the very start that the horse would be the main motive power. Outside of that one certainty, they started from scratch.

First of all they needed publicity. The promoters of the Chesapeake and Ohio Canal arranged for a grand cornerstone laying for their undertaking on July 4, 1827, and persuaded the President of the United States, John Quincy Adams, to wield the trowel. The Baltimore and Ohio, thus forced to turn parochial, called on Charles Carroll of Carrollton, surviving signer of the Declaration of Independence, for the same ritual and set the same date for their show. Despite the competition in Washington, they made a gala day of it and had a "huge concourse" of people. The "first stone" which Mr. Carroll laid was on Mount Clare, the estate of his cousin, the Barrister, which John Adams had visited during the Revolution. The main shops of the Baltimore and Ohio are still called Mount Clare shops, and the little brick building which was the original terminus of the road still stands.

The first section of the road was to run for about nine miles, more or less, along the valley of the Patapsco falls to a point near Elk Ridge Landing where there was to be a "relay" for the changing of horses. The Relay House still stands and is in daily use as a way station. The grade was very slight. The tracks were crossties with pine stringers topped with wrought-iron straps. The space between the tracks had to be surfaced so that the horses could trot on it. Several streams of considerable width had to be crossed on even this short section, and there was a terrific argument as between stone and wooden viaducts. Both were tried, but the stone ones, made of great blocks of granite quarried in the neighborhood, are still in use. The iron for the tracks was a special problem because it had to be imported from England. The projectors hoped that they would be able to get it in duty-free, but the Congress, which had committed Federal money to the canal project, would hear of no such thing. The cost, in consequence, was much greater than the stockholders had hoped.

There were labor troubles too. During the first summer the workmen—many of them were Irishmen newly arrived—took violently to liquor to relieve the distress caused by the unaccustomed heat. Frequent quarrels between bosses and men culminated in a riot in which one man was killed and several wounded and the house of a contractor was ransacked. Only one of the labor camps seems to have been relatively peaceful. Its contractor forbade the possession or sale of spirits within it and in addition, he employed only German labor, brought down from York County, Pa., that perennial source of so much of Baltimore's strength. These men worked hard, saved their money, and became in many instances permanent residents of Baltimore and its environs.

All the problems were surmounted after a fashion. On January 1, 1830, less than seventeen months after the laying of the first stone, a party of twenty-four ladies and gentlemen, including William Wirt, now postmaster general, who had come over from Washington for the purpose, got in a carriage and were drawn by a single horse from the city terminus all the way to Carrollton Viaduct, the stone bridge across Gwynns Falls, in six minutes. This works out, according to contemporary calculation, to "the astonishing rate of *fifteen miles an hour!*"

On January 7, after due advertisement, the road offered a similar ride to the general public, nine cents for one way or three tickets for twenty-five cents. This is the very first time in the United States that a railroad operated as a common carrier. Five months later the line was open all the way to Ellicott's Mills, running passenger trains—still horse-drawn—on a regular schedule. Relay House was fulfilling the function to which its name entitled it.

Ross Winans, a New Jersey horse dealer who had come to Baltimore to sell motive power to the new road, was largely responsible for the success of these early undertakings, for it was he who designed the flanged wheels which were of one piece with their axles and which turned in outside housings. This device so reduced friction that one horse could draw four carriages. Evan Thomas, the imaginative, whose tales about English roads had really inspired the whole undertaking, let his fancy take wings once more and built a carriage propelled by a sail. Called the *Aeolus*, it was given a serious trial but it obeyed the laws of physics and refused to move against the wind.

Peter Cooper, the New York philanthropist, comes into the story at this point. The building of the railroad had provoked a great wave of speculation in the city, and all sorts of roseate dreams about its future were being dreamed. Some visionaries remembered John O'Donnell's tract called Canton, lying just east of Fells Point. They got an option on it, formed a company, and then went to New York looking for capital. "I was drawn into this speculation," wrote Cooper in his autobiography, "by two men who represented they had large means, and we bought together three thousand acres for $105,000, taking the whole shore from Fells Point dock for three miles. After paying in my part of the money I soon found that I had paid all that had been paid upon the property. . . ."

Cooper wanted to make this speculation good, so he came down to Baltimore to see for himself how the railroad was doing and what its prospects were. His tale differs considerably from those of other contemporaries, but it is a fact, nevertheless, that Cooper did build a tiny experimental locomotive which could do one thing which the British locomotives then available could not do; his *Tom Thumb*, the B. & O.'s first steam engine, could negotiate the short radius curves of the new railroad. Despite the oft-told tale of its defeat in the race with a little gray horse, there was little doubt after its test that steam was to provide the motive power for the new undertaking.

The first commercially practical locomotive for the road was built in York, Pa., by Phineas Davis, a watchmaker. It was hauled to Baltimore over the York pike, to the great astonishment and scorn of the drovers who, in their Conestoga wagons, thronged that thoroughfare. The *York*, as Davis called his engine, had four driving wheels and, despite its awkwardness, got up a speed, in tests, that approached thirty miles an hour. For this performance he won a prize offered by the company. A few improvements, and the *York* was hauling a passenger train regularly to Frederick, to which western Maryland metropolis the road opened service in December 1831.

The Baltimore and Ohio Railroad was now a going proposition, carrying freight and passengers regularly to and from the heart of the Maryland wheat country and bringing the fine flour of the brothers Ellicott to the very ship side, for the city had finally given it permission to extend its tracks to the water front. The Ohio River and the vast market of the West seemed just over the hill.

It wasn't a big money-maker, of course, for all this experimentation had cost much more than the projectors had originally estimated. But it was recognized everywhere by this time that it was a solid enterprise. By 1835 the rail-building fever was on in full swing all over the country. The *American Railroad Journal* had been established and was a clearinghouse for information. In one of its early issues it carried the ninth annual report of the Baltimore and Ohio. The editor commented upon this document in these terms:

We . . . cannot refrain from here expressing our own, and we believe the thanks of the entire railroad community as well in Europe as in America, for the candid business-like liberal manner, in which they annually lay before the world the result of their experience . . . It will not be saying too much, we are sure, to nominate them the Railroad University of the United States. . . . They have published annually the results . . . that the world might be cautioned by their errors and instructed by their discoveries. Their reports have in truth gone forth as a text-book, and their road and workshops have been a lecture room to thousands who are now practising and improving upon their experience. This country owes to the enterprise, public spirit and perseverance of the citizens of Baltimore, a debt of gratitude of no ordinary magnitude. . . .

High praise perhaps, with certain overtones of flattery. But Mr. Philip Thomas and his associates were, in fact, competent, resourceful, and determined American businessmen of a type relatively new in those days. At the risk of their own reputations, they gathered together a great aggregation of private capital and used it for the general good. Of course they hoped for profit. But the profit motive does not entirely explain the spirit which animated them. Men are driven to do useful things, and the drive is stronger when the results seem likely to be big and impressive. Profits are pleasant when they come, but the doing is the main thing.

CHAPTER XXII

The Mills of the Gods

THE CENSUS OF 1830 told much of the hopes and fears of the Baltimore of that day. By the figures, the town stood second only to New York. That metropolis, thanks to the Erie Canal, had 202,589 inhabitants. Baltimore had 80,625, Philadelphia 80,462, and Boston 61,292, but the crude statistics did not show the real nature of the situation. New York wasn't a single city but the nucleus of a collection of cities. The same thing was true of Boston, though to a lesser degree. Philadelphia also was overflowing its boundaries into the surrounding territory. Baltimore was hoping to grow up to the territory already acquired.

The hopes and aspirations which resulted in the Baltimore and Ohio Railroad were not exhausted by that venture. Another group of citizens organized and built the Baltimore and Susquehanna Railroad to bring the products of York, Lancaster, and Harrisburg and of the whole Susquehanna Valley to Baltimore by the new mechanical means. The long-delayed Chesapeake and Delaware Canal was finally undertaken and carried to swift completion by the joint support of the three states most affected. It wasn't much of a canal. Its depth was but seven and a half feet, and three locks were necessary to carry it over the low rise between the two bays. It was not until recent years that the United States government took it over from the private corporation and made it into a major link in the system of inland waterways. Today vessels drawing twenty-five feet use it regularly.

Inspired by the philanthropy of men like McKim, whom we have already noticed, and Robert Oliver, a passionate Irishman, the city fathers were finally persuaded to set up a system of public schools. The beginnings were modest, but it wasn't long before the educational appropriation was one of the biggest items in the municipal budget. More clubs, learned societies, theaters were built. More bridges were thrown across the troublesome Falls. Every week the Baltimore and Ohio reported further progress toward Cumberland, its last stop before tackling the great divide.

But despite all this activity, or perhaps because of it, things were not going exactly right. The oldest and one of the largest banks in the city was the Bank of Maryland. It had always been a "progressive" bank, and its notes of issue were accepted everywhere. Its officers and directors were among the elect, at least in the popular estimation. It was these men who announced on March 24, 1834, six months after President Jackson had withdrawn the public funds, that the concern was no longer able to prosecute its business.

Other bankers in the town had been fearing if not expecting such an announcement from their overbold competitor and they were ready with an organization to liquidate its tangled affairs. Its officers and directors made a deed of trust in favor of William Ellicott, and he was advised by all the leaders of the community to accept it. The trusteeship was turned over to a committee, of which Mr. Ellicott was chairman, and under his leadership an apparently conscientious effort was made to find out the situation and turn the assets, such as they were, into cash.

This committee worked for seventeen months and still found itself unable to give any accounting or even to explain to the community the nature of the problem. The officers, some of whose activities may not have been wholly untinged with fraud, took advantage, for their own protection, of every device the law afforded for obstruction and delay. They were carrying on at the same time a public dispute by means of advertisements and pamphlets. In the meantime several smaller banks and institutions, including one savings bank and an insurance company, were forced to close their doors.

On Monday, August 3, a very hot day, Mr. Evan Poultney, who had been president of the Bank of Maryland, issued another pamphlet. The people had been muttering for some time, and this finally exhausted their patience. The disaffected turned their anger first upon Reverdy Johnson, the bank's counsel and a man of complete integrity who had been misguided enough to try to "save" the bank before it went down. Mr. Johnson's house was in Monument Square, in the very shadow of the Battle Monument raised in memory of the attack on the city by the British. The crowd surrounded this imposing residence and, on this first occasion, contented themselves with hurling paving stones through the windows.

Jesse Hunt was mayor. He was remarkable neither for

BALTIMORE ABOUT 1834

Made at the height of the romantic period and usually called "the French view," this picture was the basis for any number of lithographs and engravings and is still occasionally seen in old travel books and reference works. The most realistic feature is the representation of Federal Hill, with its obsevratory, but even this is deliberately exaggerated as to height.

judgment nor ability. Instead of calling out the police he called a meeting. This meeting passed a resolution calling upon the trustees to surrender their office, thereby giving the town the impression that an effort was being made to give the management an out. That night—it was a Friday—the mob again assembled before Johnson's house, and this time it was larger and more unruly.

During the next day the mayor bustled about, talking about the steps he had taken to secure Mr. Johnson's property, the size of the guard he had assembled, and so on, so that the whole town was on the *qui vive* for the excitement of Saturday night. The guard was there, all right, but the mob by now numbered hundreds if not thousands. Somehow a spirit of unity was infused into it, and when the guards about the Johnson house stood firm a section of the mass of men and boys moved up to the Charles Street house of John Glenn, another of the counsel, which was not guarded. Some of the guard trailed behind but too late to prevent the complete gutting of the substantial residence.

Sunday morning the assault on the same house began again, and by midafternoon its very walls were being torn down, the guard meanwhile making an occasional noisy but futile assault from the rear.

By now the lust for destruction had taken complete possession. The crowd again rushed back to the Reverdy Johnson house, broke into it, threw its contents, including a valuable library, into the street, and set fire to them. Then they began tearing the house itself to pieces, even toppling over the marble columns of the characteristic Greek portico which adorned it. Other smaller mobs were, meantime, going to the houses of other directors and officers, looting them, and burning the contents. It was a somewhat sentimental mob, at that, for it was turned away from several of its objects by appeals of various sorts, including one by a builder that the owner hadn't yet paid him for the house.

The guard itself was by this time demoralized. To protect it against the clubs and brickbats of the mob it had been armed with muskets. Now and then a desultory shot was fired. The mayor was given blame for this, and his house was the next object of attack. He issued a panic-stricken statement in which he said that although those of the guard who used firearms were authorized to do so the order "was not issued by me."

Affairs were now in a state of complete anarchy. Hundreds of residents left town, and others sent their families away. The merchants and leading citizens finally managed to call a meeting at the Exchange. By common consent, General Sam Smith, now 83 years old but still vigorous, was made chairman. He asked for no wordy resolutions but for volunteers. Behind him a parade of determined men marched through the street to Howard's Park and in the shadow of the Washington Monument received their instructions. They were to arm themselves and meet the general at the City Hall.

The procession, with the American flag at its head, had already thrown consternation into the rioters. The assembly at the City Hall, its numbers augmented by the volunteer fire companies and their apparatus, demanded and received the resignation of the mayor. The president of the First Branch of the City Council, General Anthony Miltenberger, another veteran of the war, became mayor *ex officio*. The volunteers were organized into squads and set to patrolling the streets, muskets in their hands. One hundred regulars from Washington and a detachment from Fort Severn, Annapolis, were brought in. They were not needed. The resolute spirit first displayed by General Smith had communicated itself to all the substantial people of the community. Doubtless some members of the late mob allowed themselves to be enrolled as custodians of law and order to re-establish their status.

Followed a quiet night after nearly a week of rioting. The next day the proscribed citizens who had fled the town began to trickle back. Warrants were issued for the leaders of the rioters, and they were arrested and fined or given jail terms. All of them, curiously enough, were pardoned by the governor. But the courts decided that the city was responsible for the damage done to property and allowed some rather generous claims. One of those who collected was J. J. Audubon, who received $120 for some drawings of his which were ruined in the attack on Mr. Johnson's house. Betsy Patterson got $400. Old Sam Smith, as politically alert as ever, had himself elected mayor in a special election held in September.

These troubles came earlier than those of the other big cities but they were a symptom of a widespread disease about to break out in full virulence. The rage for "internal improvements" had overreached itself. The country was overextended, and the inevitable reaction had begun.

In Baltimore, thanks to the wisdom and prudence of a few citizens, among whom the sons of Alexander Brown were notable, the long deflation, though costly and wearing, was, on the whole, carried out in an orderly manner. The mob, having once been put into subjection for a while, took the recurring blows with resignation if not with fortitude.

Baltimore on the Chesapeake

The merchants more and more turned from mercantile ventures to private banking, following a tendency general all over the Western world. The tariff pretty well eliminated the roving clipper looking for general cargo. Foreign trade became more and more a question of ingenuity. Baltimore, less able than New York to absorb and distribute general imports, had to find special fields for her maritime enterprise.

One of these special fields was exceedingly profitable for many years. Its origin was romantic. When, following the disorders which began in the French Revolution, the heir apparent of Portugal, Dom Pedro, fled to Brazil most of his court accompanied him or·trickled over afterward. A little later Brazil was an independent constitutional empire, with Dom Pedro as Pedro I.

The native Brazilians had had no use for white bread but when well-to-do whites moved over in numbers they brought their taste for that staple with them. A growing market was thus provided for American flour, and it transpired that that made from the winter wheat of the country surrounding Baltimore was best suited for transport to Brazil and for keeping in that hot climate. Here was a new outlet for Baltimore's chief product and a new use for the clippers.

In the early days of this trade there was a great difficulty in finding a return cargo. Frequently the ships unloaded their flour in Rio, took specie or London drafts to the West Indies, and there picked up sugar and coffee. After a while they could get at least a part of a cargo in the form of hides, thus bringing about the early development of the tannery business in Baltimore. But when Brazil took up the growing of coffee on a considerable scale the clippers, taking out flour, came back loaded, or nearly loaded, with coffee. In an uncertain and irregular form some of this trade still persists, but for a long while it was one of the chief mainstays of the port of Baltimore. Ships—at first schooners but later on more often brigs, brigantines, and barques—were especially built to engage in it. In Baltimore it is still talked of as the "coffee trade," though it should be called, from Baltimore's point of view, at least, the "flour trade."

Considerable attention has been given this exchange by students, and they have been hard put to it to find the reason for its decline. Dr. Frank R. Rutter (in whose study, *The South American Trade of Baltimore*, Johns Hopkins Press, September 1897, the detailed statistics are carefully examined) is inclined to believe that the coming of the steamship was chiefly responsible.

While the trade lasted it was highly profitable. The characteristic smell of the Baltimore water front during the whole period from 1825 to the turn of the century was that of roasting coffee. There was a growing taste for the beverage all over the country. New York and Baltimore ran neck and neck in developing and exploiting it, with Baltimore keeping the edge for quite a long time, because her flour surpassed that from the West, which was what New York had to offer. As a matter of fact, the New Yorkers, to compete, had to make their Brazilian voyages three-cornered. In their home port they put aboard what general cargo was available, sailed around to Baltimore for flour, and then rolled down to Rio. Baltimore's difficulty, and one that told in the long run, was that New York was constantly gaining on her in the matter of inland distribution of the coffee and hence could offer better prices for a larger supply.

Other highly specialized trades were that in copper ore and guano from the West Coast of South America. From the days of John O'Donnell's famous trip to Canton an occasional Baltimore clipper had ventured around the Horn. The skippers had to work out elaborate trading operations to make these voyages profitable. One method was to take a cargo of flour, trimmed out with dry goods, to Chile or Peru. Because of the restrictions imposed by the Spanish government the trade had to be surreptitious, and the clippers were frequently chased away from the coast by the Spanish cruisers. The natives wanted to trade, however, and the coast was long. Hence there was little chance that the Spaniards could block it entirely.

The flour and other products were traded for specie, usually silver. Sometimes if the market wasn't good enough in South America the vessels would coast all the way up to California and even Oregon, trading as they went. In the latter area they frequently procured from the Indians otter skins which were especially prized in China.

Supplied with silver and with skins, the ship would cross the Pacific to the Orient, getting spices in the Indies and tea and knickknacks in Canton. Thus laden, they would proceed across the Indian Ocean, rounding Good Hope, and so through the trades and back to the Chesapeake. There were variations in this route, of course, depending on the exigencies of opportunity. The China trade was never particularly well established in Baltimore, again because of the difficulty in those early days of distributing such large quantities of tea and spices. What Baltimore needed was a commodity for the return trip which she could use in her own vicinity.

That commodity was found, for a while, in copper ore,

and the development of the exchange was helped by a series of droughts in Chile and earthquakes in Peru which pretty well paralyzed the economies of those two countries. Peru needed Baltimore flour and needed it badly. It had copper ore to offer in exchange.

This situation, so happy from the point of view of Baltimore, was responsible for the building of what many consider the most beautiful, as she was almost certainly one of the fastest, sailing vessels ever built. In 1831 Mr. Isaac McKim, merchant, politician, philanthropist, commissioned Messrs. Kennard and Williamson to build for him in their shipyard on the Point the biggest Baltimore clipper ever conceived and one of the biggest merchantmen of her day. She was to be 143 feet long, with a beam of 31 feet—much narrower than was conventional—and she was to be rigged as a ship. They were to spare no expense in her construction, using only the finest materials. Captain James Curtis was appointed by the owners to inspect and pass or reject everything that went into her.

Captain Curtis saw to it that she was a luxurious vessel. Her frame was of live oak, and she was sheathed with copper, which was also used for all her fastenings. Her trim was of Spanish mahogany. Twelve brass cannons were mounted on her deck, and her bells and fittings were likewise of gleaming yellow metal. She was launched in June 1833 and named after the wife of her owner, *Ann McKim.*

Loaded with thirty-five hundred barrels of Baltimore's best, the *Ann McKim* sailed on August 30 under command of Captain Walker. Ninety-five days later, after a rough passage around the Horn, she was unloading her cargo in Callao, still more or less disorganized from the recent successful revolt against Spanish rule. It took months for her to get together a cargo of ore for the return trip. But she made the passage from Huasco, Chile, to the Chesapeake Bay in seventy-two days. She arrived in Baltimore June 16, 1834, just before the rumors of difficulties of the Bank of Maryland began to run around the town.

Baltimore had a copper-smelting industry of a sort before the *Ann McKim*. In a hilly area some miles north of the town—called the Bare Hills because of an almost complete absence of trees on their summit—a green stone was early found to bear some copper. Excavation unearthed a vein worth working, and furnaces for its extraction were built. The skills were thus available for the use of the Peruvian and Chilean ores, and in a very few years Baltimore had two copper-smelting companies. They flourished mightily for a while, but the tariff imposed on ore in 1869 caused them to close down. They were reorganized and in 1872 went to work on domestic ores.

After the slow recovery from the depression which began in 1834 and continued for nearly ten years farmers began for the first time to use prepared fertilizers in place of the manures produced on the farm. It was about time, for the soils had been badly treated for years. Tobacco growers were getting desperate all over the South, and even the wheat fields were beginning to show the need of some sort of rejuvenation.

Synthetic fertilizers were unknown, but the English had discovered that on the Chincha Islands off the coast of Peru there were vast deposits of the excrement of various types of aquatic birds, called "guano." A small lot of this substance was brought into Baltimore in 1824, but, because the farmers knew nothing about it, it found only a slow sale. However, the need was great, and in the early forties a brisk trade began. Realizing that it had a valuable commodity of only limited supply, the Peruvian government established a monopoly and made its deals with a single firm of merchants. Several agents in turn held the contract, one of the most successful and important ones being that of Barreda and Brother. The Barredas and their relatives, the Barrils, were important Peruvian families—they still are— but their associations with Baltimore, started at that period, are still vigorous. The vast Drum Point Estate, where the broad and deep estuary of the Patuxent River meets the bay, is still in possession of the allied families. For a long time all Marylanders thought that a great new port was to be built at the mouth of the Patuxent and that the Barril y Barreda clan would dominate it.

The guano trade kept a number of Baltimore ships busy for two or three decades. But it was bedeviled by the politicians at both ends from the very start, and when Chile recovered from its drought and began the growing of wheat again it became harder and harder to sell Baltimore flour to the Peruvians. Thus the direct exchange was no longer possible, and this business, too, gradually dropped into the lap of New York, which could provide a more varied cargo of American products for sale to the West Coast.

However, the guano trade did Baltimore a permanent good turn. It was the South which especially needed fertilizer, and Baltimore, with coasting lines running to all the Southern ports, including those on the gulf, was by far the best distributing point for the bulk material. Even after the New York ships were carrying it they had to bring it into Baltimore for distribution, thus establishing a fertilizer business which still survives and grows. Guano found in other places than Peru was brought to Baltimore. The chemical examination of soils and the discovery of other lacks led to the beginning of bone meal manufacture and finally to the production of synthetics. Baltimore still remains one of the chief centers for the manufacture of chemical fertilizers, some of them highly odorous, and all of them profitable.

CHAPTER XXIII

Desperate Evasions

THERE WAS SOMETHING almost miraculous about the vitality of Baltimore in the 1850s. The vicissitudes of the thirties and forties were a stimulant, and the city emerged from them more buoyant than ever. Though New York was gradually taking over control of her foreign shipping, making Baltimore a way station, however important, in the main stream of commerce, her manufacturers were profiting, and so was her domestic trade, whether water-borne or carried on rails. Her volunteers had taken a gallant part in the Mexican War, and she had sent more than her quota of ships and men to California in the gold rush. The surviving clippers distinguished themselves in that great hegira. With the South especially, thanks to the growing use of cotton in her mills and the return demand for the fertilizer from her factories, her commercial ties were growing. More and more her merchants and bankers became the purveyors, not of goods alone, but, more importantly, of credit for the whole Southern littoral. The tobacco trade, still mostly in German or Dutch hands, centered in a few warehouses—now operated by the state —along the Light Street water front.

Thus, despite the growing pressures and the frequent explosions of passion in the closely built-up city, there was always enough activity to enable it to survive and even to grow. The Baltimore and Ohio pushed regularly westward, opening new markets. In 1842 its line had reached Cumberland, as we have seen. On Christmas Eve, 1852, the last section of track between the Chesapeake Bay and the Ohio River was laid, and at long last Baltimore acquired that on which her dreams had been set almost from the beginning. By her own efforts and at her own expense she had direct access, by the shortest route and the easiest grades, to the watercourses of the whole Mississippi Valley.

To complement this achievement she had provided the impetus and most of the capital for a whole network of coastal freight and passenger lines. There were steamboats running from Light Street Wharf to every river on the bay, from Elk, at its very head, to Elizabeth at its foot. Every river was spotted at intervals of a few miles with substantial wharves at which the "Baltimore boat" made its daily, or, at least, its thrice-weekly, landing. One could go by boat from Baltimore to Washington, the trip taking two nights and a day. One could go overnight from Baltimore to Norfolk.

Nor did these services stop at the capes. The influx of hides from Brazil and the river Plate, brought in usually by the coffee clippers, had developed a tanning industry. Boston, as the center of the shoe trade, was the great consumer of leather. Benjamin Deford, one of the chief leather manufacturers, persuaded a group of Baltimoreans to put up $120,000 and got his Boston connection to add $80,000. With this sum they acquired a steamboat and began service to Boston. This was the Merchants and Miners Transportation Company, usually known as the Boston Line. It began operations in 1854 and is still running, though now it has absorbed or developed Southern lines as well and serves not only New England but Norfolk, Savannah, Jacksonville, and Miami.

It is necessary to bear all these things in mind while considering the internal story of Baltimore during the turbulent fifties. Politics and political passion seem to dominate it and at times they seem almost to paralyze it. But the ships sailed regularly; the Baltimore and Ohio and the other railroads carried on their services without interruption; the merchants, manufacturers, and bankers sat at their desks and gave their orders, and thousands of honest, hardworking men and women, more or less content with their lot, performed their daily tasks and received and spent their due wages.

There was enough left over for a certain inviting of the spirit. The city acquired an increasing number of squares and parks, culminating in the magnificent Druid Hill. George Peabody, who had laid the foundation of his fortune in Baltimore, made his first gift of $300,000 to the Peabody Institute, which was designed to cover the whole field of the fine arts.

But man is a political animal, and in this decade every one of the mighty forces at work in the nation seemed somehow to come into conflict in Baltimore. After a while the riots and anarchies seemed to have almost no direct relation with what was going on outside. They were a resultant, of course, but the thrusts which made them were too numerous and too subtle to be easily tagged with a name.

During the thirties and forties there had been a constantly increasing flood of immigration, mostly from Germany and Ireland. To a large extent this immigration was Catholic. To the politician every immigrant was a potential voter. Both the main parties, the Democrats and the Whigs, vied with each other in heaping flattery on the newcomers in order to get their suffrages. This was not true in Baltimore alone. It was true all over the country and it was especially true in the big cities on the Eastern coast.

The immigrants, thus wooed, acquired an inflated opinion of themselves and tended to give their political support to the highest bidder. The Germans, clannish by nature, gathered themselves together into societies and presented formal demands to the parties. They especially wanted to be permitted and maybe even paid to keep their own culture and language. They maneuvered, and in Baltimore their maneuverings were successful, to have German put on the same basis as English in certain public schools. Indeed, Baltimore had German schools in full operation up to 1914.

The Irish immigrants were almost wholly Catholic. Politically their demands were less vociferous than those of the Germans. They were taxed, like everyone else, to support the public schools, but, by tradition and by ecclesiastical persuasion, their children attended parochial schools. Their demand, in effect, was either that the taxes they paid be used to support the parochial schools or else that they be relieved of school taxes altogether.

Neither of the issues thus developed was of major importance. The country had a much more dangerous internal schism to face. The Missouri compromise had broken down, and the abolitionists on the one hand and the slavery advocates on the other were growing ever more extreme in their arguments and threats. Perhaps it was because the country feared, above all things, to face this tragic issue that it found an outlet for its emotions in this lesser quarrel with its recent immigrants. Perhaps it was because Baltimore, at the very northernmost edge of the slave territory, realized that she would be destroyed should blood be shed over the fundamental issue that she took such a passionate concern in the lesser one. Men have deceived themselves before and since in just such a fashion.

In any event, Know-Nothingism, which was essentially anti-foreign and anti-Catholic in its poorly formulated creed, achieved its greatest strength and committed its most outrageous depredations in the Baltimore of the fifties. The census of 1850, which gave the city a population of 169,054, showed also that almost 25 per cent of them were foreign-born, the Germans outnumbering the Irish by about two to one. Both groups were closely organized, and either or both could swing a close election.

In the beginning Know-Nothingism was pressure politics, pure and simple, and it operated very much like the Ku-Klux Klan of the 1920s. Later its methods were more like those of the Anti-Saloon League. It began as a secret order whose members knew each other by certain signs, grips, and passwords. With chapters or clubs established in strategic locations and a newspaper organ to express its desires, it put pressure on the various candidates, regardless of party, to force them to give public allegiance to its principles. The candidate who thus truckled received the votes of the members of the society. In addition, the clubs did everything in their power to keep supporters of his opponent away from the polls.

Growing bolder, the members of the society came out into the open, formed themselves into an avowed political organization, called it the American party, and nominated their candidates at more or less public conventions. From the very beginning the American party did a complete straddle on the slavery issue. In Baltimore it managed to write a platform plank which sounded pro-slavery to the friends of slavery and abolitionist to the opponents of slavery. From this golden mean it shaded off in both directions as it operated to the North or to the South.

The volunteer firemen of Baltimore, like volunteer firemen everywhere, had always been a source of trouble. Some of them were native, some foreign. There was a long series of bad fires in the late forties and early fifties, several of which got out of control because the fire companies became locked in battle before reaching the scene. Firemen were the special wards of the politicians, and little effort was made to control them. Indeed, it often seemed that incendiaries started fires just to provide an opportunity for a street battle between firemen. On the night of November 28, 1847, there were five fires and five riots. The very next night when an alarm was sent in from Federal Hill the company stationed in that neighborhood waited until its rival came whooping down Light Street and then proceeded to dump the apparatus into the river.

That summer another riot of a different sort took place. An excursion boat was chartered by a political club and started down the bay crowded to the gunwales. The bay was rough that day, so instead of crossing it and making for St. Michaels, on the Eastern Shore, as had been planned,

RICH AND PROUD IN 1850

This view, from a lithograph by E. Sachse, shows the city when Mt. Vernon Place, bordering the Washington Monument, had become established as the social center of the community. The view, probably taken from the roof of the Abell house (later the Baltimore Club and now a hotel), is directly south on Charles Street, for a hundred years the fashionable promenade of the town.

the captain put into Annapolis instead. A few of the male passengers went ashore and proceeded to get into a fight with some young fellows of the town. They were chased back aboard the boat. Then ensued a long-range battle, the youths on the wharf throwing sticks, bricks, and even heavier missiles at the crowd on the boat. Some of these struck women and children, whereupon the excursionists rushed the gun room of the vessel, took out rifles, loaded them with ball, and fired into the crowd onshore, wounding five persons. The rejoinder from the shore was of an even more desperate character, for in a few minutes the Annapolitans had procured two small cannon and were preparing to bombard the steamboat. Fortunately a couple of coolheaded citizens of the little capital stood before the pieces and refused to move. The captain of the steamboat meantime managed to cast her loose and backed into the river.

This was the mood in the community into which Know-Nothingism insinuated itself. Its first overt act was to call a mass meeting in Monument Square for the evening of August 18, 1853. Some five thousand persons attended and heard foreigners in general and Irish Catholics in particular roundly denounced. Clubs which had been formed all over the city marched to the appointed place, carrying transparencies on which their names were inscribed. There were the Black Snakes, the Tigers, the Rough Skins, the Red Necks, the Thunderbolts, the Gladiators, the Ranters, the Eubolts, the Little Fellows, the Ashland Club (how mild!), the Rip Raps, the Screw Boats, the Stay Lates, the Hard Times, the Dips, the Plug Uglies, and the Blood Tubs.

Lest it be thought that all the ruffianism was the property of the American party, here are the names of some of the clubs organized by the Democrats: the Bloody Eights (from the Eighth Ward, almost solidly Irish), the Double Pumps, the Calithumpians, the Ferry Road Hunters, the Gumballs, the Peelers, the Pluckers, the Shad Hoes (Roes?), the Bloats, and the Butt Enders.

The mass meeting in Monument Square was a sign, had the Democrats but known it, that they had a new and powerful political opponent in place of the disintegrating Whigs. They began to be frightened about the middle of September and started a denunciation of the Know-Nothings. But their task was difficult, because that party had as yet put up no candidate. It wasn't until September 27 that the local organ of the new group announced its candidate, one Samuel Hinks, formerly a Whig. The Democrats tried all their usual tricks to beat him at the polls and when trickery failed tried highhanded methods. The Know-Nothings responded in kind. There was a pitched battle, with firearms as well as clubs and stones, at the corner of Fayette and Exeter streets in Old Town, which was once Jones Town.

The battle was indecisive, but the election was not. The Know-Nothings elected their mayor and a controlling majority in both branches of the city council. Their jubilation was so great that they paraded the streets that night with two cannon which were constantly halted for the firing of salutes to victory.

Next year there was an election for the legislature and some state-wide offices. The campaign was as bloody as it was noisy. The Plug Uglies invaded the meetings of the Bloody Eights, and the latter retaliated. If they couldn't break them up by shouting they resorted to violence. The most absurd stories were shouted from the rostrum. One was that every Catholic church had been designed for use as a fort in case of necessity. Another was that the Federal government had sent over five hundred horse pistols for the Democrats. Pistols were on display to prove this one. The Know-Nothings carried Baltimore City and thirteen out of the twenty-one counties. Only the oldest and most conservative of the tobacco counties stood out against it.

That session of the legislature was a constant battle between the governor, a surviving Democrat, and the Know-Nothing majority in the lower house. The Know-Nothings, who had pretty well absorbed the remnants of the Whigs, introduced a number of measures aimed at the Catholics and especially at nunneries, which were their particular bane, but it soon became apparent that they were more interested in spoils than in principles. The anti-Catholic agitation was good campaign material with which to inflame the mob, but jobs were the true concern, and most of the parliamentary maneuverings had places for the faithful as their objective.

Now came on the presidential campaign of 1856 which overlapped that for a new mayor of Baltimore. Thus there were double stresses and double excitements. The new Republican party tried to hold a meeting in Baltimore. Only about forty or fifty persons showed up, but a mob of at least two thousand howled outside the door and made it impossible for even that small group to hear the speaker. There were riots nearly every night, culminating in a pitched battle in Marsh Market Space, where the Democrats defended their stronghold with a swivel gun.

The mayoralty election took place first, and on that day the chief streets and markets of the town were given over entirely to fighting between gangs, now always armed like soldiers. One battle took place on the hillside of Monument Street, just below the Washington Monument. The bloodiest of the day was between the Rip Raps and the Plug Uglies, representing the Know-Nothings and the New Market Fire Company, stationed at Lexington Market. No one knows how many were wounded in this two-hour fight, but at least four men were killed.

The object of these battles, of course, was to control the polling places and the approaches thereto. The outcome seems to indicate that the Know-Nothings were the better fighters. Their candidate for mayor, Thomas Swann, a former president of the Baltimore and Ohio and undoubtedly an able man, was elected by a majority of more than two thousand.

Passions were by no means exhausted by this display, for the presidential election was due in two months. The rioting continued daily, and the more respectable citizens, foreseeing anarchy complete, begged the Know-Nothing mayor to take steps to keep order. He claimed that there was no danger and refused to act. The governor then stepped in and offered the services of the state militia. But the mayor coolly refused the suggestion of a political opponent, and the governor retired discomfited.

On Election Day Belair Market was the main fortress of the Know-Nothings. They had mounted cannon in advance and expected to be able to hold it against any force. But the Democrats, made desperate by approaching defeat at the polls, charged with such determination that they finally captured the armament and carried it off. In this fighting ten were killed and more than one hundred and fifty wounded.

Desperate Evasions

It is significant that in Maryland alone were the Know-Nothings successful in this, their first and only national campaign. In the rest of the country the fact that its nativist protestations were a futile avoidance of the issue had become apparent. Baltimore and Maryland clung to them and supported them longer than the rest of the country for the reason that I have suggested before: the tragic truth about the real division in the country and the approaching internecine war was too terrible to be faced.

Thus the Know-Nothings continued in power. In the spring of 1857 they sent emissaries to Washington to help in a municipal election there, and the Democrats, not to be outclassed, sent one of their own most reckless gangs along to give battle. Thus the national capital was given a display of Baltimore's political methods. The chief object of this diversion seems to have been to keep up the fighting spirit for the gubernatorial election in the fall when the Know-Nothings planned to displace Ligon, the Democratic governor.

By this time the police department, controlled in those days by the mayor, had come to be an arm of his party. Governor Ligon, to give protection to those who wanted to vote the Democratic ticket in the city, ordered the commanding officer of a division of militia to enroll six regiments of six hundred men each. Ensued a legalistic debate between him and Mayor Swann, from which the governor eventually retired. He was worsted, not so much by the superior arguments of the mayor, but, rather, because the general charged with the enrollment of the militia couldn't get volunteers. The Know-Nothings elected their candidate for governor, a man named Hicks, but they elected him only because of the thumping majority they rolled up in Baltimore City. The rest of the state had begun the retreat.

Baltimore clung to its uncomfortable delusions until the next year, when it re-elected Swann. It was in this election that the instrument which had been accepted as the symbol of the party was openly carried and used. It was, in its simplest form, a bradawl. If a non-member approached the polls and attempted to vote he was surrounded by a group of Plug Uglies who jabbed their sharp weapons into his fleshy parts until he was convinced that retreat was advisable.

Such was the regular procedure during the early hours of Election Day. By noon Colonel A. P. Shutt, an independent who had had the temerity to take the nomination after the disheartened Democrats had thrown up their hands, withdrew from the race and told his supporters not to subject themselves to any more risks. Swann received nineteen thousand votes out of twenty-four thousand cast. Only the Twelfth Ward, an Irish island in a sea of Know-Nothingism, voted against him.

This election in Baltimore was a national, even an international, scandal. Newspapers all over the country sent reporters to describe it, and it was pictured even as far away as London, where the *Illustrated London News* devoted a page to it. Such publicity finally got under the skins of the substantial citizens of the town, and they organized the first City Reform Association, the organization which was destined to drive the hoodlums from power.

One of the chief reasons they were able to accomplish this desirable end was that the Know-Nothings, having taken over the city, lock, stock, and barrel, began fighting among themselves. Nearly every appointive office was the focal point of serious dissensions. The fact that the Court of Appeals was still uncontaminated gave the reformers an opportunity to raise various legal issues with some success. They exploited also the known venality of the Criminal Court of Baltimore City, presided over at that period by a judge given to heavy drinking and light sentences for political offenses. Finally, they even managed to persuade the legislature—which had refused to seat several Know-Nothing representatives elected in Baltimore—to take the control of the city police force away from the mayor and vest it in the hands of a commission selected by the Assembly. From that day to this the police force in Baltimore City has been an arm of the state government rather than of that of the city.

By such devices, planned long ahead, the Reform Association paved the way for the municipal election of 1860. They nominated for mayor one of the best known and most respected of citizens, George William Brown. The Know-Nothings, bereft of the support of the police force, knew that they would have a thin time at the polls and found it difficult even to find a candidate. After one refusal by a reputable citizen they finally persuaded a man named Samuel Hindes to make the race.

Even heaven conspired against them, for as one of their major campaign gestures they had planned an elaborate ceremony marking the opening of Druid Hill Park, which the city had acquired under Swann's guidance. But on the appointed day a heavy northeaster, with torrents of rain, broke up the celebration, and it was not possible to hold it until after the election was over. The last trick they played was to find a man named William George Brown and put him up as an independent candidate. But this effort, patently the recourse of despair, deceived no one. William George received but twenty votes.

The election was quiet and orderly. Brown was elected by a vote of almost two to one, and the whole reform ticket went in with him.

It was about time. No longer was it possible even for Baltimoreans to deceive themselves into thinking that the real decision could be any longer postponed. The reform victory meant that the city went into the long and almost mortal struggle with men of good intent in charge of public affairs.

CHAPTER XXIV

Occupied Territory

MR. LINCOLN as campaigner was an unimpressive figure to Baltimore. Breckinridge received almost half the town's vote. Douglas and Bell together got about 47 per cent. The Republican got a bare 3 per cent. With this figure staring him in the face, the President-elect decided that the plan whereby he was to come to Baltimore on the Baltimore and Susquehanna Railroad (now renamed the Northern Central) and then ride across the city to Camden Station to get the Baltimore and Ohio train to Washington wasn't the wisest plan in the world. The stories about the turbulence of Baltimore and its addiction to rioting were fresh in his mind, as they were in the national mind.

Hence it was easy for him to believe the tales he heard in Pennsylvania about a plot to wreck his train and murder him as he reached Baltimore. At the last moment he changed his route, took an earlier train via Philadelphia, and sneaked through Baltimore early in the morning of

Washington's Birthday. Mrs. Lincoln, his children, and his official party came through on the scheduled train—without incident, of course—and were greeted by a curious crowd at Calvert Station. The citizens hardly credited the story that the President was already in Washington. When it was apparent that he had indeed avoided facing a Baltimore crowd the city's chagrin took itself out in violent denunciation of him. It wasn't only Democrats whose pride was lacerated but Unionists as well.

There was little faith in the new President after this episode. "Had we had any respect for Mr. Lincoln," said *The Sun*, now become the paper which most closely reflected the prevailing opinion of the community, "his career and speeches on his way to the seat of government would have cruelly impaired it, but the final escapade by which he reached the capital would have utterly demolished it and overwhelmed us with mortification."

This view of Lincoln was the generally accepted view of the community. The citizens regarded him as a poltroon and trusted him not at all. They thought he had lost his head and that no act of his was motivated by reason.

But it should not be assumed that because of this distrust of Lincoln Baltimore was secessionist. Parts of the state were, beyond a doubt. The tobacco counties and the lower Eastern Shore were moved by precisely the same economic and political considerations as Virginia. But the country to the north and west of Baltimore was, generally speaking, as free of pro-slavery sentiment as Pennsylvania. As its citizens saw it, Baltimore's existence depended on the *status quo*. The "union as it was" was the ruling slogan. It could not conceive of itself as existing without the South. It could not conceive of itself as existing without its trade with the North and West. Mr. Lincoln seemed bent on splitting the country asunder. Baltimore wanted it held together, preferably by concession to the seceding states. The careful reader will accept these statements as the generalizations which they are and remember that it is impossible to be completely precise about such a complicated business.

In any event, Baltimore's responsible citizens realized that the town was in grave danger and they felt that it was up to them to avert that danger as far as possible. To save Baltimore was their first concern, to save the Union their second.

With reference to the first, their opportunity came speedily. The Sixth Massachusetts Regiment, bound for Washington, reached Philadelphia on April 18. There the commanding officer, hearing that he was likely to meet opposition in Baltimore, had ammunition distributed to his men and told them to keep their muskets loaded. He told them, moreover, that they were to march through the streets of Baltimore in close formation, paying no attention to insults, abuse, or even the throwing of missiles. If fired upon they were to hold return fire until the command was given by their officers and then they were to shoot only in the direction from which the attack had come. If these wise and prudent orders had been followed to the letter it is likely that the damaging events of the next day would not now be a part of history.

But when the train with the troops—now augmented by a body of Philadelphians—reached President Street Station the next day the orders were not followed. Instead of marching as a body along Pratt Street to Camden Station, where trains for Washington awaited them, the troops

were subdivided and put into horse-drawn cars holding
only a few men each. Thus their order and unified command was broken, and they were easy targets for rioters.
The second error was in not informing the city authorities
of the exact nature of their plans. Even Mayor Brown was
kept in ignorance of every detail save the bare announcement that the troops would pass through the city.

The first seven companies were moved through the
streets in their horse-drawn cars without any disorder. But
the news of the movement spread, and crowds began to as-
semble. The notion got abroad that Maryland was being
invaded. There was a variant of this which held that Maryland was being recreant to her friends in the South by permitting prospective invaders thus to use her soil. On one
of the wharves along Pratt Street there were several heavy
anchors. Some men and boys, aided, interestingly enough,
by the Negro crew of a vessel tied up there, dragged these
anchors out into the street and blocked the tracks. Seven
cars, as we have said, had already got through, but the
driver of the eighth was unable to proceed. So he unhooked
his horses, hooked them again to the rear of his vehicle, and
reversed his direction. The cars trailing behind him at
irregular intervals had to follow his example. Soon the
whole body of men, about 220 in number, was back in
President Street Station.

The officers held a hurried consultation and decided
to take their men through the streets to Camden Station
on foot. But they were all excited by this time, and the
march, instead of being orderly, was at the double-quick.
The first obstacle was the Pratt Street bridge over Jones
Falls. This was undergoing repairs, and the workmen, who
had stopped for dinner, had left the bridge half blocked

with tools and timbers. The story is that one of the soldiers, running through this debris, stumbled and discharged his musket. It is as good a tale as any perhaps. In any event, the firing began, and the riot was on.

Mayor Brown, in the meantime, had learned of the arrival of the troops and of their proposed transit by coach to Camden Station. He accompanied the new and competent marshal of police, named George P. Kane, and a strong force to that point. There was a crowd there by this time, and the police were stationed between the soldiers and the civilians to prevent any possible clash. Things were very quiet.

Word came to Mayor Brown of the fighting on Pratt Street. Bidding the marshal to follow him with police, he rushed off alone, carrying his top hat in one hand and his umbrella in the other. The middle-aged gentleman had to run at least half a mile before he came to the scene of the conflict. The mob wasn't a large one—it has been variously estimated that from 250 to 500 persons were actively engaged—but it was pursuing the troops and bombarding them with missiles of all kinds, particularly with paving stones torn out of the bed of the street. The soldiers were running desperately, turning now and then to fire at their pursuers and, on occasion, firing ahead at groups of observers which they suspected of hostile intent.

Into this bedlam the mayor thrust himself. A very polite man, he first introduced himself to the captain in command. Then he suggested that the double-quick was an error and perhaps it would be better if the men resumed regular marching order. The captain was impressed, and so was the crowd, by the spectacle of this man, armed only with a hat and an umbrella, facing both soldiers and mob and taking control of things. For a few minutes there was something very much like order.

The appeasement, however, was only temporary. The raw soldiers were thoroughly frightened and could not be restrained from firing at any group they saw. The crowd, aroused, fired back. Men began falling on both sides, and there was still perhaps a third of a mile to go.

At this juncture Marshal Kane arrived with his police force, their revolvers drawn. He had left only ten men at the station and had forty with him. They surrounded the soldiers as well as they could, putting most of their number in the rear of the troops to fend off the pursuers. Marshal Kane himself arrested one young hothead who disobeyed his order to stand back.

The troops reached the station without further molestation. In the course of their passage they had lost four killed and thirty-six wounded. Their fire had killed eleven civilians and wounded a much larger number.

The whole incident had taken about an hour, and by one o'clock the soldiers were in the trains bound for Washington. Just outside the city a man alongside the track shook his fist at the passing cars. There was a shot from a window, and he fell dead. He was Robert W. Davis, a well-to-do merchant of the town, of known Southern sympathies, who happened to be inspecting a piece of property he intended to buy.

This incident, tragic as it was, did not divide Baltimore. Instead it united it. Hicks, the Know-Nothing governor was, of course, a pronounced Unionist but he issued a statement in which he said, "I love my state and I love the Union, but I will suffer my right arm to be torn from my body before I will raise it to strike a sister state." He and

Mayor Brown joined in a telegram to the President asking that no more Federal volunteers be sent through the city. Brown followed this with a personal letter, committed to the hands of three of the city's leading figures, repeating in the most earnest terms the request that the troops be kept away. Lincoln delayed replying, and, hearing rumors of further troop movements, the governor, the mayor, and the police board decided on the radical step of destroying all the railroad bridges to the north and east, thus making it impossible for Northern soldiers to come upon the city unawares.

Such measures seem rather childish now, but the officials of Baltimore were not in a position at that time to survey and adjudicate. The problem was one of self-preservation, and they took the steps which seemed to meet the momentary situation. Their determination had the effect of drawing from the President, in a conference he called, with a committee headed by Mayor Brown, a statement that the troops which might be sent through the city would be used only to protect the capital itself from assault.

While this delegation was still in Washington the mayor received from John W. Garrett, president of the Baltimore and Ohio Railroad and certainly no troublemaker, a telegram that three thousand Federal troops were in Cockeysville, about fifteen miles north of the city, and were about to march in. Whereupon the delegation returned to the White House and this time got from Lincoln, in the presence of General Scott, the definite promise that the troops would march around the town.

Thus for a few days the city managed to preserve itself. But the measures taken were costly, for the trade with the South was already practically stopped, and the destruction of the bridges had effectually cut off that with the North. Thus the merchants, meeting in the Corn Exchange on May 2, made a formal plea that the railroads coming in from the North be permitted to resume operations. There was opposition from those who believed that if Baltimore stood firm Washington would have to make terms with the South. But Annapolis had already been occupied by Federal troops which had come down by the ferry *Maryland* from Perryville, and the city was thus well-nigh surrounded. The legislature, meeting in special session at Frederick, played an entirely correct game and denied that it had no right to pass the ordinance of secession laid before it.

How futile such a move would have been was proved only a few days later. On the night of May 13, during the midst of a violent thunderstorm, General Benjamin F. Butler, with a sufficient number of troops and guns, came in from Annapolis and took over Federal Hill. From this eminence, with his guns pointed across the basin at the heart of the city below him, he proclaimed martial law and orally declared, according to tradition, that if there was any disorder his first target would be the Washington Monument. Thereafter Baltimore's resistance, when it made any, was clandestine and individual.

General Butler was no stickler for legal form, nor were his successors deterred by constitutional limitations. They built up almost immediately a network of spies and informers and began a series of arrests, many of which were without any justification whatever. The military put a censor in every newspaper office, and on one occasion their minions arrested C. C. Fulton, the publisher and editor of the chief Unionist organ of the town, the *American*. It took all Mr. Fulton's influence in Washington to get him out of the jam. It was this period which produced the famous case of John Merryman, in which Mr. Chief Justice Taney himself came to Baltimore to issue a writ of habeas corpus, only to have it ignored by the commanding officer of Fort McHenry.

The military next arrested and imprisoned the marshal of police, Mr. Kane, and put their own man in command. A little later they went even further and arrested not only the whole of the Baltimore delegation to the legislature but Mayor Brown himself. All of these men were locked up in Fort McHenry, now the recognized Bastille of the community.

Nor was the activity of the military confined to the arrest of imposing figures of the city and state. The little bay steamboats, carrying on their business of bringing supplies into the occupied city as best they could, were brought to the fort as a matter of routine and their passengers subjected to rigid questioning. Very often boys of fourteen or fifteen, so frightened by the interrogation that they were unable to answer coherently, were taken ashore and held in the dungeons beneath the walls of the fort until their frantic relatives learned of their plight and maneuvered their release.

There were political pressures as well. In November 1861 the Unionist party, which was the name under which the Republicans passed in Maryland at that time, nominated Augustus Williamson Bradford as governor. Bradford was a slave-holder but a coercionist too. The military, having enlisted the old Know-Nothing rabble in his support, saw to it that he was elected. During the whole of the war the course of government in Maryland was precisely that which was dictated from Washington, even including the formulation and adoption of a new abolitionist constitution for the state.

Our concern, however, is mainly with industry and trade, and, as to that, with one exception, there is little that is exciting to report. Save for local traffic, the port was almost immediately closed. During the early days, as we have noted, the railroad connections with the North were completely severed. There was no trade whatever with the South. Great numbers of people were thrown out of work, and the well-to-do opened soup houses to supply food for them. Many men of Southern sympathies managed to slip through the lines and enlist in the Confederate armies. Voluntary enlistment and the draft took other thousands into the Union forces. More than once Marylanders faced Marylanders and Baltimoreans faced Baltimoreans in bloody battle.

In the biographies of Baltimore merchants and industrialists there are many lapses at this period. Some of them, we know, put politics or principle above business and devoted their all to the effort to save the South. Some slipped through the lines and were never heard of again. Some shook the dust of the warring country from their feet and spent the long years in Europe. Some moved North and tried to conduct their business with foreign countries from a new headquarters. New York, Philadelphia, and Boston profited greatly by Baltimore's troubles at this time. But the majority adjusted themselves to the exigencies of the occasion and, grudgingly or enthusiastically, according to their tempers, did what they could to survive and prosper. Some magnificent fortunes were made in Baltimore during the Civil War.

It was the Unionists, naturally enough, who took the lead in such endeavors. One of the first was William J. Albert, of German background, who had been one of the founders of a company engaged in smelting Cuban copper ores. He was dispatched to Washington as the head of a committee to plead with Lincoln for a little of the business which was being passed out. The mission was eminently successful. The contracts were forthcoming, and Mr. Albert thereafter stood high in the councils of the Lincoln administration and was able to help the businessmen of the city in many ways.

Another Baltimorean who brought business in from the government was Horace Abbott, a Massachusetts blacksmith who had come to Baltimore in the thirties and bought the Canton Iron Works, established by Peter Cooper, builder of the Baltimore and Ohio Railroad's first locomotive. As an expert in heavy wrought iron Abbott made a great reputation for himself and his company, a reputation which was climaxed when he forged for the Russian frigate *Kamchatka* a shaft of the then unheard-of weight of 26,000 pounds. In 1850 he had enlarged his works by adding a rolling mill bigger than any ever seen before in this country.

To Abbott's works the government almost immediately gave large contracts, and he increased the size of his plant and the number of his employees to take care of them. In 1863 he turned out an order for 250,000 pounds of rolled iron in forty-eight hours. When it was decided to build the *Monitor* Abbott got the contract for the armor which withstood so successfully the pounding of the heavy guns of the *Virginia*.

The cotton mills of the community were likewise called

upon to do their best, and the owners and employees profited accordingly. The Gambrills, the Hoopers, and the Garys provided a large proportion of the tents which the Union army used.

But the biggest asset of Baltimore during all this period was the Baltimore and Ohio Railroad. In the Revolutionary War and in the War of 1812 the city's concern had been with the sea most of all. Her solid men were merchants, her heroes sailors. The two, working in combination, had enabled her to survive and to prosper and to win glory as well. But now her eyes were turned inland. For twenty-five years her chief concern had been to win her share, and more if possible, of the great market to the west and south-west of her. The Baltimore and Ohio was her chief weapon in that struggle. And just as she had devoted her energies in those early days to keeping the flag flying on the sea, so now, when the test came, the achievement in which she could take the greatest pride, without regard to political bias, was the operation of her railroad.

John W. Garrett, who was president of the road at this time, was probably as torn in his sympathies as most Balti-moreans. Because of his position in the town he could hardly have been wholly lacking in understanding of the South and its special problems. His firm had been estab-lished by his father Robert early in the century. Like many another, it had abandoned trade for private banking. For a while, at least, it held the honored position of Baltimore correspondent for George Peabody and Company of Lon-don. The commodities in which the Garretts were chiefly interested were, of course, grain and tobacco.

It was largely because he was disgusted with the constant efforts of warring political factions to dominate the B. & O.

that Mr. Garrett accepted a place on its board of directors and finally, in 1859, at the solicitation of Johns Hopkins, agreed to become its chief executive. This background is ample evidence of his close relationship with the business and financial life of the community and of his understanding of its special problems with relation to the war between the states.

In his meticulous centennial history of the Baltimore and Ohio Railroad Mr. Edward Hungerford tells the story of Mr. Garrett, the road, and the Civil War with skill and gusto.

One of the first acts of General Ben Butler, in command of the troops which had been ferried from Perryville to Annapolis, was to march an artillery detachment to the Relay House and set up guns commanding the line leading out from Baltimore. Garrett's first task after the battle of Pratt Street was to persuade Butler to let his trains pass. His argument was a simple one: Washington depended on this line for food and supplies, more so than ever now that troops were pouring into the city by the Annapolis route at the rate of thousands every day. Butler was convinced, and the very next day a train of thirty-six cars loaded with provisions moved from Baltimore to Washington.

Thus was the way paved for closer relations. Garrett knew E. M. Stanton, Lincoln's Secretary of War. He cultivated that acquaintance until it grew into a friendship, and the friendship expanded until it included Abraham Lincoln as well. In a little while Garrett was in a position to offer the services of his road to the government. There may have been shrewdness as well as patriotism in the offer, for other roads, less cooperative, were simply seized and operated by the military. The Baltimore and Ohio remained under its own management during the whole of the four-year war. Instead of being told what to do Garrett was asked.

He was a genius at organization. His line ran along the very border between North and South. For a few miles the people living along its route might be predominantly Federal in their sympathies. Along the next few miles they might be entirely Southern. The Southern commanders knew this as well as Garrett and they took advantage of it. It was a simple thing for them to stage a foray from one side of the Potomac or the other and cut the line. They did it, not once, but a hundred times.

To Garrett this was a problem, not of politics, but of organization. His solution, roughly, was to set up the road in such a fashion that whenever one part was cut off from the parent stem it had an independent life of its own and could continue to function within its limits until its circulation from the main body was restored. This meant, of course, that the company had to have a corps of employees whose loyalty at all times was not to the North or to the South but to the Baltimore and Ohio Railroad. Such employees were acquired. During the whole of the conflict the Baltimore and Ohio treated the burning of bridges, the tearing up of track, the deliberate derailing of trains, the theft of locomotives, and the destruction of rolling stock, not as if these things were the work of willful enemies, but, rather, as if they were the result of the convulsions of nature. The bridge at Harpers Ferry was rebuilt five times during the period.

Most of the necessary fabricating was done in the Mount Clare shops, the great building and repair plant which the company had developed on the land which used to be part of the park of Charles Carroll, the barrister, and which John Adams had so much admired eighty-odd years before.

In 1863 a writer in the *American Railroad Journal* visited Mount Clare to see what he could see. He reported that 525 cars had been built there since the outbreak of hostilities and that at that moment 200 more, with iron trucks, were about to be constructed. Then he went on to say:

Among the curiosities of the Mount Clare depot are the debris of the rails, locomotives, etc., which were destroyed by the rebels. There are successive piles of twisted rails, sections and rods of bridges, bolts, screens, car wheels, and boilers of excellent locomotives, fragments of coal cars, axles, and demolished tenders.

These articles having fallen into the hands of the rebels, they seem to have adopted the most effective means of destroying them. The rails, some of which are of the finest quality of English iron, after having been torn from the roadbed, were laid upon piles of crossties and fire applied to the latter. Whilst in heated state they were dragged off by tongs and twisted and turned in almost every conceivable manner. . . . There are millions of pounds of damaged iron, but it is not lost to the company, for no matter how small the piece, it is collected, placed into melting furnaces and again wrought into such parts of engines and cars as are required. . . .

Garrett's relationship with the administration developed as the war progressed and as his ability to deliver was more and more impressed upon the men in Washington. After a while his influence was great, and he used it more than once to help effect the release of some fellow townsman whose zeal for the Southern cause had outrun his discretion and who had found himself under arrest in consequence.

His road was the first to transport troops in great numbers. He planned, in fact, much of the famous movement of twenty thousand men from the army of the Potomac, to the relief of Rosecrans, after Chickamauga and carried out his part of it almost without a hitch. He saw that supplies were constantly carried to Washington. Sometimes he was the recipient of a personal appeal from the President, as witness this letter, written hastily in the Lincoln scrawl:

Executive Mansion
Washington, Jan. 10, 1865

Mr. J. W. GARRETT
MY DEAR SIR:

It is said we shall soon all be in the dark here, unless *you can* bring coal to make gas—I suppose you would do this without my interference, if you could; and I only write now to say *it is very important to us;* and not to say you must *stop* supplying the army to make room to carry coal—— Do all you can for us in *both matters.*

Yours truly,
A. LINCOLN.

So during all the four years of the war the Union needed Baltimore and Baltimore needed the Union and both needed the Baltimore and Ohio. The triple symbiosis made for the survival of all three. Geography once more exerted its dominance over the passions and prejudices of men. Even the fact that Lincoln was done to death by a crazed Baltimorean, thereby arousing the passions of the North once more against the unhappy city, could not alter the fundamentals.

Baltimore takes pride in the fact that it survived the Civil

FEDERAL HILL DURING THE CIVIL WAR

Immediately after the beginning of the Civil War, which deserved that name in Baltimore, Union troops occupied Federal Hill, fortified it and trained its heavy guns on the turbulent city below. During most of the war Baltimore was under martial law and its leaders imprisoned.

War as well as it did. The basis of its pride should be in the circumstance that when the testing time came there were a few men, John W. Garrett especially, who put the job ahead of politics. Those smart gamblers who saw the opportunity provided by the combination of Baltimore's geographical position and the clipper ship are rightly regarded as worthy men. By the same sort of judgment the Baltimoreans who used the geographical position of their city and the tools it had built to keep it going through this even greater crisis are equally to be admired.

CHAPTER XXV

Pride and Prejudice

IF THIS WERE a social history of a community it would be proper to devote this chapter to a description of the effort of the Southern sympathizers in Baltimore to adjust themselves to living peacefully with those whose allegiance had been given to the victorious North.

It doesn't take much imagination to see that the situation was difficult. Baltimore in those days immediately following the war was emotionally as riven as Madrid after the triumph of Franco. The people in the North had the catharsis which comes from overwhelming victory. Those of the South had at least the consolation that they had devoted themselves wholeheartedly and heroically to a cause which they believed noble. Baltimore, as a community, had no such compensations. It had survived, and that was all. Both sides were suspicious of it; both doubted its good faith. It had no sure faith of its own.

But, except incidentally, this is not a social history. It is our function to spy out, as far as possible, the economic bases of the town and to narrate the activities of those individuals and groups whose energies were given to the fabrication and distribution of goods. The political and sentimental emotions of individuals and groups play roles in the commercial drama, of course, but enterprise, ambition, and occasionally greed are the chief actors.

Despite sentimental chroniclers, Baltimore was not ruined by the Civil War. In the period preceding that war it was coming to be one of the credit reservoirs of the South, its commission merchant. The war broke off that business. It left the South financially prostrate, economically profoundly altered. But it left the South also with a disciplined manhood and womanhood and precisely the same natural resources which it had had before. The people of the South had a job to do. They had to be clothed and fed while they were doing it. The food and clothes had to be provided, at a price. The houses and barns had to be rebuilt, the communications re-established.

Forty years before, Baltimore had decided that its primary job was to win its share of the Western market. Now, with almost equal alacrity, it decided that its primary job was to help the South get back on its feet in a business way.

For this new task it was as well equipped as it had been for the earlier one. Perhaps it was even better equipped. Just as it was the nearest of the big cities to the West, so it was the nearest to the South. But it had a subtler advantage. Its leading merchants had, to some extent, the manners and attitudes of Southerners, thanks to their long association with the manorial lords of Maryland. They seemed less alien than the harsh, overbearing men of the North. That made the approach easy. Prior knowledge is as great an advantage in a commercial campaign as in a military one.

More important than this perhaps was the fact that the Southerner, on his side, still believed, or wanted to believe, that if Maryland could have made a free choice its troops would have fought at his side. As a matter of fact, thousands of Marylanders did fight in Southern armies. It is not necessary to be entirely cynical about Baltimore's role in the rehabilitation of the South.

But, above all these advantages, Baltimore had in profusion the primary commodity in the campaign she was about to undertake. She had capital.

The war had supplied that essential on a scale the city had hardly dreamed of in its callow days. The great government contracts for cotton, for flour, for iron and steel, for armor plate, for ships had left profits in the hands of many Baltimoreans. A new generation of rich men had come into being, for this was before the days of income and excess-profit taxes. Their takings were largely invested in government bonds. When the sale of the bonds lagged in 1863 the Federal banking law was amended to make the organization of national banks profitable by permitting them to issue notes based on Federal bonds purchased at ninety. In 1865 the law was amended once again to put a tax of 10 per cent on the notes of issue of state banks. That amendment made it practically impossible for the state banks to issue more notes, and thus almost all banks of issue were forced to nationalize themselves.

Baltimore's First National Bank was organized almost immediately after the amendment of 1863. One of the first men to see the significance of that amendment was Johns Hopkins, and it was he who persuaded a group of Baltimoreans to go in with him on the venture. If he foresaw the opportunities that the ending of the war would provide it would not be the first time that he had displayed uncanny foresight, for Hopkins was a man whose instincts were those of the born trader.

His family were Anne Arundel County Quakers. At first they had been slaveholders, but when the Quakers generally turned against slavery Samuel Hopkins, Johns's father, followed the dictates of the society and turned his Negroes loose. Johns was a small boy at the time and for a while he worked in the fields alongside the freed Negroes. But the city lured him, and he moved to Baltimore to work in the wholesale grocery house of his uncle, Gerard. Only a little later, with his brother as a partner, he had an establishment of his own and was in the business of distributing supplies of all kinds along the line of the Baltimore and Ohio but particularly on that branch line which led down through the Shenandoah Valley. His business capacity, plus the fact that as a heavy shipper he became interested in the development of the road, resulted in his being elected one of its directors in 1847.

During the trying times of the fifties he twice pledged his resources for the support of the company and emerged finally as one of its chief stockholders. Excess funds he utilized in banks particularly but also in real-estate ventures. He built a number of large warehouses and leased them to merchants like himself whose primary interest was the distribution of goods. Thus during the whole of the Civil War he was one of the chief commercial and financial figures and prospered greatly. He never married, and the money piled up. He was more interested in making it than in spending it for his own pleasures.

The example of the First National Bank, under Hopkins' shrewd direction, was followed by other groups of a finan-

cial turn of mind, especially in 1865, after the extra tax
had been placed on the state banks. The Farmers and
Planters Bank, established in 1836, nationalized itself in
1865. Its guiding spirit was a Massachusetts-born money-
making genius by the name of Enoch Pratt. Pratt, after an
apprenticeship in New York, came to Baltimore in 1831 and
set up for himself as a commission merchant. His business
career almost paralleled that of Johns Hopkins, but his allegiance was given, not to the Baltimore and Ohio, but to
the Philadelphia, Wilmington and Baltimore, the chief railroad link with the North. He was as shrewd as Hopkins
and made perhaps almost as much money. But he married,
was more genial, and devoted himself more easily to interests outside the countinghouse. Perhaps because of his New
England origin he willingly accepted public responsibility
and served on various boards, exerted himself in behalf of
the unfortunate, and for a while even acted as finance com-
missioner of the city. This was an unusual arrangement on
both sides, for after the war the city consistently voted
Democratic, whereas Pratt was as consistently Republican.

It was men of the quality of Johns Hopkins and Enoch
Pratt who determined the course that Baltimore was to
follow after the war. The wisdom of the course they suggested was so apparent that it became almost a religion with
Baltimoreans to regard themselves as the appointed guardi-
ans of Southern economic welfare. Maryland, as a state,
barely escaped being included in the "reconstruction"
program of the South and fought hard against being subjected to carpetbag rule. If that fight had been lost it would
have been impossible for Baltimore to play the role in the
South it was determined to play. But it was won, and thereafter the South, or at least Virginia, the Carolinas, and

Georgia, had in Baltimore a sort of social and economic mediator between their needs and the venomous greed of the Northern extremists.

That the merchants of the city played their role wisely almost any informed Southerner can testify. The method was relatively simple. The Baltimore merchants knew well all the merchants of the near-by South. They knew which of them were competent and which were honest. They knew, that is, the business risks involved. Thus they were willing and able to supply goods on credit and carry at least a part of the load while the favored retailers established themselves. Those retailers knew their individual customers, in turn, and were careful in their selections.

Because the better men of the South realized their situation and knew that they had to work or perish the business which was thus set up was profitable. The commission merchants of Baltimore leased or built new warehouses and stocked them with a vast array of wares, from farm tools to millinery. The big mercantile names of the Baltimore of this period are not those of shipowners or shipbuilders or men who took daring chances in elaborate trading ventures at sea. They are, rather, those of the heads of the wholesale houses—the Hursts, the Millers, the Armstrongs, the Cators, the Woodwards, the Baldwins, and a score of others. These are the men who sold the goods and also acted as directors of the banks which stood behind their ventures. Their chief assets, aside from capital, were geography and their intimate knowledge of the Southern merchants with whom they dealt.

Such undertakings as these, however admirable in the great scheme of things, however productive of profit, drain off something from the men who direct them. One doesn't ordinarily find, among men whose eyes are focused from dawn until sunset upon the profit and loss and account any great ebullience of spirit, any magnificent spilling over into colorful adventure. One searches the record in vain to discover a Joshua Barney or even a William Lux among these solid citizens.

But they made money. They built churches and they worshiped according to their lights. Occasionally they sent their sons to college. These youngsters, returning to the drab city, sometimes found it dull and tried to enliven it. But the livening, for the most part, expressed itself, as always before, in mimicking—perhaps "re-establishing" is a better word—the life of the old country gentry. When the Northern Central Railroad was building toward York it had been stopped for a while by a complicated lawsuit. During the delay a branch line was run through the length of one of those charming little valleys which are characteristic of the country north of Baltimore. This one, called the Green Spring Valley, was especially lush, and in order to stimulate passenger travel on the line the railroad had built a summer hotel at its terminus. In their annual flight from the city many of the bankers and merchants used this hotel as a refuge. They discovered, as previous generations had discovered before them, the charm of country life. After a while they began to buy land along the route and to build houses upon it. Their youngsters, growing up in such agreeable surroundings, took to the old country sports—riding to hounds, point-to-point racing, and even that most clandestine of all aristocratic games, cockfighting. The wealthy newcomers could carry on such sports on a scale that the older county families, with rare exceptions, could not hope to attain.

[294]

But this was by the way. There were still a few men among the merchants who had the old flair for reaching out. They fought against great odds, for the whole attention of the country was turned inland, and the love of the sea had dried up in the hearts of men. John W. Garrett, still scheming to develop his beloved railroad, persuaded a group of citizens to join with him in 1865 in establishing a connection with Liverpool. They actually bought six fair-sized steamships and started the line. Its success was not notable, and it was soon abandoned.

Undaunted by his first failure, Mr. Garrett tried again. This time, however, he was careful to avoid too-heavy commitments. Instead he made a deal with the North German Lloyd. In return for certain concessions that famous corporation agreed to keep at least two first-class passenger and freight vessels on the Baltimore run for five years. The enterprise was more than successful. The tobacco, wheat, and flour of Baltimore provided an adequate cargo eastward. Minor German manufactures, notably toys, plus thousands of immigrants, supported the westward trip. Baltimore became a main immigration port, receiving newcomers not only from Germany but from Austria, Hungary, and Eastern Europe as well. The city had always had a broad German streak in it. That streak now became even broader. The elite of the city had always had a special fondness for Hanoverians. The frequent ships from Bremen produced a new tie with Germans of this type, and they became important factors in the social and business life. The line endured—and prospered, in fact—until the outbreak of the first World War.

There was plenty of trade in the port, but the ships to carry it gradually slipped out of the hands of those who formerly owned and directed them. The English established a line from Baltimore to Liverpool in 1870, and by 1880 there were three such lines. Another under the red ensign ran to the Continental ports of the Channel and the North Sea. Grain for the Mediterranean was carried in tramps, either sail or steam, which came when they heard of a possible cargo. Under Baltimore flags only the coffee clippers, which had by now become barques for the most part, continued to carry Baltimore flour to the islands and to Rio, bringing back, when they could get it, a cargo of coffee, more often than not for New York account. The port was busy but it was humdrum. It was humdrum because the men who brought the products from the interior to its wharves no longer found it profitable to use the additional energy and run the additional risks necessary to get those products across the sea. They let George and Fritz and Hendrik and Ole do it. Acting merely as agents, they took their commission in this endeavor as they took it in their Southern business.

In 1867 Johns Hopkins was seventy-two years old. He had piled up many millions and he knew that Baltimoreans regarded him as a moneygrubber. He began to wonder as the end approached what he should do with all that money. Before him was the example of George Peabody, a man who had laid the foundation of his fortune in Baltimore and who, as his end drew near, thought more and more nostalgically of his early association. The Peabody Institute was the result, and because it was established as a going concern before his death he had been widely acclaimed.

Pondering on this and kindred subjects, Johns Hopkins called a group of his business intimates together and outlined a scheme to them. His suggestion was that they form a corporation to be known as the Johns Hopkins University for the Promotion of Education in the State of Maryland. They agreed, and from that time forth the aging man devoted most of his energies to getting his affairs in such order that the institution could be started. He died in 1873, before the idea was fully matured, but in his will he left detailed plans for the undertaking. The endowment for the university alone amounted to more than three millions.

The trustees, with the help of the president of Harvard, settled on Daniel Coit Gilman, formerly of Yale but at the time president of the University of California. How closely Gilman's idea of the function of a university tallied with that of Johns Hopkins is still a matter of dispute. But it is a fact, nevertheless, that the university, as Gilman envisaged it and as he built it, changed the whole course of higher education in the United States, taking the emphasis for good and all away from the old theoclassical routine and placing it upon untrammeled research. Today he would be a bold man who would deny that the Johns Hopkins University, under Gilman and his successors, has not been one of the major influences on learning in the United States.

But the university was only half of Johns Hopkins' plan. The other half laid down instructions for the building of a hospital for the poor of the city and the operation of a medical school in connection therewith. For many reasons, most of them financial, the hospital was not opened until 1889. But when it did open Gilman proved that he was as capable of selecting distinctive men in medicine as he was in the arts and sciences. The "big four"—Osler, Kelly, Welch, and Halstead—these were the nucleus of his staff. It was added to year after year as superior men emerged here and abroad. In a little while the medical school was turning out graduates trained in its own methods, and these students, in turn, were staffing other medical schools. Gilman's university had worked a revolution in the natural sciences but it was not more complete than the revolution which Gilman's medical school worked in its turn.

Enoch Pratt was likewise childless. But, as we have seen, he had an expansive nature once he was out of his counting-house. His wealth piled up like that of Johns Hopkins. Some of it he used as he went along in helping build up or improve various charitable institutions, particularly those devoted to the care of children. In the early eighties, with Hopkins' example before him, as Peabody's had been before Hopkins, he organized a corporation called the Enoch Pratt Free Library of Baltimore City and put in its hands securities to the value of $1,445,833.33. The library was opened to the public in 1886, and Pratt had ten years during which to enjoy the encomiums of the city for his generosity. His library has since been the recipient of many other gifts, notably from Andrew Carnegie. Latterly, the municipality has tended to regard it as akin to the public-school system and makes regular and usually increasing appropriations toward its operations. Housed in a fine new building and with a competent staff, it is frequently held up as a model public library.

There is a paradox in the circumstance that at the very period when individuals were being most lavish in their gifts to the city, the city itself, as an organized entity, was most laggard. There was physical growth, of course. In 1860 the population was 212,418. In 1900 it reached

508,957. New streets extended in every direction, most of them in the checkerboard pattern which was the sole recourse of city planners of the period. Almost without exception these streets were lined on both sides with narrow row houses two or three stories high, each precisely like its neighbor and differing hardly at all from the house across the street or in the next block.

These streets, though monotonous, were not and are not unpleasant to look upon. They were all built of brick, and Baltimore brick has a charming reddish-pink color and weathers well. The sidewalks were likewise of brick, laid in intricate but well-established patterns. Because of the survival of a tradition the proportions of the windows and doors and their spacing in the walls were intelligent. Every house had either a stoop painted white (Baltimoreans call their stoop "the front steps") or, more frequently, similar steps of white marble from the quarries to the north of the city. There was an obligation, accepted by nearly everyone, to keep the front steps gleaming white, and special soaps and soft polishing stones were kept on hand in order that the ritual might be correctly celebrated.

Such houses were and are almost always owned by their occupants. The contractors who built them usually kept title to the land, putting an arbitrary value upon it and demanding an annual payment, called the "ground rent," from the occupant. Ground rents were negotiable and formed one of the main investments of the thrifty. The effect of the ground rent was to reduce the purchase price of the house, and there were neighborhood building-and-loan associations to step in and help the purchaser by making large loans upon the "improvement," as the house was called. In the period we are discussing the ground rent was permanent. Now the owner of the house has a right to purchase the ground outright after five years, and thus the owner thereof is no longer assured of a permanent income.

Thus the immediate outward aspect of the Baltimore of this era was not unpleasing. Downtown, in the business district, most of the ramshackle houses of the very early days had been replaced by more substantial warehouses, most of them built with a fair regard for the gracious tradition of colonial times. Baltimore Street, Lombard Street, Gay Street, South Street, and all the others in the neighborhood had a pleasant uniformity. The main office of the Baltimore and Ohio Railroad, at the corner of Baltimore and Calvert streets, with the astonishing height of seven stories, towered over its neighbors in symbolic assertion of the importance of the corporation it housed.

The railroad itself had taken over most of old Whetstone Point—excepting, of course, the very tip, which was occupied by Fort McHenry—and also the neighboring area, called Locust Point. Here were its vast tidewater terminals, its docks and piers for the North German Lloyd and other lines, its immigration station, and, more important than anything else, its grain elevators.

On the other side of the harbor, between Fells Point and Canton, the Philadelphia, Wilmington and Baltimore Railroad, now an integral part of the Pennsylvania system, had duplicated most of the facilities of the B. & O. Canton itself was beginning to attract industries, intrigued by the notion of having water transportation at their front doors and rail transportation at the back.

Thus there was growth and activity even during the protracted hard times of the seventies and eighties. But there were obvious lacks as well. The visitor, first attracted by the neat houses with their red bricks and their white steps, was likely soon to notice that the streets were badly paved with the roughest and most irregular cobblestones. Only where the streetcars ran would he find decent paving. The law required that the rails be laid with precisely the gauge of the ordinary wagon and buggy and that the space between them be kept well paved.

But more unpleasant, and perhaps to the visitor more revealing, would be the open sewers which ran along the curbs of nearly every street. In every back yard of the period there was a cesspool. All other waste water found its way into the gutters, whence eventually it might be let into a storm-water drain. Such drains all emptied either into Jones Falls or directly into the basin. The Falls thus became a great open sewer—often tinted a sickly blue on Monday—discharging its malodorous contents into the inner harbor whose waters bubbled constantly as they engendered the noxious gases of putrefaction.

Nor was that the worst of the situation. The visitor could not see the water-supply system. That was both insufficient and impure. Most of it came from an artificial lake created at the lower end of the Green Spring Valley by the damming of Jones Falls. All the wastes from the great houses in the valley thus drained into the lake and contaminated it. There was no filtration plant. Baltimore had the highest typhoid rate of any big city in the country.

The apologist for Baltimore has here his greatest difficulty. How can he explain this neglect of the most elementary needs of a great city? How can he explain (for he cannot condone) the indifference of the leading men of the community, not to its physical shortcomings alone, but even to the political corruption which ever and anon was all too manifest?

Perhaps there is no satisfactory explanation. But there are factors which will have to be taken into account by the scientific historian if ever the attempt is made to show why Baltimore, a relatively prosperous city, should have lagged so far behind other and often less fortunate communities.

One factor was the Southern influence. Because Baltimore had allied itself economically with the South, because it insisted upon its sympathy with and understanding of the South it adopted quite easily the casual indifference of the South. From the South, too, there came a great rush of immigration. Families by the thousands found the task of re-establishing their agricultural life too much for them and came to Baltimore to find new opportunities. Many of these newcomers were superior men. As lawyers, physicians, and businessmen they enriched the life of the community. But the great majority were but average people looking for jobs, with no urban experience or understanding. They gave the city a more Southern cast than it had ever had before but they provided a reservoir of labor which tended to depress the wage scale.

But the biggest factor of all, it is fair to guess, was the influx of Negroes, released from thralldom and free for the first time to follow their inclinations. To the Negroes, anxious to get away from the hard labor and low estate of the South, Baltimore was North. It was the city of which they had heard their old masters talk. To reach it used up most of their not extravagant ambitions. Drab and slow-going as it was compared to the larger towns, to them it was the "city of gold."

Housing these black newcomers provided a special problem and a special opportunity for the use of capital. As the new streets were extended in checkerboard squares the interior spaces behind the small back yards of the row houses were subdivided by narrow alleys, and thousands of tiny brick dwellings, with four rooms normally and the most primitive of sanitary arrangements, were erected. Thus nearly every one of the fair blocks of row houses was the outer wall behind which were hidden labyrinths of hovels, each swarming with from two to half a dozen proliferating family groups.

Every Saturday night such communities were the scene of fights and brawls, with frequent stabbings and even murders. On Sunday morning, either in the streets or in some room turned into a gospel tabernacle, the evangelists would hold forth in interminable sermons and the congregations join in moaning spirituals. Most of the children had rickets and sore eyes, while tuberculosis was as common as measles.

This was a special burden which few communities could have shouldered with equanimity. Baltimore did not know what to do about it. To eliminate these foci of infection was far beyond its fiscal powers. It had no authority to control the Negro influx. Having one clearly insoluble problem on its hands, it found it consoling to say that all urban problems were equally insoluble. So it did almost nothing.

CHAPTER XXVI

The Iniquities of the Fathers

SUNDAY MORNING, February 7, 1904, was a very cold day in Baltimore. February is always the most wintry month, and this was a typical February day. The skies were clear, but a biting northwest wind was blowing across the city. Uptown those so inclined were on their way to their churches. The downtown districts, as was natural on Sunday morning, were deserted by all but watchmen and an occasional policeman sheltering himself from the icy blast in a doorway on the windward side of the street.

Archibald McAllister, a private watchman employed by a number of the big wholesalers to keep an eye on their warehouses, was passing the corner of German Street and Hopkins Place when he saw a puff of smoke emerge from a grating in the sidewalk before the stuffed warehouse of John E. Hurst and Company, one of the major establishments in the Southern trade. He immediately sounded a fire alarm. Another alarm had already been sounded from the automatic system in the building. Firemen were on the scene in a few minutes and prepared to fight what they thought was an ordinary basement fire.

But this was not an ordinary fire. Already it had gained headway among the inflammable dry goods piled up in the building in preparation for the spring visit of the Southern buyers. The gases engendered had to find an outlet. They got it by blowing out the front wall of the building in the very faces of the leisurely firemen. Thus they were made to realize they had something major on their hands and called out more equipment. Before this could be put into action the fire had complete possession of the Hurst building and had begun to spread. Frantically the firemen sounded still more alarms.

They had no chance of controlling it. Even after special trains had brought apparatus from Washington, then Wilmington and then Philadelphia and New York—and, of course, from York and Hanover in Pennsylvania—the flames roared on, paying no attention to the thin streams of water from the innumerable hoses which the firemen hooked to the hydrants. Every new hose meant a lessening of the water pressure, never high enough to make an effective weapon against a first-class fire. The flames, whipped by the winds, leapt clear over the buildings upon which the firemen were concentrating their efforts and often hemmed them in so that they were forced to flee for their lives, leaving their equipment behind.

Some said that the fire could be stopped by dynamite, and experts were brought in to try this method. Building after building toppled before this roaring assault, but the flames leapt across the gaps created and started afresh on the leeward side.

Not many Baltimoreans slept that night. From Federal

Hill, where thousands gathered, the whole extent of the lurid panorama was visible. The warehouses, from that height, would be intact one minute and the next great torches, sending roaring flames hundreds of feet in the air. Large sections of wooden roof or cornice, caught in the upward blast, would fall perhaps a quarter of a mile away and start a new blaze where they landed.

In the threatened streets employers directed clerks in the frantic effort to save records and other valuables before the fire came upon them. In some instances they were in time, but because it was Sunday sufficient volunteers were not immediately available. Oftener than not the would-be salvagers arrived too late to get at the threatened building.

On a front almost half a mile wide the flames rushed eastward. New tall buildings with steel frames and brick curtain walls were no less vulnerable than the old solid brick structures whose fronts, in imitation of that of *The Sun's* famous iron building, had been plated with cast-iron columns.

The new courthouse, of Beaver Dam marble, stood as a bulwark on the left flank of the advance and though it crumbled a bit, still it saved the post office and the City Hall. Here and there, scattered through the district, there were low and solidly built banking houses. Over these, in a few instances, the flames leapt impatiently. The little building of Alexander Brown & Sons was one of those which escaped, because it was small and compact and because its roof could withstand the rain of blazing debris. But everything else went.

By Monday evening the destroying enemy reached the Falls. The wind had died down, and, save for a few dying thrusts at the lumberyards across the stream, he made no

further conquests. From Liberty Street east to the Falls
and from the basin north to Lexington Street little was left
save the segment protected by the courthouse. Every major
wholesale warehouse, every major downtown hotel, most
of the banks, all the newspapers save one small one, and
all save one or two office buildings had gone down. The
official count said that 1343 buildings had been burned in
an area of 139.9 acres. The damage could hardly be estimated. The accepted figure is $150,000,000. Readers of
this book will perhaps get some idea of the extent of the
destruction when they are told that all save a tiny corner
of the original town was burned out and that the fire took
all within an area more than twice that size.

Baltimore had never suffered a calamity like this before.
Some were so overwhelmed that they said immediately
that the city might as well be abandoned. The mayor, an
amiable and competent young man of good position, fell
into a depression and finally shot himself. Such pessimists
had something on their side, for a number of the local fire-
insurance companies caved in under the pressure and could
make only partial payments on their policies. The companies outside the city paid in full, however, and thus there
was capital available to begin at least part of the rebuilding. Thus it was soon possible to silence the pessimists and
to contemplate realistically the task that had to be done.

After all, it could have been much worse. The fire was
confined to the business district. People were not made
homeless. Major transportation had not suffered, and supplies could be brought in. There were no deaths surely at-
tributable to the fire, and hence there was none of that
personal agony usually associated with such conflagrations.
Baltimore was able to decline with thanks the offers of

financial and other assistance which came pouring in from all over the country. The problem, as the town saw it, was a business problem.

Baltimore in normal times often seems to lack outstanding figures. But there has never been a crisis in the city's history when leaders did not emerge to assume the burdens and responsibilities of action. Before the ruins were cold the legislature, called into special session, had empowered the mayor to appoint a Burnt District Commission clothed with extraordinary powers. To be head of the commission he appointed Colonel Sherlock Swann, not a brilliant man perhaps but a determined one. In a few days, working with funds the city had borrowed, he had crews of men carting debris from the streets and dumping it on the mud flats where the falls of the Patapsco empty into Middle Branch, not far from Moales Point, where Baltimore might have been. Thus new land was made, and, what may have been more important, one more breeding ground for malarial mosquitoes was reduced in size.

With this example of official vigor before them, individual property owners began to show their resourcefulness. In a few days most of the important firms had found temporary offices. The newspapers made arrangements with their Washington colleagues for temporary use of their mechanical facilities, and special trains were bringing the papers over to Baltimore and distributing them promptly. *The Sun* did not miss an edition. The number of pages in all the papers began to swell as more and more of the businessmen found quarters—even the parish houses of churches were requisitioned—and announced their new locations and their plans for the future in large advertisements. After the ruins cooled sufficiently they began to dig about in their own debris and make plans for the fine buildings which were to arise.

Right here trouble began, for the Burnt District Commission, hearkening to a general demand, began to make plans for widening and straightening some of the narrow and uncertain streets. It transpired that every property owner was in favor of all such plans save the one proposed for his block. Christopher Wren had much the same experience when he tried to redesign London after the fire of 1666. The result was a poor compromise, with the Burnt District Commission managing to get about 25 per cent of what it asked for. Its biggest achievement was the widening of Captain Lux's Light Street which, despite its commercial importance, had been an alley in the beginning and had remained an alley ever since. It transpired, further, that E. Clay Timanus, the president of the City Council, who succeeded the dead mayor *ex officio*, was an able and vigorous man, although he was a Republican and hence held office only by accident.

Thus Baltimore rose from its ashes more quickly and more splendidly than anyone had believed possible. The new buildings were larger, lighter, and airier. But they were not more beautiful, alas! The old colonial tradition had spent itself, and the architectural style that was to replace it had not yet been found. Taller buildings were possible, thanks to steel construction, and wide arches and great windows. But every designer had his own notions as to how the new methods were to be used, and most of them were so busy that they didn't make even formal protest against the vagaries of their clients. Thus the new Baltimore had none of the satisfactory uniformity of the old but instead grew up higgledy-piggledy, with each new structure warring in height and in design and color with its neighbors. The only charm in the new downtown area was the charm of variety, which can easily be overdone.

Energy begets energy, and the enthusiasm released when the people of Baltimore discovered that they had actually survived the fire and were to be better off in lots of ways sought almost immediately for new outlets. To reconstruct its business area the municipality had forgotten its old conservatism and gone into debt. To reconstruct their own warehouses the merchants likewise had assumed mortgages. Thus familiar with what had previously been a hideous specter and finding it endurable, the citizens came almost to love it. They demanded further improvements and enthusiastically voted new debts to pay for them. One of their first decisions was in favor of a proper sewage system and a disposal plant. This meant the eliminaton of the old cesspools and the stinking gutters. They voted that the city take over and rebuild for lessees all the piers in the inner harbor, bringing order into what had previously been very like chaos. When this money was used up they voted another harbor loan for still more elaborate improvements. More important than anything perhaps, they voted for an extension and improvement of the water supply and included in their authorizations the money for a filtration plant. Typhoid fever almost immediately became a well-nigh forgotten disease. The elimination of cesspools and stagnant puddles in the streets reduced the number of mosquitoes and the prevalence of malaria. Most remarkable of all perhaps, they voted a paving loan, and there was talk of eliminating all cobblestones from the streets. Impossible as that seemed at the time, it has been all but accomplished.

The Iniquities of the Fathers

From some points of view, this outburst of energy is the most interesting phenomenon in Baltimore's history. For forty years the town, though individuals in it had prospered mightily, had adopted a fatalistic attitude toward its community existence. It had found an excuse for its shortcomings, and the excuse was so generally accepted that it made no major effort at self-improvement. The fatalism sometimes degenerated into self-pity, the most destructive of emotions.

Yet when disaster came and the choice was between aggressive action or dissolution the decision and the energy to make the choice and to implement it welled up from some deep springs of being. The old Baltimore was dead. Long live the new!

CHAPTER XXVII

Life Goes On

IT HAS BEEN almost forty years since the last flame
of the great fire flickered and died. In that perspective
it is possible to see that there was something symbolic in
the blaze which started in the well-filled warehouse of one
of the greatest of the local merchants.

Baltimore had always had a way of devoting itself to
some special task. There was the business of flour which
brought its first boom. There was the business of privateering and blockade running which carried it through the
Revolution and the War of 1812. There was railroad
building in the mid-century. There was the Civil War
and after that there was the opportunity to rehabilitate
the South. All these undertakings were interconnected, of
course, and in some senses each grew out of the other. It
is an obvious oversimplification to state them as they are
stated here and so, too, it is an obvious oversimplification to
say that the fire ended an era.

But this much can be said: that if the fire had not wiped
out those great distributing firms, then they would have

been destroyed by other forces less spectacular but no less irresistible.

The restoration of the South, in the sense that Baltimore conceived that operation, could never have been a permanent job. If the new South had continued precisely like the old one—overwhelmingly agricultural and manorial—then the business of supplying its consumption goods could well have gone on indefinitely. But the South was altered as well as prostrated by the war. When it arose, with the calculating help of Baltimore, it was a different community. Its new leaders were not the farmer-statesmen who had ruled its destinies from the time of Washington to the time of Lee. Instead they were often harsh, grasping men, sprung from a stock different from that which had produced the earlier heroes. These new men made the new South in their own image, and the economic and social organization which they erected did not resemble that upon which even the shrewdest of Baltimore's merchants and bankers based his faintly sentimental plans.

There was another reason why the business of supplying and financing the Southern retailers could not have been permanent. Baltimore did these things best for the first decades after the war chiefly because Baltimore was the nucleus of the only effective transportation system which fed the South. It owned the first railroad to enter Washington. One of its financiers, William T. Walters—he was one of those Baltimoreans who for personal reasons spent the whole period of the Civil War in Europe, buying pictures —had assembled and developed the Atlantic Coast Line, which ran along the Southern littoral. The coastal shipping lines which served the Southern ports found their Northern terminal in Baltimore. As far as the physical distribution of goods went, Baltimore controlled the mouth of the funnel.

But other approaches were possible, and after the war energetic and aggressive men swarmed down from the Middle West to get a share of the Southern business. They were handicapped at first by lack of knowledge and lack of transportation, but as the years went on these lacks were remedied. From Cincinnati, from St. Louis, even from Chicago new rail connections were developed, and merchants arose able to make use of them. The South built up its own distributing points, and the wholesalers established in them were able to pick and choose between offers and even, on occasion, to buy directly from the manufacturers who might be located anywhere from Boston to Akron.

The special credit knowledge which Baltimore possessed could not be kept a permanent secret. The merchants of New York finally acquired a comparable knowledge and developed at the same time transportation routes over both sea and land to put their knowledge to use. Thus, for a variety of reasons hard to measure accurately and put in their proper sequence, Baltimore's strong position was gradually undermined. At the time of the fire her wholesalers were feeling the strain and were going to extraordinary lengths to attract the buyers to their emporiums.

When Baltimore was fighting its way out of the ruins of the fire some of the merchants rebuilt as if they expected the Southern trade to be permanent, but in their hearts they must have known that a great change was in the offing. They had to admit it when the big houses began to have financial trouble. Inside very few years many of them failed outright. Some will always survive, but one of the melancholy sights of present-day Baltimore is that of those bulky brick structures deserted by their proud occupants and now standing vacant or else divided up between perhaps half a dozen small clothing manufacturers. Johns Hopkins had left many such properties to his hospital, and it suffered sharply when the business which made them valuable withered away.

It is possible to say that the merchants themselves suspected that a change was impending, because soon after the excitement of the fire had died down they began to organize among themselves and argue about means for increasing trade. Half a dozen proposals, all of them almost purely fanciful, were adopted by as many different groups, each of which poured money into its selection in the endeavor to make it work. One slick promoter from somewhere in the West showed up and proved, to the satisfaction of his hearers, presumably sensible businessmen, that the prosperity of a community was in direct mathematical relation to the amount of money that community spent in advertising itself. He had a whole series of charts and graphs—always impressive to a worried businessman—which demonstrated that for every thousand dollars spent by community advertising almost exactly half a million in new trade was produced. In Portland, Ore., the expenditure of each thousand produced $547,083.62 in new trade; in Kenosha, Wis., it produced $493,875.06, and so on and so on.

The merchants in the group gave this fellow a fat fee for imparting this information and, at his suggestion, raised an initial fund of $100,000 to test out his theory locally. To direct the campaign they employed, also at his suggestion, a young man trained in his office. Most of that $100,000 was spent in the bars of Baltimore by the young man and the long series of "advisers" he brought to the city. But the trade which the merchants had hoped to increase continued to dwindle away. As the dominant group in the community they were in the decline.

No comparable group to take their places was produced spontaneously. In fact, Baltimore was never again to be the concern of Baltimoreans only, nor was it to be molded and directed exclusively by them. The whole nation was becoming financially and economically integrated as it had never been before. Great corporations, financed by national rather than local savings and operating on a national rather than on a regional scale, were coming to dominate the country. The fundamental job before Baltimore was not that of preserving its past activities but, instead, that of integrating itself or being integrated with the new national economy.

Some Baltimoreans had felt this in a vague sort of way for a long time. The railroad wars of the eighties had been hard on the city, because the lines serving New York and Philadelphia and even Boston had ignored the facts of geography and cut rates violently in order to attract freight and stimulate the use of their terminals. The Baltimore and Ohio was forced to meet this unreasonable competition and lost heavily in the process. The struggle was ended by an agreement, and the agreement, in turn, produced finally the Interstate Commerce Commission.

Under the benign suasion of this regulatory body geography was given its proper consideration, and the rates from Baltimore to Western points were based on the undeniable fact that the haul from Baltimore to Chicago, Buffalo, Cleveland, or almost any interior point is miles shorter than the haul from Boston, New York, or Philadelphia to those points. The rate differential enjoyed by Baltimore ranges from one to three cents per hundred pounds on freight bound East and from three to eight cents per hundred pounds on freight bound West. It has been maintained at those figures, despite almost annual efforts by the other ports, acting singly or in combination, to reduce or eliminate it.

Such an advantage is useful to all forms of enterprise. It would not be overlooked, for instance, by ship operators anxious to coal their ships at the lowest possible cost per ton. It would not be overlooked by fabricators of goods dependent in any degree upon bulky imported materials. The combination of cheap water transport and cheap rail rates is a powerful one.

To these advantages, the result of geography, Baltimore now had another one, not to be left out of the equation. Those thousands upon thousands of Negroes who poured into the city during the last quarter of the nineteenth century and the other thousands waiting to come from Virginia and the Carolinas were labor of a poor and uncertain quality perhaps, but the quantity was unlimited. The individual Negro might find more than two consecutive days of hard labor beneath his dignity, but if a great surplus of such individuals was hired enough would turn up any given day to do the work that had to be done. Moreover, their presence and especially their numbers were like a sword suspended over the heads of unskilled white workers and tended to keep wages down and even to prevent the growth of unions in all save the most aristocratic trades. Low wages are not an unmixed blessing, but it is hard to prove it to the man who has a pay roll to meet.

These were the new bases on which Baltimore was now to grow, but the growth had gone far before the dominating figures of the community realized it. It was not until the wholesale houses began to collapse that the bankers began to preach the doctrine of industrialization, but, in fact, that industrialization had already progressed a long way. All the plants along the B. & O., as it followed the shore of Spring Gardens and flowered in its Locust Point terminals, were profiting for the reasons we have listed. Mr. Abbott's rolling mill in Canton and the Pennsylvania Steel Company on Sparrows Point, a little way down the river, had seen the prospect toward the close of the Civil War. The shipyards at the foot of Federal Hill began fabricating vessels of iron at the same period and continued to operate successfully during all the years that followed. So that when the community itself was finally convinced what really happened was a change of emphasis.

The West Indian trade and that in coffee with Brazil had pretty well dried up before the turn of the century, but the opening of the Panama Canal gave a fillip to Baltimore's port for reasons a glance at the map will show. In preparation for it, the city importuned the Federal government to widen and deepen its channel. By slow degrees this was accomplished. With the authorization of 1905, the year after the fire, a permanent depth of thirty-five feet was maintained in the main channel and thirty feet in most of its various branches. The city backed this up with loan funds with which it prepared to build new facilities, including docks and channels, for water-front industries locating within its borders. At the beginning of World War I twelve overseas shipping lines, all under foreign flags, were operating out of Baltimore. The Beth-

AIRPLANE VIEW OF MODERN BALTIMORE

Compare this with the picture of Baltimore in 1850. If you look very closely you will see certain features which have survived the onslaught of time.

lehem Steel Company, successor of the Pennsylvania Steel Company, had multiplied the capacity of its plant and was hauling ore all the way from Chile and Peru via the new canal. Tankers were bringing crude oil from the Gulf ports and Mexico to the refineries on the south shore of the river. New fertilizer and chemical plants were belching acrid smokes and vapors over Curtis Bay, which only a few years before had been a pleasant little indentation known chiefly to yachtsmen and week-end canoeists.

All these undertakings expanded with a roar when the United States entered that first great war. The existing steel companies, the refineries, and the chemical plants doubled, trebled, and quadrupled their capacity. Agents for out-of-town corporations swarmed into the city, bought up and enlarged the little local plants built for regional needs, integrated them with great national corporations, and put the new type of peripatetic manager in charge. He shouted his demands for workers, enrolled them by the thousands, paid them undreamed-of wages, and the town zoomed into its new role in thoughtless exaltation.

Thus our tale is told. If more were added it would be but to pile on detail. The process of industrialization has moved in these last two decades in precise conformity with the industrial ups and downs of the country as a whole. Every year more national corporations have found Baltimore a convenient and economical location for their undertakings and have contributed to the wealth of the city while at the same time taking away more and more of its self-sufficiency. Each new corporation has sent in its manager to administer its properties and to make the adjustments to the local habits and customs necessary to get the most profitable results.

Each newcomer, hoping to make a good record and so earn advancement to another and larger plant in some other city, complains at the start that Baltimore is a strange and difficult town. If he stays more than two years the chances are that he forgets his earlier desire to move on and pulls what wires he can to lengthen his time among us. Baltimore may not own or dominate the great industries which use it but it has its ways of taking over and dominating the hired overseers of those industries.

To answer the question which this statement implies the self-appointed historian, wearied after long months of reading and pondering his all-too-elusive subject, asks the right, in these few closing pages, to make a few remarks drawn, not from his mind, but from his heart. Reading back over his words, he sees that he has been almost exclusively concerned with the business of Baltimore, and little of the legendary and picturesque has found a place. Only a few personalities have emerged. Partly that was by original intention. But it became a sort of obsession as he went on, because it seemed to him that he was traveling a path which only a few had trod before him and none at such length. In order to finish this course he had to resist the temptation to turn aside into other and more colorful pathways. Several times he was not strong enough to resist this temptation, as such long side journeys as those through the development of the Baltimore clipper and the minutes of the Delphian Club attest. For these sins he offers no apology. A case can be made for including them in an economic history. But this method leaves out something essential. It does not disclose the soul of the town.

Life Goes On

The saddest part of our story, I think, is the wresting away from Baltimore of the control of its own destiny. There was no way of avoiding that. The integration process, in business as in government, is a process it would be perilous to resist. But it is trying to see the sons and grandsons of men who were dominant and successful in their own right, who said the final yea and nay in their own business now working as salaried clerks and minor executives in corporations whose control is vested in a hundred thousand stockholders scattered from El Paso to Buffalo. There is not much sustenance in being a provincial if the status does not carry independence with it. Perhaps that is why so many of the present descendants of the tough old merchants flock into the professions, where a man is still his own boss in a sense.

Another disheartening aspect of the present era is the extent to which the old compact city has been deserted by those who formerly dwelt in it. This is a tendency all over the country, of course, and it is glibly but inadequately explained in terms of automotive transportation. In the early days only the rich and powerful could afford to live in the country many miles from their offices. In the case of Baltimore they had special reasons for leaving, especially during the summer, for summer in Baltimore is likely to be a stifling time, and in the early days the man who was forced to stay had to endure the ravages of mosquitoes and flies and to take his chances with the various plagues. But now the middle classes, whose character determines the character of the city, likewise move to the hills and give their allegiance to the remoter suburbs or to the county. In order to be truly urban in outlook people have to live close together. They have to know by daily observation and contact the life of their neighbors. Streets have to be more than mere thoroughfares to them.

In present-day Baltimore the old compact city is given over more and more to the very poor white workers and the Negroes. Houses built to be the spacious homes of single families have been turned into cheap lodgings for half a dozen or even a dozen families. Such people, living close to the subsistence level and at every period of depression falling below it, are not likely to have the time, the energy, or the capacity to contribute much to the community. They tend to become dependents rather than citizens.

The rich and powerful of Baltimore have never done as much for the city as they should have done. When you have listed Peabody, Hopkins, Pratt, and, recently, the younger Walters, who gave his father's magnificent art collection to the city and provided at the same time a gallery to house it and an endowment to support it, you have almost exhausted the list of major donors. The middle classes, moving to the suburbs, are losing their intimate concern with the town's needs. No one can justly demand much of the poor. Thus, from this single point of view, it is legitimate to view the future with certain forebodings.

But there are other points of view from which the picture is brighter, gayer, and more stimulating. For those who can command a relatively modest income life in Baltimore can be very pleasant. All of the suburbs, save those to the east and southeast, are on high rolling ground, with rich soil often sprinkled with original forest trees. The man with the patience to spend half an hour or less in his car, morning and night, can buy a few acres for the price of a city lot, build himself a house, and be a country gentleman, over the week end at least. Or, if his taste runs that way, he may acquire a small piece of land fronting on any one of a hundred creeks and rivers or on the bay itself and spend his week ends fishing and sailing. The oystermen have done terrible things to the original oyster bars on which they subsisted for many years, and the long nets have played havoc with the shad, but the lesser fish—perch, hardheads, trout, and even bluefish—are still plentiful and provide both sport and food. Children can still catch a dozen or two dozen crabs during a patient morning. Thousands of workmen own or rent little shacks along the rivers near Baltimore and come back to their shops on Monday morning boasting of their sunburn. Even yachting isn't the sport of the rich alone. There are at least twenty modest clubs which hold their week-end racing series and their annual regattas.

The bay still looks busy, and it isn't only the ore carriers, the tankers, and the steamship lines which make it so. The little steamboats which used to run up the rivers and gather the produce of the countryside are almost all gone, but the nightly boats to Norfolk still survive and make their glittering passages as they have done for a hundred years. When the river lines passed out local enterprisers in such towns as Cambridge, Chestertown, Crisfield, the oyster-and-crab metropolis, and Solomon's Island, the fisherman's paradise, built or acquired smaller motor-driven freighters which constantly run up and down the bay, taking grain, produce, and canned goods to Baltimore and bringing back fertilizer and other local needs. When watermelons are running they still pile up around the little quays of the basin and give it the fetid smell and color of the tropics. The surviving bugeyes and the innumerable skipjacks haul bulk freight during the summer and spend the R months tacking back and forth across the oyster bars, dragging their destructive dredges behind them. Now and then they still poach on forbidden territory—for the state is engaged in an earnest effort to bring the oyster crop back to something like its old size—and have a sharp encounter with the patrol boats of the conservation commission. Maryland still maintains its armed oyster navy, but it has been many years since it fought a pitched battle with the oyster fleet. The last battle was not with the oystermen but with the Virginia menhaden fishermen who had the temerity to pursue a school into Maryland waters. A furious cannonading, mostly in the air, drove them back.

Most of these vessels use the port of Baltimore several times during the year for one reason or another. They give it a constant sense of bustle. In the calendar year 1936 the record showed that 157,273 vessels used the port. The figures on New York are not available, but San Francisco could count only 38,976 and Philadelphia but 18,066. These figures, set down formally in the statistical tables, are hard to credit, but the man who spends a morning on Fort McHenry watching the harbor from its ramparts finds them about what he expected. They certainly make it apparent that the port is in no immediate danger of drying up.

Nearly every year brings its own proof that the city, however integrated with the nation, still produces its characteristic sort of citizen, of enterprise, eccentricity, or glamour, all compact. In the boom days of the twenties, for instance, there arose a man who was haunted because no great line of passenger ships, Baltimore-financed and of Baltimore registry, was sailing regularly to European ports. He was a dreamer of dreams, this man, but he had energy and drive as well. After a while his dream came true, and there was a line of ships, with "Baltimore" on their sterns, carrying passengers and freight regularly to Britain, Holland, and Germany. The depression and a change in the Federal subsidy policy did away with the Baltimore Mail Line, but it was a pleasant and enlivening thing while it lasted, and Europe-bound Baltimoreans and a good many Southerners as well used it as a matter of course.

It was this same man who persuaded, or helped to persuade, Glenn L. Martin to move his airplane factory to Baltimore. That was a modest venture at the start, too, but events treated it more kindly than they treated the Baltimore Mail Line, and now it is one of the city's greatest industries, employing perhaps twenty thousand men and turning out flying boats and deadly bombers by the scores and hundreds.

Eccentrics are so common in Baltimore they are almost normal. There was a case not long ago of a man who resented a misquotation on the statue to Edgar Allan Poe and announced that unless it was officially changed he would change it himself. The offending line was:

Dreaming dreams no mortals ever dared to dream before.

When he had finished with his hammer and his chisel the extra s was gone, but the police were on hand, and he was sent to the watchhouse. But the town on the whole approved his action, and he was set free. Maybe it is wrong to call such a man an eccentric.

There was a wealthy bachelor, domiciled in the old University Club, whose twin enthusiasms were Madeira wine and the belles of old Baltimore. He died finally, and when his will was read it transpired that he had left a large sum to the Johns Hopkins University to build a lecture hall, provided the university agreed, among other things, to have the walls of the hall covered with murals containing portraits of Baltimore beauties of the previous generation, beauties whom he listed and most of whom were still living. The ladies were embarrassed, naturally, but the university accepted the gift with the string attached.

It is almost superfluous to mention Miss Wallis Warfield, descendant of one of the merchant-planter families, whose allure won her a king-emperor and lost him a throne. The shade of Betsy Patterson must have turned green at that news. . . .

One could go on with such instances. There is the case of the Baltimore airport. Back in the late twenties, when the Lindbergh flight made the country air-conscious, Baltimore decided to have the greatest airport. The politicians, with engineering backing, decided the place for it was the water front but because all the available near-by land was bespoke by the new industries they decided to make land as the Ellicott brothers had made it a hundred and fifty years before—by dredging the mud and silt from the river bottom and using it as fill behind great bulwarks. On a scale measured in square feet such a scheme is eminently feasible. On a scale measured by the hundreds of acres it has certain shortcomings, of which the chief is that after the mud on the top of the fill has dried out and formed an insubstantial skin to the depth of a few inches the result is a perfect seal against further evaporation of the moisture beneath. The great airport, in brief, refused to jell. Now, more than thirteen years later, after millions upon millions have been lavished upon it, it is still unfinished. But Baltimore continues to hope and to believe that before the next snow flies it will be the regular stopping place of the whole roster of air lines, most of which now avoid the city because of the limitations of the temporary field. To be wholly fair, the new airport is already the alternate terminus of Pan-American's trans-Atlantic and Bermuda services and the regular terminus and service depot of the British-owned line. Baltimore has much less ice, snow, and fog than New York, and the big clippers of the air use it when New York is unsafe.

Such things keep the town in a state of suspense, mild excitement, and laughter. Baltimore grows apace but it no longer cherishes any hope of surpassing either New York or Philadelphia in size and wealth. Its ambitions are modest. Because its place is secure and it knows that its survival is certain it can afford to laugh at itself and even enjoy the comments of newcomers who regularly call it a "hick town."

It is drab perhaps but it is relatively clean, relatively healthy, and its economy is sound. Its ups and downs, so dramatic in its early days, have been flattened out. The wartime booms which come upon it—the middle-aged of today have seen two of them, of course—are recognized for what they are and change to no great degree the habits and attitudes of its permanent citizenry. When depressions come and its more spectacular banks go down mobs no longer roam the streets seeking vengeance. There hasn't been a real mob since the turn of the century. There have been a few strikes but little violence.

One hears talk of Baltimore food, especially sea food, and, in truth, it is very good. But there are only a few first-class restaurants. Save in the racing season—which, to be sure, lasts for almost a third of the year—there are few spendthrift transients. Most Baltimoreans prefer to dine at home or with friends. The expensive restaurant has a hard time.

Nowadays the theaters have a hard time too, though Baltimore is a good tryout town and some producers think it lucky to bring their new plays to the ancient Ford's Theatre or to the gaudy Maryland. Music fares better than drama. The town's symphony orchestra is not a national organization, like the Philadelphia Orchestra, for instance, but it goes its substantial way year after year. It doesn't have to worry about finances because it is regularly provided for in the municipal budget, just as the art museum is. Baltimore is the only town in the country which considers a symphony orchestra as a proper charge against the taxpayer. Perhaps this, like so many other characteristics of the town, is the result of the German influence.

Baltimore was never a Southern city. But it is not a Northern city either. The old conflict is still there. Though the economy is Northern, or national, the social organization remains Southern. Rural leisure is the mild ambition of almost all Baltimoreans, and for an extraordinary percentage of them it is attainable. Even the Western-born manager of a national industrial corporation, under pressure to break production records, finds it hard to resist the lure of the countryside when it is so sensuously beautiful and so close at hand. On a hot summer day in Baltimore nothing is easier to find than a rational excuse for not working. Even the man who has no eye for well-groomed nature can still feel the attraction of an afternoon mint julep on his own terrace when there is a black servitor in the pantry yearning to exercise his immemorial art.

I wouldn't go so far as to say that the julep explains Baltimore. But it is the evidence of a spirit which does explain Baltimore. Useful, yet leisurely, urban but not sophisticated, prosperous but not harassed—all these may be said of our city. If driving ambition plays but a small role with us in these later days, what boots it?

Index

Index

Index

Index

Index

of flax, 109; of flour and tobacco before the Revolution, 69–79; of flour and tobacco after the Revolution, 133–5, 138–9, 150, 187, 221–3, 250–6; re-exporting, 140. *See also* Commerce, Harbor, Merchants, Ships, Tobacco, Wheat

F

Farmers and Planters Bank, 292
Fearnaught (vessel), 100
Federal Hill, 5–6, 9, 136, 262, 278, 305–6, 318
Federal Republican (newspaper), 162–5
Federalism, 135, 151, 162–7, 186
Federalist (vessel), 136–7
Fell, Edward (brother of William), 27, 42
Fell, Edward (son of William), 46–7
Fell, William, 27, 45–6, 54
Fells Point, 27, 30, 37, 43, 45, 46–9, 99, 129, 136, 142, 240, 253, 300
Fire of 1904, 116, 304–11, 312–3
Firemen, Volunteer, 262, 266
Fires in 1840s and 50s, 262
First National Bank, 290, 291
First Presbyterian Church, 39
Fishing, 323
Fite, Jacob, 110
Flanigan, Mr. (shipwright), 188
Fleming, John, 25
Flour trade, *see* Wheat-growing
Fly (brig), 181
Fly (sloop), 113
Food, 327–8
Ford's Theater, 328
Foreign-born; *see* Immigration
Forests, 23, 55
Fort Babcock, 189, 194, 202
Fort Covington, 189, 194, 199, 202
Fort McHenry, 150, 189, 194, 197, 199, 200, 202, 229, 279, 300, 324
Founding of Baltimore Town, 25–8
Fountain Inn, 124
Frederick, 132–3, 200, 237, 241, 278
French aid in the Revolution, 121–4
French and Indian War, 75
French at war with English after American Revolution, 139, 142–3

French hostilities against United States, 145–9
French immigrants from Haiti, 143
French Revolution, influence on Baltimore, 152
French settlers, 43–4, 69, 120, 143
French take British ship in Chesapeake Bay,. War of 1812, 159
Frenchtown, 44, 136, 188
Friendship (vessel), 100
Fulton, C. C., 278–9

G

Gaither family, 163
Gale, Doctor, 164
Gale, George, 142
Gambrill family, 282
Garrett, John W., 277, 282–7, 295
Garrett, Robert, 282
Gary family, 282
Gas plant, 216
General Assembly of Maryland, 118, 119, 135, 153, 155, 167, 269, 308
General Monk (vessel), 136
Georgetown, 129–30, 163, 232
George Washington (vessel), 173
German influence on schools, 260
German merchants, 134–5, 140, 257, 281
German settlers, 17, 33, 36, 42, 69, 218, 239, 260–1, 295, 328; anti-German feeling in nineteenth century, 260–1
Gibson Island, 131
Gilman, Daniel Coit, 297
Gilmor family, 127
Gist, Richard, 25
Glenn, John, 247
Glenn L. Martin airplane factory, 325
Goddard, William and Mary, 81, 109, 113–5, 134, 201
Godefroy, Maximilian, 217
Gold rush, 257
Goliath (vessel), 142, 146
"Goodrich's pirates," 116, 120
"Graces, The Baltimore" (Elizabeth, Louisa, and Mary Grace), 141
Great Eastern Road, 31, 131, 132
Grecian (vessel), 61

[335]

Index

Index

Index

McKim, Alexander, 161
McKim, Isaac, 161, 237, 245, 253
McKim, John, 217-8
McMahon, John V. L., 234, 236
Madison, Pres. James, 161, 162
Malaria, 308, 310
Manufacturing, *see* Industry
Marine Committee of the Continental Congress, 103-4, 110, 116-7
Marine insurance company, The first, 139
Markets, 227-8, 233, 265-6
Marquis of Cornwallis (vessel), 179-80
Marsh Market, Political battle in, 265
Maryland (ferry), 278
Maryland (sloop-of-war), 151
Maryland Gazette, 30
Maryland Historical Society, 144
Maryland Theater, 328
Matthews, General, 116
Matthews, Mr. (manufacturer), 109
Medical school founded in 1816, 217
Medical School, Johns Hopkins, 297-8
Men of Marque (book), 178
Merchants, 42, 242-3, 248, 321; after Civil War, 289-90, 293, 294; after fire of 1904, 310; after the Revolution, 125-49; after War of 1812, 220-1, 226, 233, 242-3, 250; associations, 139,. 315; before Civil War, 257, 259; Dutch and German, 134-5, 140; in relation to Civil War, 278, 280; in relation to the Revolution, 80-96, 97-8, 100-1, 109-10, 112, 123; in relation to the War of 1812, 159-60, 167-8. *See also* Banking, Commerce, Exports, Imports, Railroads, Ships, Tobacco, Wheat
Merchants Bank, 233
Merchants & Miners Transportation Company, 259
Merrimac (vessel), 172
Merryman, John, 279
Mexican War, 257
Middle class of present-day Baltimore, 321-2
Miller family, 293
Miltenberger, Gen. Anthony, 248

Mining, 23, 24
Moale, John, 24-5, 27, 32
Moales Point, 24, 27, 72, 308
Mobs, *see* Riots
Molly (vessel), 100
Monitor (vessel), 281
Monument Square, 246, 263-4
Monuments, 226, 227, 228, 233, 246, 325
Morris, John B., 237
Morris, Robert, 89, 120, 126
Mount Clare shops of B. & O., 238, 284-5
Mount Vernon Place, 227
Muir, Adam, 55
Mumma, Mr. (lyncher), 165
Municipal Museum of the City of Baltimore, 216
Murray family, 163
Museum and Gallery of Fine Arts, 216
Museum of the City of Baltimore, Municipal, 216
Music, 328
Musquidobit (vessel), 62-4

N

Nancy (vessel), 89
Napoleon's objection to marriage of Betsy Patterson and Jerome Bonaparte, 153
Navigation Acts (of Britain), 69, 86
Neal, John, 219
Negroes, 3, 138, 214, 274, 291, 302-3, 317, 322. *See also* Abolitionism, African Colonization Society, Anti-slavery, Slavery
Nelson, Benjamin, 48
Nesbit (privateer), 122
Newspapers, 218, 278, 307, 308. *See also Baltimore American, Federal Republican, Journal and Commercial Advertiser, Sun*
Newton (vessel), 175
Nichols, Henry, 141
Nicholson, Capt. James, 98-9, 103-6, 114, 122, 146, 149
Nicholson, Judge Joseph H., 201
Niles, Hezekiah, 190
Nonesuch (vessel), 161
Non-importation agreement (of Revolution), 82-5, 90, 91

Index

[339]

Index

Index

Index